Managing Reform in Universities

Issues in Higher Education

Titles include:

Jürgen Enders and Egbert de Weert (*editors*)
THE CHANGING FACE OF ACADEMIC LIFE
Analytical and Comparative Perspectives

John Harpur
INNOVATION, PROFIT AND THE COMMON GOOD IN HIGHER EDUCATION
The New Alchemy

Tamsin Hinton-Smith
WIDENING PARTICIPATION IN HIGHER EDUCATION
Casting the Net Wide?

V. Lynn Meek
HIGHER EDUCATION, RESEARCH, AND KNOWLEDGE IN THE
ASIA-PACIFIC REGION

Guy Neave
THE EUROPEAN RESEARCH UNIVERSITY

Guy Neave
THE EVALUATIVE STATE, INSTITUTIONAL AUTONOMY AND
RE-ENGINEERING HIGHER EDUCATION IN WESTERN EUROPE
The Prince and His Pleasure

Mary Ann Danowitz Sagaria
WOMEN, UNIVERSITIES, AND CHANGE

Snejana Slantcheva
PRIVATE HIGHER EDUCATION IN POST-COMMUNIST EUROPE

Sverker Sörlin
KNOWLEDGE SOCIETY VS. KNOWLEDGE ECONOMY

Bjørn Stensaker, Jussi Välimaa, Cláudia S. Sarrico (*editors*)
MANAGING REFORM IN UNIVERSITIES
The Dynamics of Culture, Identity and Organizational Change

Voldemar Tomusk
THE OPEN WORLD AND CLOSED SOCIETIES

Issues in Higher Education
Series Standing Order ISBN 978–0–230–57816–6 (hardback)
(*outside North America only*)

You can receive future titles in this series as they are published by placing a standing order. Please contact your bookseller or, in case of difficulty, write to us at the address below with your name and address, the title of the series and the ISBN quoted above.

Customer Services Department, Macmillan Distribution Ltd, Houndmills, Basingstoke, Hampshire RG21 6XS, England

---

Managing Reform in Universities

The Dynamics of Culture, Identity and Organizational Change

Edited by

Bjørn Stensaker
University of Oslo, Norway

Jussi Välimaa
University of Jyväskylä, Finland

and

Cláudia S. Sarrico
ISEG – School of Economics and Management,
Technical University of Lisbon, Portugal

First published 2012 by
PALGRAVE MACMILLAN

Palgrave Macmillan in the UK is an imprint of Macmillan Publishers Limited,
registered in England, company number 785998, of Houndmills, Basingstoke,
Hampshire RG21 6XS.

Palgrave Macmillan in the US is a division of St Martin's Press LLC,
175 Fifth Avenue, New York, NY 10010.

Palgrave Macmillan is the global academic imprint of the above companies
and has companies and representatives throughout the world.

Palgrave® and Macmillan® are registered trademarks in the United States,
the United Kingdom, Europe and other countries.

ISBN 978–0–230–30037–8

This book is printed on paper suitable for recycling and made from fully
managed and sustained forest sources. Logging, pulping and manufacturing
processes are expected to conform to the environmental regulations of the
country of origin.

A catalogue record for this book is available from the British Library.

A catalog record for this book is available from the Library of Congress.

10   9   8   7   6   5   4   3   2   1
21   20   19   18   17   16   15   14   13   12

Printed and bound in Great Britain by
CPI Antony Rowe, Chippenham and Eastbourne

Contents

Figures and Tables

Figures

Tables

Contributors

Alberto Amaral is Head of the Portuguese Quality Agency. He is a professor at the University of Porto and a researcher at the Centre for Research in Higher Education Policies. He is a member of the editorial board of *Quality Assurance in Education and Higher Education Dynamics*.

Sónia Cardoso is currently with the Development and Analysis Office of the Agency for Assessment and Accreditation of Higher Education, Portugal. She is a researcher at the Centre for Research in Higher Education Policies. She has written and published on the participation of students in quality activities in higher education.

David D. Dill is Professor Emeritus of Public Policy, University of North Carolina at Chapel Hill, USA. His interests are public policy analysis, ethics and higher education policy. His books include (with Maarja Beerkens) *Public Policy for Academic Quality* (2010) and (with Frans van Vught) *National Innovation and the Academic Research Enterprise* (2010).

Nicoline Frølich is a research professor at the Nordic Institute for Studies in Innovation, Research and Education, Oslo, Norway. Her research interests are related to public administration reform, governance, leadership and funding in higher education. She has published in *Public Administration, Higher Education, European Journal of Education* and *International Journal of Education Management*.

Mary Henkel was a professor in the Department of Government, Politics and History, Brunel University, UK. She has published books and articles in the fields of evaluation, higher education and science policy. Her main research interests are in the academic profession, and academic values and conceptions of knowledge.

Ana I. Melo is an assistant professor at the University of Aveiro. She is currently the coordinator of the degree in public and municipal management. Her research interests lie in the areas of public management reform, triple helix collaborative arrangements, and performance measurement and management in public services.

Amy Scott Metcalfe is an associate professor in the Department of Educational Studies at the University of British Columbia. Her main research interest is research policy, particularly inter-organizational and international linkages related to research, employment policy and the lived experiences of academic researchers, and the role of research universities in society.

Guy Neave, Professor Emeritus at the Centre for Higher Education Policy Studies, Twente University, the Netherlands, is currently Director of Research at the Centre for Research in Higher Education Policies, Matosinhos, Portugal. A foreign associate of the National Academy of Education of the United States of America, he is an historian by training. He jointly edited with Burton R Clark the *Encyclopedia of Higher Education* (1992). He lives in St Germain en Laye in France.

Keijo Räsänen is Professor of Organization and Management at the Aalto University School of Economics, Helsinki. He is a member of the research group Management Education Research Initiative, which does participatory research in the practical activities of academics and students (http://management.aalto.fi/en/research/groups/meri/). He has also studied developmental work in work organizations.

Maria J. Rosa is an assistant professor at the University of Aveiro and a researcher at the Centre for Research in Higher Education Policies, Portugal. Her research interests are in quality management, especially issues of quality assurance in higher education. She is a member of the Consortium of Higher Education Researchers and of the Executive Committee of the European Association of Institutional Research.

Taina Saarinen is a researcher and adjunct professor at the Centre for Applied Language Studies, University of Jyväskylä, Finland. Her main research interests are higher education policy, internationalization and language policy, currently from a Nordic and European perspective.

Kerstin Sahlin is Professor of Management in the Department of Business Studies at Uppsala University, Sweden. In the years 2006–2011 she was the Deputy Vice-Chancellor of Uppsala University.

Her research interests include transnational governance, public management reforms, management ideas and their circulation, and the role of corporations in global society.

Cláudia S. Sarrico is an associate professor in the School of Economics and Management, Technical University of Lisbon, and a researcher at the Centre for Research in Higher Education Policies, Portugal. Her main research interests are in public management, especially issues of performance management and governance in education and higher education.

Bjørn Stensaker is Professor of Higher Education in the Department of Educational Research, University of Oslo, Norway. He is also a research professor at the Nordic Institute for Studies in Innovation, Research and Education, Oslo. His research interests are related to governance, leadership and organizational change in higher education. He has published more than 150 articles, book chapters, reports and books in these areas.

Jussi Välimaa is Professor of Higher Education at the Finnish Institute for Educational Research, University of Jyväskylä. His main research interests focus on academic work, disciplinary cultures and identities, and social theory of higher education.

1
Introduction: How Is Change in Higher Education Managed?

Bjørn Stensaker, Mary Henkel,
Jussi Välimaa & Cláudia S. Sarrico

It is an understatement to argue that the previous two decades have been characterized by an interest in reform and change of higher education. It is thus difficult to find an area of the sector that has not been exposed to policy initiatives aimed not only at changing the surrounding structures, but also at the ways in which teaching and research are organized and function. Reform initiatives have been taken at the supra-national level (exemplified by the Bologna Process in Europe), at the national level and at the institutional level (Gornitzka et al., 2005).

However, the studies conducted so far provide mixed evidence with respect to the impact of all these initiatives at the shop-floor level of higher education. Without doubt, it is not hard to find evidence of change in the way that higher education system study programmes are structured and organized, in the way that governance arrangements are different from before and in the way that new funding systems influence the behaviour of universities and colleges. Most noticeable, perhaps, is the build-up of new forms of accountability, pushed by the growing numbers of ranking lists and performance indicator schemes (e.g. see Kehm & Stensaker, 2009). Moreover, increased institutional autonomy has contributed to more strategic institutions, resulting sometimes in mergers, new collaborative initiatives and much more internationally oriented institutions. Available macro-data also show that productivity and performance of higher education at the system level is increasing in a number of countries, not least in research-intensive universities (Halffman & Leydesdorff, 2010).

While 'change' in the sector can indeed be said to be easily identified, this does not mean that the impact and outcomes of the 'changes' are equally easy to explain. For example, although the Bologna Process has indeed contributed to change in the study structure and the ways in which quality assurance is conducted in many countries, there is scarce evidence that new study structures or quality assurance processes have radically changed the fundamental ways that teaching and learning is conducted (Witte, 2006). Studies of reform attempts that aim to change governance structures within higher education systems, and within institutions, also indicate that structural reforms do not always contribute to changing the behaviour of academics (Maassen, 1996; Henkel, 2000). Hence, while performance of the sector may have improved, one still faces some challenges in explaining how 'change' takes place at the institutional level and what the consequences of these changes are in universities and colleges (Sarrico et al., 2010).

The themes and content of this book

The current book addresses the challenge of explaining change by employing a threefold strategy. In the first section of the book we problematize and discuss in more depth how we can and should understand the concept of 'change' in higher education. As suggested above, change is a broad and multifaceted concept that goes beyond mere political initiatives and reform attempts to transform higher education. Change also includes the more organic developments in higher education that are triggered by both extrinsic and intrinsic factors, such as demography, technological breakthroughs, globalization, disciplinary developments and how knowledge is organized within the university. As pointed out by Guy Neave in Chapter 2, 'change' can sometimes be unexpected – even for politicians – and brings with it a certain dynamic – changes caused by previous changes – that is part of the explanation for why we currently seem to face a constant stream of new political initiatives and measures trying to keep up with the whole process. How we should – on this basis, and from a more methodological perspective – understand and analyse the concept of change is the theme addressed in Chapter 3. Here, Taina Saarinen and Jussi Välimaa briefly review different ways in which the concept of change has been addressed in previous research. They point out that we may apply different perspectives for grasping and describing change before arguing that we also need to examine critically how 'change' itself can be exposed to discursive power games. Hence, to understand the impacts of changes, we should also bear in mind the ideological power related to 'change' as a concept.

In the Part II of the book, our intention is to provide a broad coverage of areas in which 'change' has occurred within higher education and how we can interpret and understand the impact of these changes. This part starts by analysing how new administrative and managerial tools are taken up by the institutions. In Chapter 4, Nicoline Frølich and Bjørn Stensaker study the ways in which higher education institutions are adapting to expectations of behaving more like strategic actors. In the following chapter, Cláudia Sarrico and Ana Melo analyse another novel tool in the university – that of performance measurement– and discuss whether the characteristics of such processes can be said to relate to the central characteristics of academic work. Chapters 6 and 7 focus on yet another modern driver for change in higher education – quality and quality assurance. In Chapter 6, Sónia Cardoso takes a closer look at how students perceive quality assurance and whether such instruments change their attitudes and values with respect to student learning. In the next chapter, Maria J. Rosa and Alberto Amaral develop this issue further to look at academic staff and discuss whether there actually is a bridge between being engaged in quality work and being exposed to more formal quality assurances processes. Keeping the focus on the academic staff, in Chapter 8, Amy Scott Metcalfe sets out to examine how we can understand and provide meaning to changes in the research culture of higher education. Finally, in Chapter 9, we take an in-depth look at how academic identities are tackling turbulent times in higher education. Here, Mary Henkel provides a sweeping overview of developments carrying continuity, change and ambiguity, and how academic identities are evolving as a result. Some common denominators of the contributions in this part of the book are questions challenging our – often intuitive – assumptions of how we should understand change in the specific areas addressed, but also that the effects of the changes that have taken place can be quite surprising and unexpected. A core message coming out of all the chapters in this section is that change is an open-ended process – and that this process carries with it both threats and opportunities.

In the final part of our book, we turn to what can be said to be more 'pro-active' contributions for dealing with change. Our starting point for this section is that the ambivalence and ambiguity associated with the changes taking place within the sector can be seen as potential room for manoeuvre by those wanting to cater for the central values and norms of higher education. Hence, a more optimistic picture is offered as to how higher education can play a more prominent and distinct role when exposed to change processes which academics only have partial control over. In Chapter 10, Keijo Räsänen argues against the belief that change in higher education can only be externally initiated. Instead, it is suggested that a renewed focus on academic practices can address many of the issues the sector is confronted with by more critical voices. In a similar vein, Kerstin Sahlin, in the following chapter, suggests that the constant flow of externally driven organizational trends can be translated into functional and relevant concepts in higher education, but that this is very much dependent on the capability for translation and subtle leadership skills. The latter point is also underlined in the final chapter of this section, in which David Dill critically examines the current conditions for upholding what we – for lack of a better word – can call the 'glue' of higher education: the ideals of collegiality, but perhaps more importantly, the integrity of academic work.

The unpredictability and ambiguity of reform attempts

Hence, while change certainly takes place in higher education, it is also easy to identify many initiatives to manage change at the institutional level. As noticed in a number of the contributions to the book, such attempts to manage change are often characterized by a high degree of instrumentality and intention, as a carefully planned and highly organized process of instigating reform within the institutions. Hence, in modern universities the capability of reforming themselves can be said to have increased considerably in recent decades. It has been argued that the university is no longer a 'republic of scholars', but is steadily being transformed into an organizational actor, fully capable of behaving more strategically within the emerging higher education 'market' (Bonaccorsi et al., 2010). Part of the reason for this is related to a systematic build-up of analytical and organizational capacity for organizing and implementing internal reform through increased professionalization (Gornitzka et al., 1998), centralization (Stensaker, 2003) and other developments in governance arrangements (Sarrico, 2010). While this development certainly can be labelled as a distinct 'reform' of the university, the prime ambition is still that such 'first-order' reforms should only pave the way for 'second-order' reforms – in which teaching, research and innovative capacity should also be transformed.

However, as institutions with the purpose of organizing knowledge, universities have for centuries demonstrated their ability for persistence and path-dependency. There are several factors that contribute to this emphasis on continuity. First, reform attempts always carry an element of unpredictability, especially in organizations that have as their prime purpose the development, provision, but also questioning, of knowledge. As Weick (1976) and others have pointed out, universities are – even in a more streamlined design – organizations where much authority is decentralized and with very powerful individuals. Reforming such organizations is not only about changing formal structures, but also about mindsets and the values of individuals.

Second, since universities are organized around knowledge, the knowledge basis for reform ideas tends to be questioned and discussed in the same way as other knowledge domains. Hence, reform ideas concerning 'quality', 'autonomy' or 'internationalization' will often be confronted with a critical attitude by those affected, questioning the logic and arguments provided in favour of reform. In other words, changing mindsets and values of individuals is not a straightforward task.

Third, even when reform ideas are accepted they still have to be implemented and there is much research pointing out that ideas might be transformed as they are translated (Czarniawska & Joerges, 1996) or edited (Sahlin-Andersson, 1996) to fit with the specificities of a given organization or a particular reform setting. Such processes often open up the original ideas to new interpretations and new meanings that can sometimes create ambiguity and paradoxical situations.

The common denominator underlying all of these arguments is that in order to understand the conditions for reform we need to understand better the intangible aspects of the university (Dill, 1982) and the role this dimension plays during reform. In other words, we need to understand better the role culture and identity play during reform.

Culture – change promoter or change preventer?

The intangible aspects of higher education have for several decades been an important object of study in the sector (see Välimaa, 1995; Maassen, 1996, for an overview). Some of the classical studies in the field address how higher education institutions have developed certain cultural characteristics and traits that have made them unique compared to others and how cultural characteristics have also made these institutions more effective and relevant to society (Clark,1970; 1972).

Burton Clark's interpretation of culture was rooted in the belief that norms and values of the organization were embedded in an almost seamless way, connecting structure and culture, and making the organization into an institution in itself (see Selznick, 1957). Hence, in this version culture was understood as something 'real' and 'deep'. This tradition can be said to belong to a Durkheimian perspective where individual behaviour aggregates into a holistic and institutionalized organizational entity. The development of such a specific culture was believed to take time and although there certainly could be influential individuals making an impact on the direction of the organization, change was seen mainly as a collective effort in which incremental actions, history and traditions played a vital role. This way of interpreting culture can be said to characterize the analysis conducted by Clark throughout his career. In one of his latest contributions to the field, he wrote:

> Organizational culture is the realm of the ideas, beliefs and asserted values, the symbolic side of the material component [...] Always ephemeral, often wispy to the touch, it escapes easy empirical identification. But it is there.
>
> (2004, p. 177)

However, this conception of culture is not the only one dominating the literature. Attempting to create an overview of the whole area of organizational culture in higher education, Tierney (1988, p. 8) suggested that those interested in analysing culture should pay particular attention to certain elements within an organization and among these, missions, strategies and leadership. While these elements are far from the only ones Tierney mentioned influencing the organizational culture, the identification of such elements make strong hints that organizational culture is closely intertwined with and influenced by formal structure and hierarchy. This implies a conception that change can be strongly affected by rational action and decision-making, and is dependent on how one uses organizational resources to implement these processes:

> administrators will be in a better position to change elements in the institution that are at variance with the culture.
>
> (Tierney, 1988, p. 19)

This conception of organizational culture can also be found, to some extent, in the 'Quality Culture' project of the European Universities Association (EUA), a project that ran between 2002 and 2006. The quality culture project can be regarded as a spin-off from the Bologna Process with its emphasis on quality assurance and was instigated by the EUA with economic support from the European Commission (EUA, 2006). While the formal description of the project emphasized its bottom-up approach in which the higher education institutions and those working within these institutions should have a voice and be invited to engage in discussions on how to 'establish a quality culture' (EUA, 2006, p. 4), the project also has a clear instrumental side. For example, the quality culture project should increase awareness of the need to develop an internal quality culture in universities, ensure the wide dissemination of existing best practices in the field and promote the introduction of internal quality management. What this suggests is that a culture can be 'introduced', it can be copied and transferred to another setting – processes that imply that it is even 'manageable'.

Hence, in principle, one can argue that the classical divide between these two conceptions is rooted in their views about how changes occur and to what extent culture is open for manipulation – whether culture is 'manageable'. Is it 'deep' and inseparable from the organization in question or is it an 'attachment' to the organization, an element that can be changed in a more instrumental way?

In posing these questions, studies in higher education echo similar debates within other disciplinary fields studying culture. Thus, since the 1980s studies of culture in organizations have often been divided into two basic camps (Alvesson & Berg, 1992): on the one side, those seeing culture as something an organization *has*, that is, culture as a potentially identifiable and manipulative factor; on the other side, those seeing culture as something an organization *is*, that is, culture as an integrated product of social interaction and organizational life, impossible to differentiate from other factors. In the latter version, culture is an integrated dimension of (most often) sociological and anthropological research into social behaviour. In the former version, culture is emphasized as the new organizational instrument by reformers, consultants and management gurus – sometimes because they had simply 'run out of specifics' (Kogan, 1999, p. 64). According to Maurice Kogan, a long-time observer of higher education, culture often became the umbrella term for all possible intangible factors in organizational life.

At this point, it is tempting to argue that within higher education, the two conceptions have continued to live separate lives. While the conception of culture that *is* organization has continued to inspire academic research, emphasizing pluralism with respect to acknowledging the importance of disciplinary culture, academic cultures, and professional and academic identities (see Välimaa & Ylijoki, 2008; Gordon & Whitchurch, 2010), for some recent contributions, the example from the EUA project suggests that the belief that an organization *has* culture still dominates the political realm and the reform agenda in many countries with its emphasis on the need to change the functioning of higher education. The interest in culture as an instrument for improving organizational performance is still a dominant theme in many policy-statements on the need for reform and change in higher education

(Maassen & Olsen, 2007). In essence, the general message is that values and norms in an organization have a substantial role in securing the interest of shareholders or stakeholders in making a profit or enhancing organizational survival and that such values and norms are 'manageable' (e.g. Stratton, 2006).

Taking one step back, one could easily agree with the argument that those advocating a cultural and more symbolic perspective for understanding social and organizational behaviour are reacting against the functionalist (and political) neglect of how rationalist meaning is constructed in modern societies (Pondy et al., 1983). If our assumption is correct in that different conceptions of culture have different stakeholders, it is perhaps not surprising that culture also is a controversial issue during reform. While those advocating reform tend to see culture as an element preventing the needed change in the sector, those opposing reform tend to see culture as an element promoting inherent values and norms for the sector – which must be nurtured despite any reform attempts. In this politicized environment, culture then becomes the dependent variable for those advocating reform, while it is seen as an independent variable by those opposing it.

From culture to identity, and beyond

Although the previous section almost portrays research on organizational culture as a stalemate between two extreme positions, more recent developments can be seen as a valuable attempt to overcome this dichotomy. Not least, studies in organizational symbolism (Alvesson & Berg, 1992) and organizational identities (Czarniawska & Sevón, 1996) have been important and led to the establishment of new arenas for more interdisciplinary and cognitive approaches to the notions of culture where the distinction between the two categories (*having* or *being*) has become increasingly blurred (e.g. see Schultz et al., 2000).

In an attempt to find a concept that incorporates such cognitive changes in higher education, Välimaa (1995; 1998) and Henkel (2000) have suggested that 'identity' may be a promising concept, not least in that it can be used to build a bridge between structure and actor, between the policy context, the institution, the profession, the discipline and the individual academic (Henkel, 2000, p. 22). This integrating capability of the concept of identity is of special interest for our book, which aims to analyse how universities and colleges, units within these institutions and also individuals are all trying to make sense of and cope with external demands at the same time as they are faithful to the values and norms they believe in. In principle, one can distinguish between two types of identities: those related to the organization or an organizational unit and those related to the individual person.

Academic identity

These two identities are related to each other because they can combine structural elements (higher education institutions) with individual conceptions of self. Academic identities can be described as belonging to post-industrial or post-modern identity construction, which may be described as a process based on dialogue where the development and change of identity is based on continuous dialogue with significant others (Taylor, 1991). Quite naturally these significant others may change during a lifetime even though the questions 'Who am I?', 'Where do I belong?' structure our self-understanding throughout our lifetime whether we like it or not (see also Sennett, 2006). The same is true with academic identities, which may be described as interactive processes between an individual and various significant others. These reference groups can be disciplinary-based communities (national and international colleagues), professional communities (colleagues and/or professional organizations in one's own institution and/or at the national level), institutional-level communities (colleagues from other departments), institutional traditions (like organizational sagas or institutional memories) and national culture (as a reference group: friends, relatives). In addition to these significant others we also would like to emphasize the role of intellectual traditions in the making of academic identities, even though they cannot always be identified as persons or as reference groups. These different epistemic traditions may have strong influence on the ways academics see the world, how they define relationships between human beings and what they see as important things in life. Translated into disciplinary cultures these epistemic traditions have influence on ways of organizing academic work (teaching and research), communicating with other academics (through publications and/or face-to-face communication) and defining principles for practical matters, such as academic leadership. In other words, disciplinary-based cultural assumptions and values often translate into actions and processes in universities. However, a crucial matter in the interplay with different academic significant others is the fact that, depending on the reform or change concerned, these groups may also, and do, change (see Välimaa, 1998). Academic identities, then, can have multiple starting points for either supporting or resisting changes – or both of them simultaneously – in higher education, depending on how the reforms are defined and what their objectives are.

Organizational identities

The concept of identity has also been used for the analysis of cultural change at the institutional level. As a starting point, organizational identity can be defined as collectively held perceptions and beliefs about the distinctiveness of a given organization (Albert & Whetten, 1985). As such, organizational identity can be regarded as one of several possible cultural artefacts in an organization (Alvesson & Berg, 1992; Hatch & Schultz, 1997) and has in recent years attracted renewed interest both within organizational studies in general (Weick, 1995; du Gay, 1996; Whetten & Godfrey, 1998; Albert et al., 2000; Gioia et al., 2000) and in higher education studies more particularly (Välimaa, 1995; Stensaker, 2004).

Indicating that organizational identity is one of several possible cultural artefacts in an organization suggests that it is a narrower concept than, for example, organizational culture. While conventional definitions of the latter often highlight that organizational culture can be managed and manipulated, resulting in changes in the collective behaviour of the members of the organization (Alvesson & Berg, 1992), a provisional definition of organizational identity would emphasize the symbolic, mythological and cognitive sides of the organization. The construction of organizational reality through the use of symbols and myths that blur the distinction between truth and lies is important here (Strati, 1998, p. 1380). In other words, organizational identity should be understood as a socially constructed concept of what the organization is, rather than how it acts. This does not mean that behaviour is unimportant. Symbols and myths may interact in numerous ways with organizational behaviour (Pondy et al. , 1983). The point is that a focus on organizational identity is more interested in how organizations are constructed as meaningful entities. The focus is not so much on how people act as on how they try to make sense of their actions (through the use of cognition, symbols, language and emotions).

Henkel (2000, p. 22) has pinpointed the danger of this position by claiming that, as a consequence, analysis may ignore the reality of academic working lives and instead overemphasizes the influence of abstract epistemologies, symbols and language. However, what a focus on organizational identity does is acknowledge that symbols, myths and language exert great social power in that they stimulate fresh ideas, change attitudes and provide new cognitive frames for action (Scott, 1995, p. 129).

Focusing on organizational identity can also be particularly beneficial when studying change processes in general. Organizations are never 'frozen' entities, they move and change constantly. In complex organizations, such as higher education institutions, changes can also occur in contradictory and diffuse ways, where the direction and meaning of the change process can be difficult to identify. By emphasizing organizational identity, pinpointing change can be easier as the identity concept provides a lens where the 'essential' elements in these change processes are distilled.

If organizational identity describes what the organization is, then the consequence is that identity would be understood as something 'real' and 'deep' and as an expression of the true 'self' of a given organization. This tradition can be said to belong to a Durkheimian perspective where individual behaviour aggregates into a holistic and institutionalized organizational entity. As such it links the organizational identity concept to more conventional understandings of organizational culture emphasizing values, norms and behaviour. As already noted, Burton Clark is a consistent representative of this perspective in higher education research (Clark, 1970; 1972; 2004).

Interestingly, it was also a higher education setting that triggered Stuart Albert and David Whetten to develop their interpretations of the organizational identity concept in the 1980s (Albert & Whetten, 1985). As business administration professors involved in a cutback operation at the University of Illinois, they experienced the financial strain in their own university as marginal compared to cutbacks in the industrial sector. The university was not planning to shut down departments, reduce the number of faculty or downsize core academic programmes. Still, the proposed cutbacks triggered internal discussions on whether the university could maintain its profile as a research institution if a few programmes were reduced and heated debates were initiated on whether university legitimacy had been lost. In other words, what seemed to be a marginal budget cut by state legislators, escalated into a full-blown identity crisis for the university.

That event formed the basis for the article 'Organisational Identity' in which Albert and Whetten (1985) proposed that the type of commitment shown by the faculty was rather fundamental. The questions asked at the institutional level were those such as 'Who are we?' and 'What sort of organization is this?' – questions closely related to religious beliefs. At least the observations could not be reduced to factors such as distress, anger or incredulity (Albert, 1998, p. 2). Rather, the factors that seemed to influence the university debate were those of affection, emotions and search for meaning – summed up in what they termed organizational identity – a form of uniqueness related to the university. In trying to generalize from their case study, Albert and Whetten (1985) suggested that this uniqueness consisted of three aspects: (1) central character, (2) temporal continuity and (3) distinctiveness. The first notion – central character – distinguishes the organization on the basis of something important and essential. Temporal continuity means that the identification includes features that exhibit some degree of sameness or continuity over time and distinctiveness implies a classification that identifies the organization as recognizably different from others.

However, Stensaker (2004) has argued that organizational identity may be a much more fluid concept than usually conceived. The argument is that organizational identity is dependent on the degree of consistency between the image of a given organization (the view from the significant others) and the identity of the organization (traditions and historical values and norms constructing self). If there is too much divergence between the image and the identity of an organization, the organization will try to bridge this gap. The process that enables bridges to be built is based on the fact that organizational identities are expressed as specific labels ('being entrepreneurial', 'modern' and so on) and that change takes place as the meanings of these labels are translated or re-interpreted over time to fit external demands and expectations (Stensaker, 2004, p. 211). Thus, in order to obtain legitimacy from the environment, organizations compose themselves into a whole (Czarniawska, 2000, p. 273). An implication is that the organization then becomes a metaphor – a 'super-person' who 'exposes' an identity (Czarniawska & Sevón, 1996). Instead of a conception of identity emerging from deep inside the organization, identity is rather located in the formal structure and becomes a 'chameleon-like imitation of images prevailing in the post-modern marketplace' (Gioia et al., 2000, p. 72). Hence, organizational identity is transformed from a stable, distinct and enduring characteristic to a more fluent and more easily changeable organizational entity.

Beyond identity

While we would argue that the concept of identity is vital in improving our understanding of how higher education is changing, one could still criticize the emphasis on identity as focusing too much on the cultural aspects of organizational life – once again ignoring the structural dimensions. In general the latter focus is well covered in recent contributions on changing governance, funding and quality assurance structures being implemented in the sector (e.g. see Amaral et al., 2003; Teixeira et al., 2004; Gornitzka et al., 2005). What has received less coverage is how the manifestations of the new structures are culturally interpreted in the sector. In other words, what is the meaning given to new practices and procedures, and how are new rules and routines culturally embedded and translated into universities and colleges? To research such questions we need to dig into the micro-processes of academic life.

A culture-as-practice approach to organizational change

In recent years and much inspired by research in the sociology of science (Knorr Cetina, 2007), one can witness a renewed interest for more anthropological and ethnographic inspired studies within the social sciences. Some examples are the interest in analysing institutional work within neo-institutional theory (Lawrence et al., 2009), the emphasis on studying strategy-as-practice in the field of management (Whittington, 2006) or the use of the concept of epistemic cultures in the sociology of knowledge (Knorr Cetina, 2007). Even in higher education, some empirical studies have been conducted in which strategic processes have been analysed more closely (Jarzabkowski, 2005).

The common denominator for all these contributions is an attempt to identify and investigate the 'machineries of knowledge construction' (Knorr Cetina, 2007, p. 363). Such machineries contain not only social structures, but also material structures such as technology, budgetary and evaluation arrangements and requirements, or managerial tools (performance and management information systems). While such material structures are often seen as 'technical' arrangements to which culture and identity is attached, we agree with Knorr Cetina (2007) in that culture and identity is an integrated part of how the social and material structure is constituted through practice. In this process, we are in particular focusing on how those working in universities and colleges manage and try to control their lives, and how in doing this they also contribute to change and influence the realities they are facing. As Emirbayer and Mische (1998, p. 962) have pointed out, human agency can be described as a temporally embedded process of social engagement, informed by the past, but also oriented towards the future (as a 'projective' capacity to imagine alternative possibilities) and towards the present (as a 'practical-evaluative' capacity to contextualize past habits and future projects within the contingencies of the moment).

We would argue that such an understanding of agency combined with a careful consideration of the surrounding social and material structures at the micro-level is well equipped to analyse how reform is managed in higher education. As such, in this book we are more interested in addressing and uncovering the dynamic, mediatory and interactive role of culture than in portraying it just as either a preventive or promotional force during reform.

References

Albert, S. (1998) 'The Definition and Meta-definition of Identity', in Whetten, D. A. & P. C. Godfrey (eds), *Identity in Organizations. Building Theory Through Conversations*. London: Sage Publications.

Albert, S., B. E. Ashforth & J. E. Dutton (2000) 'Organizational Identity and Identification: Charting New Waters and Building New Bridges', *Academy of Management Review*, 25, pp. 13–17.

Albert, S. & D. A. Whetten (1985) 'Organizational Identity', *Research in Organizational Behavior*, 7, pp. 263–295.

Alvesson, M. & P. O. Berg (1992) *Corporate Culture and Organizational Symbolism*. New York: Walter de Gruyter.

Amaral, A., L. Meek & I. M. Larsen (2003) *The Higher Education Managerial Revolution?* Dordrecht: Kluwer Academic Press.

Bonaccorsi, A., D. Cinzia & A. Geuna (2010) 'Universities in the New Knowledge Landscape: Tensions, Challenges, Change – An Introduction', *Minerva* 48: 1–4.

Clark, B. R. (1970) *The Distinctive College*. Chicago: Aldine.

Clark, B. R. (1972) 'The Organizational Saga in Higher Education', *Administrative Science Quarterly*, 17, pp. 178–184.

Clark, B. R. (2004) *Sustaining Change in Universities. Continuities in Case Studies and Concepts*. Berkshire: Open University Press.

Czarniawska, B. (2000) 'Identity Lost or Identity Found? Celebration and Lamentation over the Postmodern View of Identity in Social Science and Fiction', in Schultz, M., M. J. Hatch & M. Holten Larsen (eds), *The Expressive Organization. Linking Identity, Reputation and the Corporate Brand*. Oxford: Oxford University Press.

Czarniawska, B. & B. Joerges (1996) 'Travels of Ideas', in Czarniavska, B. & G. Sevón (eds), *Translating Organizational Change*. Berlin: Walter de Gruyter.

Czarniawska, B. & G. Sevón (1996) *Translating Organizational Change*. New York: Walter de Gruyter.

Dill, D. D. (1982) 'The Management of Academic Culture: Notes on the Management of Meaning and Social Integration', *Higher Education*, 11, pp. 303–320.

du Gay, P. (1996) 'Organizing Identity. Entrepreneurial Governance and Public Management', in Hall, S. & P. du Gay (eds), *Questions of Cultural Identity*. London: Sage Publications.

Emirbayer, M. & A. Mische (1998) 'What Is Agency?' *American Journal of Sociology*, 4, pp. 962–1023.

EUA (2006) *Quality Culture in European Universities: A Bottom-up Approach*. Brussels: European University Association.

Gioia, D. A., M. Schultz & K. G. Corley (2000) 'Organizational Identity, Image and Adaptive Instability', *Academy of Management Review*, 25, pp. 63–81.

Gordon, G. & C. Whitchurch (eds) (2010) *Academic and Professional Identities in Higher Education*. New York: Routledge.

Gornitzka, Å., S. Kyvik & I. M. Larsen (1998) 'The Bureaucratization of Universities', *Minerva*, 36(1), pp. 21–47.

Gornitzka, Å., S. Kyvik & B. Stensaker (2005) 'Implementation Analysis in Higher Education', in Gornitzka, Å., M. Kogan & A. Amaral (eds), *Reform and Change in Higher Education*. Dordrecht: Springer.

Halffman, W. & L. Leydesdorff (2010) 'Is Inequality Among Universities Increasing? Gini Coefficients and the Elusive Rise of Elite Universities', *Minerva*, 48, pp. 55–72.

Hatch, M. J. & M. Schultz (1997) 'Relations Between Organizational Identity and Image', *European Journal of Marketing*, 31, pp. 356–365.

Henkel, M. (2000) *Academic Identities and Policy Change in Higher Education*. London: Jessica Kingsley Publishers.

Jarzabkowski, P. (2005) *Strategy as Practice. An Activity-Based Approach*. Sage: London.

Kehm, B. & B. Stensaker (eds) (2009) *University Rankings, Diversity, and the New Landscape of Higher Education*. Rotterdam: Sense Publishers.

Knorr Cetina, K. (2007) 'Culture in Global Knowledge Societies: Knowledge Cultures and Epistemic Cultures', *Interdisciplinary Science Reviews*, 32, pp. 361–375.

Kogan, M. (1999) 'The Culture of Academe', *Minerva*, 37, pp. 63–74.

Lawrence, T., R. Suddaby & B. Leca (eds) (2009) *Institutional Work*. Cambridge: Cambridge University Press.

Maassen, P. A. M. (1996) *Governmental Steering and the Academic Culture. The Intangibility of the Human Factor in Dutch and German Universities*. Enschede: CHEPS, University of Twente.

Maassen, P. & J. P. Olsen (2007) *University Dynamics and European Integration*. Dordrecht: Springer.

Pondy, L. R., P. J. Frost, G. Morgan & R. M. James (1983) *Organizational Symbolism*. Greenwich: JAI Press.

Sahlin-Andersson, K. (1996) 'Imitating by Editing Success: The Construction of Organizational Fields', in Czarniavska, B. & G. Sevón (eds), *Translating Organizational Change*. Berlin: Walter de Gruyter.

Sarrico, C. S. (2010) 'On Performance in Higher Education: Towards Performance Governance?', *Tertiary Education and Management*, 16, pp. 145–158.

Sarrico, C. S., M. J. Rosa, P. N. Teixeira & M. F. Cardoso (2010) 'Assessing Quality and Evaluating Performance in Higher Education: Worlds Apart or Complementary Views?', *Minerva*, 48, pp. 35–54.

Schultz, M., M. J. Hatch & M. Holten Larsen (eds) (2000) *The Expressive Organization. Linking Identity, Reputation and the Corporate Brand*. Oxford: Oxford University Press.

Scott, W. R. (1995) *Institutions and Organizations*. Thousand Oaks: Sage Publications.

Selznick, P. (1957) *Leadership in Administration. A Sociological Interpretation*. New York: Harper & Row.

Sennett, R. (2006) *The Culture of the New Capitalism*. New Haven: Yale University.

Stensaker, B. (2003) 'Trance, Transparency and Transformation: The Impact of External Quality Monitoring in Higher Education', *Quality in Higher Education*, 9(2), pp. 151–159.

Stensaker, B. (2004) *The Transformation of Organizational Identities*. Enschede: CHEPS, University of Twente.

Strati, A. (1998) 'Organizational Symbolism as a Social Construction: A Perspective from the Sociology of Knowledge', *Human Relations*, 51, pp. 1379–1402.

Stratton, R. (2006) *The Earned Value Management Maturity Model*. Vienna: Management Concepts.

Taylor, C. (1991) *The Ethics of Authenticity*. Cambridge, Mass.: Harvard University Press.

Teixeira, P., B. Jongbloe, D. D. Dill & A. Amaral (2004) *Markets in Higher Education. Rhetoric or Reality?*. Dordrecht: Kluwer Academic Publishers.

Tierney, W. (1988) 'Organizational Culture in Higher Education: Defining the Essentials', *Journal of Higher Education*, 59, pp. 2–12.

Välimaa, J. (1995) 'Higher Education Cultural Approach', *Studies in Education, Psychology and Social Research*, 113, Jyväskylä: University of Jyväskylä.

Välimaa, J. (1998) 'Culture and Identity in Higher Education Research', *Higher Education*, 36, pp. 119–138.

Välimaa, J. & O-H. Ylijoki (eds) (2008) *Cultural Perspectives on Higher Education*. Dodrecht: Springer.

Weick, K. E. (1976) 'Educational Organizations as Loosely Coupled Systems', *Administrative Science Quarterly*, 21, pp. 1–19.

Weick, K. E. (1995) *Sensemaking in Organizations*. London: Sage Publications.

Whetten, D. A. & P. C. Godfrey (eds) (1998) *Identity in Organizations. Building Theory Through Conversations*. London: Sage Publications.

Whittington, R. (2006) 'Completing the Practice Turn in Strategy', *Organization Studies*, 27, pp. 613–634.

Witte, J. K. (2006) *Change of Degrees and Degrees of Change: Comparing Adaptations of European Higher Education Systems in the Context of the Bologna Process*. Enschede: CHEPS, University of Twente.

Part I
How to Make Sense of Change

2
Change, Leverage, Suasion and Intent: An Historical Excursion Across Three Decades of Change in Higher Education in Western Europe

Guy Neave

Introduction

In love and war, so the Ancient Romans held, *'Fortes fortuna adiuvat'* – Fortune favours the brave. Hopefully, this millennial adage is just as applicable to the study of higher education in general and, more particularly, to those hardy souls who elect to study change in higher education and its management. To continue for a moment in the world of the Classics – mythology this time – there is no topic more protean than change nor so central to our understanding the present condition of higher education and, for that matter, how it got to be in its present pass. For those untouched by the curse of a semi-classical upbringing, let me introduce an obscure metaphor, which is not inappropriate to studying change.

Proteus was a second order deity in the Greek Pantheon. In the Greek league tables of divine repute, he was a *Demiurge*, an entity somewhat beneath the gods in divine social standing. Proteus' principle feature was his ability, like change itself, to shift his shape. This he would do to avoid giving a clear answer to any question an importunate Mortal happened to pose him. If, however, the Mortal gripped him fast despite his wriggling and shifting shape, on the third time of asking, Proteus would finally tell the truth. Yet, it was not bravery he rewarded. Like scholarship, and very certainly when it comes to the study of how change has been managed in higher education, it is persistence and tenacity that are necessary, if one is to have even the slightest hint of a reward.

Proteus replies

In this chapter, at the risk of being as elusive as Proteus himself, I will highlight a number of themes and dimensions that serve to 'set the outer bounds' of our basic 'problématique', namely, change and its management. In tackling this, I will attend first of all to certain immediate and contextual aspects of change in higher education, with the purpose of providing some handle over the scale and the often seismic nature of the forces at work. I will do so by examining three themes: the dislocation of time and place in higher education, the globalization of the nation state and the collapse of Keynesianism with the subsequent rush of governments to clasp neo-liberalism to their bosom and to tighten that embrace through an instrumentality commonly alluded to as New Public Management.

As scholars engaged in dissecting change, ours, however, is a delicate position for we cannot deny that what we are studying also affects us, just as change also summons up different disciplines and scholarly cannons to tease out why higher education developed as it did, how it developed and what its consequences were – or still are, for that matter – for our own house. What we study and how we study it cannot be excluded from the very process we are studying. From this it follows that careful attention ought to be paid to the historiography of higher education studies as an equally significant, but all too often disregarded, component in the disciplinary dynamic of how managing change is understood, interpreted and presented. How has change at the macro and systems levels of higher education born down on the dynamic and fate of the fields and disciplines that explore and analyse what is fashionably alluded to today as 'the higher education enterprise'? This is no less important, if only to gain some purchase over how change has impinged on the tools of our scholarship just as it has transformed the object of our study.

Having set out the broad themes to what has altered in higher education and in its cannons of scholarship, in the third part this chapter returns to two transversal leitmotifs identified in the first part – dislocation in time and change in change. If we are to grasp the full impact change has currently wrought in higher education, in its place, status, function and identity in the Commonwealth – or Republic – of Learning (Neave, 2002a, pp. 17–35), we need to place it against a backdrop that draws explicitly on a perspective *de longue durée* and one, moreover, which proceeds from that basic and abiding core activity the university has fulfilled from its earliest times – namely, knowledge.

Boldness be our friend

That boldness is needed in addressing this topic is a banality of the highest degree, for the history of the past three decades can be written and rewritten within the boundaries of this single word – change. Indeed, to do so diminishes neither the subtlety nor the complexities to be tackled in a single system, let alone across the 27 now involved in the European Union. But for us, as students of higher education that is, those who study it, change – to use that horrid neo-business jargon that has wormed its way into our vocabulary – is singularly 'challenging'. It is singularly challenging not simply because of the evolution in higher education's purpose, in the ways of attaining that purpose and making sure that purpose has been met. It is no less 'challenging' when we consider, for instance, the fundamental shift in paradigm which over the past 30 years has seen higher education shift from its historical location in Europe as part of the political sub-system of nations. (Premfors, 1981; Shils & Daalder, 1981; Olsen, 2008). Today, higher education has been 'relocated'. It is seen as a prime instrument to 'leverage' (another ghastly phrase, this time drawn from the barbarous tongue of traders and stockbrokers) economic development, innovation and to boost national standing as evinced by international tables of performance, productivity, expenditure and output.

Two contending forces

Nor does this seismic shift stop there. There is another. It represents no less a trial by intellectual ordeal for some – though by no means all – who seek to make sense of higher education's rush to what is sometimes termed 'post-modernity'. This second dimension comes in the form of globalization, the power and leverage of which have redrawn – literally – the frontiers, outreach and place of higher education systems just as it has elevated individual universities which, while geographically and physically set down within one nation state, now exercise a 'norm-setting' function and stand as an example for emulation elsewhere.

Even so, one of the more taxing issues that fuel the general dynamic of change is less the move of higher education from the nation to being one of the prime drivers of an 'emerging world economic order', erected around the new faith of neo-liberalism. Rather, this new *Weltanschauung* poses an acute, threefold dilemma before the individual university. First, vis-à-vis both nation and globe, how may it lay down a viable and sustainable balance? Second how is that balance to be defined and operationalized within individual nation state systems of higher education? Third, within such a balance set out at macro level, how may the individual university devise an arrangement for itself that is viable, sustainable and desirable?

These two contending forces – on the one side, the physical location of higher education in a particular state and on the other, the role higher education is held to play in accelerating the international exchange of ideas, effectively non-material capital – in the application of ideas to production thereby creating technological capital – or human capital created through the trained, certified and qualified individuals who in turn generate both intellectual and technological capital – are the catalyst for transforming higher education. These two 'directions of dynamic' – within the nation or out to the globe – are then the prime elements of scale in higher education's present-day crisis, that is, a situation in which decisions can be neither delayed nor avoided. A 'crisis' – in the exact meaning of the term as opposed to its flaccid use as synonymous with 'difficulty' or as a mere moving on from previous practice – marks a powerful moment in 'reshaping' institutional identity. Reshaping institutional identity, as the experience of different European systems of higher education has shown with blinding clarity over the past decade and a half – if not longer in certain specific instances, the United Kingdom (Becher & Kogan, 1991) and the Netherlands (van Vught & Maassen, 1989) – brings equally radical change to the relationships between higher education's 'Constituent Orders' – namely, the academic, administrative and student estates (Neave, 2009, pp.15–35).

Arguably, the intensity of these two pressures varies from one university to another and from one system to another. But such variation in no way detracts from the basic fact that it is rare for either to be utterly absent. These two dimensions – and very certainly so at the present conjuncture of the incessant financial and therefore economic crisis – have a bearing weighty indeed, not merely on the self-perception that systems and individual universities have of themselves. For that very reason, they also exert a formative influence on both institutional identity, whether that identity is conceived in terms of where individual universities stand and are weighed in the scales – national or international – of repute or, in an alternative but no less significant force for shaping institutional cultures, where they would *like* to be.

A very old methodological dilemma

Yet, beneath the broad issues of change and identity – whether the latter applies to the individual university or to the 'cultures' academic, administrative and student that make up the 'institutional fabric' of higher education (Clark & Neave, 1992) – a very old issue raises its head. So old it is that I doubt whether even medieval historians, unless they are also specialists in Theology or the writings of the medieval Schoolmen, will ever have heard of it. But the arcane is not always the irrelevant. And the expansion in the range of scholarly canons employed in studying higher education stands in basic contradiction to that other methodological principle first enunciated by the Franciscan *Gelernter* William of Ockham in the 14th century (1288–c.1348). In the lingua franca of his times, William's principle stated, *'Entia non sunt multiplicanda sine necessitate'*. This has been variously rendered. By philosophers with a methodological bent, it reads 'As many as you may, but as few as you can.' In today's demotic language of the sound bite, William's injunction is somewhat shorter: 'Keep it simple, stupid.'

Both in the selection of what is to be examined, in the choice of variables that allow us to dissect the anatomy of change, identify its key dimensions, characterize systems and institutions, or for that matter the evolution in the disciplines brought to bear on this task, parsimony is the essence of our métier. Yet, given the panoply of disciplinary perspectives on which the study of higher education may draw, we seem to have joyously embarked on the first part of William's principle without always being successful in observing the second.

Changes in methodology and technique as keys in policy shift

That our fields have multiplied, however, has lead to a second trend, in part, I suspect, precisely because we as a scholarly community have maintained such a latitudinarianism, an intellectual eclecticism so great that the Prince, who qua government has for long been our patron, did not always find what we were doing corresponded to his often immediate and specific needs. Why this has been so brooks no easy answer, though it is only fair to point out that the reason for the Prince's moving in on the second part of William's principle 'as few as you can' is itself intimately connected with the phenomenon of change and was spurred on by a combination of developments, some on-going, observed and reasonably predictable, others less so.

Among the more predictable trends – and it remains with us today quite apart from being one of the fundamental forces that was a prime factor in the existence both of our domain and of its intellectual dynamism – is, of course, the massification of higher education. Today, in many of our lands, higher education is moving on towards what the late Martin Trow defined as its 'universal stage' (Trow, 1970, pp. 1–42).

Yet it is not always the predictable trend that influences the way the Prince perceives priorities or, for that matter, policy. Rather the contrary, the experience of the past three decades suggests that it is the *unexpected* which has the Prince dancing on tenterhooks. Of all the events that have shaped both the Prince's perception of what ought to be done – which is a goodly way towards stating how it should be done and who should do it – the onset of economic crisis is among the most potent. From the standpoint of the university or from the standpoint of changes to change itself, two types of crisis have shaped higher education in Western Europe. Economic *prosperity,* as we saw during the 1960s, is no less potent than the prospect of economic down-turn, though on balance, it is probably correct to see the latter as concentrating the princely mind yet more wondrously. It remains to be seen whether our current condition in Europe will be as portentous for higher learning as the break up in Western Europe of the Keynesian consensus was in the course of the 1980s (Neave, 1989, p. 163).

I will leave aside for a moment what is best set in terms of the intellectual history (*Geistesgeschichte*) of the university in Western Europe which emerged in shifts to the university's mission, purpose, (Neave, 2011, pp. 16–35) and its self-perception that both prosperity and the threat to prosperity brought about. The importance of this aspect of change is only with great difficulty under-estimated. For that reason, I will come back to it later. Here I want to pursue a little further a line of thought that is certainly well documented, though not in the context I propose to examine it.

Tickling the cutting edge of Ockham's razor

Neo-liberalism and its operational expression – New Public Management – most certainly overhauled those features and practices that long had served to identify and characterize the individual nation state higher education system in Western Europe. Both had radical consequences for the second part of William of Ockham's proposition. That is to say, its 'cutting edge'. By concentrating on the second part of the maxim, 'as few as you can' – a perspective that took shape around performance indicators – governments introduced a new dimension both for analysing higher education and for making succinct statements about the state of that institution, though in a form very far from being devoid of ambiguity. No student of higher education, and certainly not those who concentrate on the comparative and policy aspects, will bother to contest the significance, place or influence that performance indicators assumed from the early 1990s onward. In saying this and by setting such a chronological frame around the rise of this instrumentality, I am not denying its prior existence. What I am saying, however, is that previously this instrumentality neither possessed nor wielded so central a role. Nor was it so intimately welded into the process of policy-making. By tying indicators to policy, the instrumentality thus forged, refined and continually re-applied, assumed a role key, central and indispensable in determining and actively shaping the change the Prince wished to see amplified, and did so down to the smallest detail.

To parody the well-known aphorism of the Canadian communications guru, Marshal McLuhan, 'the method thus became the message' and a mode of change in its own right. What started off as a technical device to provide a synthetic account of higher education's condition, to register the state of its constituent orders in areas that presented a source of disquiet to the Prince and his servants (cost, efficiency, output, all crucial dimensions to be mastered in time of economic blizzard), moved on to become an instrument for 'steering' policy and setting its priorities.

The terms that describe this construct are legion. Not surprisingly, they reflect the myriad disciplinary perspectives our domain can muster and bring to bear on the same basic issue: 'remote steering' for the adepts of Public Administration (van Vught, 1989); the 'offloading State' for government specialists, or the Evaluative State for philosophers and historians (Henkel, 1991, pp. 121–138; Neave, 1998, pp. 265–284).

From the perspective of the historiography of the study of higher education rather than from the standpoint of the unfolding of higher education policy, the rise of indicators has lent themselves to be interpreted as a bid by national administration to assert a new coherence over the study of higher education by applying the principle of parsimony to those dimensions which, as the domain itself proliferated, the Prince saw as essential to his purposes. To put no finer point on the matter, here is an example of the ambiguous relationship our field has with the Prince, quite apart from the more obvious point that the rise of indicators represents a further stratification within our field between those fields and their attendant knowledge base that seemingly enjoy an officially recognized and enduring utility and those upheld by scholarly curiosity that may from time to time be summoned by the Prince as the spirit, the moment and his interests all move him. In short, regardless of whether such a move was intentionally seen by the Prince as putting our house in order – and personally I do not think he deliberately set out with such intent – this step nevertheless had that effect upon our domain.

Evasion and suasion

I shall not to go into the vexed and never-ending issue of whether indicators are sufficiently sensitive to reflect what those commanding them take to be reality. As one who trained in history, I would simply note that indicators are, to use a French term, simply a *constat* – a statement of condition. They tell us what is. They are rather less forthcoming on answering why. Explanative power is not always their strong point. Still, the mere registration of condition may serve other purposes, not least of which to bring a degree of moral suasion to spur further efforts on to consolidate national achievement or to avoid institutional ignominy. And, as an aside, the injection of moral suasion, as an explicit and inseparable function of indicator driven policy, is yet another example of change in change.

In effect, the injection of moral suasion into indicator-driven procedures is nothing less than imposing on technical methods and statistical procedures an interpretation that serves both a political and an ideological purpose. That purpose in its political dimension is to enforce compliance with national policy. Its ideological facet also serves to embed 'competition' as the basic and predominant value into the institutional fabric of higher education. By so doing, such procedures ensure an enforced rallying of the university around one predominant ethic – competition – as the self-proclaimed value neo-liberalism holds essential to its own perpetuation, apart from the cash nexus.

The alliance through indicators of the technical with the ideological also involves a deliberate concentration upon higher education as a temporally de-contextualized entity. It tends to boost 'short-termism' as an inseparable concomitant of change. Given the historical functions of the university, which I shall develop later, 'short-termism' was a most significant change in what may be described as 'the pace of change', not to mention the consequences the latter has for the behaviour and thus the identity of its Constituent Orders (Henkel, 2007a, pp. 87–99). Nor are the consequences of the drive to the immediate in the change of technique and method as a means of spurring on 'policy change' confined to the university. Rather they reflect a far broader shift in what Op Ed is pleased to call the 'communications society'. Some historians, who by dint of their trade tend to espouse the long-term, describe this fixation with the here and now as opposed to the medium or the long term, as the 'Historical Attention Span Deficit Disorder' – Alzheimer's disease in a bureaucratic form. Interestingly, the first examples of this administrative syndrome have been traced in Britain back to the late 1980s and early 1990s. Nor was it exclusive to higher education. On the

contrary, while seen as a consequence of introducing New Public Management, short-termism also infested some of the more sensitive areas
of the British Civil Service. (Andrew, 2009, pp. 848–849).

The changing university

Having looked broadly at some of the changes in the methods and
shifts in types of analytical purchase our domain has undergone, the
third part of this chapter turns its attention to the changes that have
taken place in the institution of higher education as opposed to the
way it is studied. As I promised earlier, we now move back into the
intellectual history of that institution. There are, however, a few pre-
liminaries to be settled before we can examine the way change in the
university has itself changed. The first of these involves what appears to
many, but not to historians, as an obscure quibbling over dates which
historian's jargon dresses up as 'periodicity', that is, the place in the
chronological framework when crucial shifts in the understanding of
change occurred. The second is a conceptual distinction. It separates
out three processes involved in the mutation of the university. These
are change, adjustment and accommodation. A third has to do with the
sources used to tease out both chronology and concept. Let us tackle
them in reverse order.

Some years ago as the previous millennium drew to its close, I examined all the speeches made at the quinquennial meetings of those
university presidents[1] who were also members of the International Association of Universities over some 50 years between 1950 and the Year of
Grace, 2000. Four dimensions in particular interested me: university values, role and mission, university government and university and society
(Neave, 2000, pp. 9–36). And it is mainly from this study of the view of
university leaders that the remarks that follow are drawn.

The dynamics of change in change

The dynamics of 'the change in change' are akin to those involved
in bankruptcy. They start very slowly. They tend to end very quickly.
The first signs of presidential unease with the issue of change in
higher education emerged around 1970 and continued across the decade
(Neave, 2000). The 1980s, however, mark a second phase with the onset
of a new reform cycle that began with initiatives undertaken in the
Netherlands and Britain, the former in the shape of a national exercise
involving the overhaul of subject provision and institutional reprofiling
in the shape of the report *Schaalvergroting, Taakverdeling en Concentratie*

Wetenschappelijk Onderwijs (1983). It was followed two years later by a second report setting out new terms for university autonomy and quality control (Ministerie van Wetenschappen en Onderwijs, 1985; Maassen, 1987, pp. 161–175). In Britain, what was later to blossom forth as an equally marked overhaul of both the structure of higher education, its funding and quality control, began with swingeing budget cuts in 1981 (Kogan & Kogan, 1983).

Though the second of these two periods is commonly identified with the rise of neo-liberalism, the elaboration of administrative reform in the shape of New Public Management (Pollitt & Bouckaert, 2004) and redefining the relationship between higher education's three Constituent Orders (sometimes couched as the rise of managerialism in the case of the administrative estate or the redefinition of the student estate as 'consumers'), what was no less evident was the recasting of change itself as an on-going, abiding feature and, for higher education, as a non-negotiable principle. Such a reconstruction of higher education as 'responding to the market' profoundly altered both its purpose and the conditions under which that purpose could be pursued. Succinctly put, the purpose of higher education was redefined as 'reactive' – adaptable, flexible and conditional upon meeting the demands of what some labelled in a catch-all of magnificent imprecision as 'external society', others as the 'stakeholder society' (Neave, 2002a, pp. 17–38).

Change, construed as evidence of institutional initiative and enterprise, contains a number of sub-components. These sub-components are neither uniform in the ways they emerge nor in the intensity and pace at which they emerge. In effect, change encompasses two other dynamic processes – Accommodation and Adjustment.

Accommodation and Adjustment

The two concepts of Accommodation and of Adjustment are each of them important and sensitive boundary markers to what Martin Trow, more than a third of a century back, alluded to as the 'public and private lives of academia' (Trow, 1976, pp. 113–127). Taken together, accommodation and adjustment stand as two processes that take place within academia's 'private life'. They form what may be presented as the 'interior dynamic' of change. Their 'interiority' lies in two aspects. First, they are part of that essentially organic evolution that takes place in knowledge and the ways it is organized, a process that the American historian of higher education, Walter Metzger, termed 'subject parturition' (Metzger, 1987), that is, the breaking down of 'disciplinary boundaries' and their re-coalescence, recombination and reorganization around the new knowledge – or knowledge paradigm – that advance brought about. Second, their intensity, take-up and pace are not a function of the disciplines alone, though obviously this varies considerably depending on which individual discipline – or combination of disciplines – one concentrates on. Pace, intensity and take-up are also a function of the place of the university in society and the role it is expected to fulfil.

That the disciplinary dynamic itself has come under scrutiny on the basic assumption that greater responsiveness to outside demands requires new patterns of knowledge organization (Gibbons et al., 1994) is, of course, a clear example of how deeply the imperative of 'meeting change' has penetrated into the heartland of academia. What Trow in the American and British universities of the mid-1970s cast as private appears in certain systems today to be rather less 'private' than it once was.

Accommodation and Adjustment: concepts whose time has come

Since both accommodation and adjustment rest on the distinction Trow drew between academia's 'public and private lives', how far are they either applicable or, for that matter, relevant to other systems of higher education where, for instance, the notion of institutional autonomy did not have the same centrality as it did in say Britain or the USA, systems with which Trow was concerned? As I will argue in a moment, issues that were taken up in these two concepts certainly posed grave problems to university leadership four decades ago, even in those systems where institutional autonomy involved a very different boundary status from its Anglo-Saxon counterpart. In other words, both activities *were* present even in those systems of higher education that, as is still largely the case in mainland Europe, are intimately and formally shaped by legal codification.

There is, however, a further development – and as such it too has no small place in the panoply of change changing. It is inseparable from that trend, as visible in France as it is in Portugal, in the Netherlands or in Norway – to wit, the Prince's gladsome tidings that he is graciously extending the boundaries of institutional self-government, though he has also made abundantly clear that greater institutional latitude will be followed by close monitoring of what his university subjects are up to. Since both accommodation and adjustment take on a new weight as responsibilities are handed off from central national administration to the individual university, there is good reason for suggesting that the analytical value of these two concepts, quite apart from their relevance, is greater today than ever it has been. Rather less clear, however, is whether the strengthening of accommodation and adjustment have the same consequences for institutional self-government across different systems or that they drive in the same direction.

Let me suggest that the difference between Accommodation and Adjustment rests on the following distinction: accommodation sees the university responding *on its own initiative* to external demands and pressures. Adjustment, by contrast, while also an autonomous process involving the university engaging in updating and overhauling its internal administrative, curricular or evaluation procedures, differs slightly but nevertheless significantly from Accommodation. It differs by dint of the university having detected and defined this situation *on its own initiative* and then having taken measures to remedy it again *on its own initiative*. To make matters even plainer, Accommodation involves the university's initiative to respond to issues already identified by outside interests. Adjustment sees the university both identifying those issues and taking the initiative to deal with them.

Issues that abide: a rapid and mercifully short foray into history

In any examination of change, there are always two basic dynamics, though the ravages the 'Historical Attention Span Deficit Disorder' has wrought on the way we construe change today tends to have us contemplating what we are faced with rather than where we have come from. That, *soit dit en passant,* is what 'short-termism' is about. However, what is forgotten in this one-sided perspective is that moving to what we are told the future holds forth – whether a place in the sun or a spot in the pit of decline and fall – have their price. Those who make too much out of this latter point leave themselves open to accusations of being reactionary, *passéiste* or unrepentantly nostalgic. Set against such slights, there is nevertheless an important methodological consideration. It is this: if we are to have the full measure of how far change has propelled us down the path of progress, we need some point of reference. Without it, unlike Neil Armstrong, we can never fully know whether the step we are about to take – or, for that matter, those we have taken – is a small one for man, woman or insect and certainly not whether it is a large one for humanity, the nation or its citizens. In short, without this datum, we are ill-equipped to know whether what has been achieved is banal or truly amazing. That is why the long-term perspective is important.

Autres temps, autres mentalités

As we look at the way presidential opinion perceived what was happening in the university from the early 1970s onward – as a kind of vicarious participant observation of the moment – there are certain features we have to bear in mind. The first is that the elite university was very marginally concerned with change. Rather its basic mission, which had been with it since the earliest days in 12th-century Italy, was the transmission of knowledge and the upholding of a social order (Ruegg, 1992). Only later was 'scientific' as opposed to 'authoritative' knowledge added to its abiding mission. This was the work of the 18th-century Enlightenment (Ben David, 1978). Nor did the impact the Enlightenment had on the university stop there. As Sheldon Rothblatt has pointed out with his customary verve and incisiveness (Rothblatt, 2007), the Enlightenment added further dimensions to the abiding task of the university. Among them, the valuation of knowledge, merit, worth and last, but not least, the advancement, registration and onward transmission of those achievements – intellectual, linguistic, historic, legal, literary and scientific – came in the course of the 19th century to be the bedrock on which the nation set its self-proclaimed identity.

This is not to say that in the absence of change, the universities stagnated, though some of them – even those that later were to figure among 'the best' – were often strangely immobile. One has only to think of Edmund Gibbon's sorrowful description of late 18th-century Oxford or the railings of the young Byron at the goings on of dons and students in his Cambridge college to see that, even two centuries remove, the absence of Adjustment and Accommodation was not always been looked upon with complacency.

Even so, the notion of advancement was largely conceived within a humanistic perspective. The basic intellectual mission of the university was, in the words of that most tedious among clichés, 'to preserve the best of the old along with the best of the new'. The elite university did not preserve the lessons, knowledge and values of the past because they were of the past. Rather it operated a gradual system of *triage*. Knowledge of the past was to be valued not because it was, in the phrase of England's arch conservative, Edmund Burke, 'the wisdom of our ancestors' but because it was knowledge that had retained its appropriateness. It was valued and worth retaining because its survival proved its 'sustainability'. What counted in knowledge lay not its usefulness alone, but the fact that it had withstood the test of time. This mental set, which elsewhere I have called 'the Voices of Constancy' (Neave, 2000, p. 15), owed much to the religious origins of the university. And the university, like the knowledge it handed on, was seen as transcendental. It too had borne up under the test of time.[2] From this it followed that change was organic to the university itself, filtered over the long term rather than being induced externally.

Valuation of knowledge as an abiding task

Several consequences flow from the way knowledge was thus construed as that which had abiding value because it had endured over time; first, not all knowledge has this status; second, knowledge that was to be accorded this standing was wholly a matter for the scholarly; third, that there was no obligation on the university to take account of the wishes of society in those domains held to be coterminous with scholarship and learning. Learning and scholarship were, by definition, the responsibility of the initiated, not the profane. Furthermore, knowledge was fragile. It had to be protected from the things of this world – industrialization not least. If we recall the writings of both John Cardinal Newman (Rothblatt, 1998) and Wilhelm von Humboldt (Nybom, 2003), it was precisely through *Einsamkeit* and *Einigkeit* that the university was able to generate, uphold, advance and sustain intellectual creativity, though neither the Cardinal nor the State Secretary used so anachronistic a phrase.

Thus, behind the modernization of the European university that proceeded throughout the 19th century, principally in its incorporation as a national and as a state supported – and state supporting – institution, a certain continuity with the religious origins of that institution persisted. In persisting, continuity also set down the terms on which change could be admitted. Key to this – and again it is powerful evidence of the hidden continuity of the religious and monastic model that had governed learning for centuries – was intellectual isolation. The university was *in* the world but not *of* it. But above all, only the initiate had sufficient grasp over the corpus of the knowledge they commanded to determine what indeed was worth taking on board and, by the same token, what was not.

Presidents Agonistes

Having briefly laid out the 'value set' of the world we have left, as our datum for the changes that came after, we now return to the issue of how change was perceived by university leadership at the onset of mass higher education in Western Europe. What concerned the presidents of the world's universities – as mayhem and uproar leapt from Berkeley to

Paris, to Berlin and beyond – was not so much the change that mass higher education brought in its wake. What worried them to the point of distraction was change penetrating to the 'private life' of higher education and setting at nought those internal and largely autonomous functions of Accommodation and Adjustment which determined the inner nature of change itself. They had good reason to be agitated. Once these two procedures are no longer within the purlieu and discretion of the university, but are part of the formal administrative procedures attendant upon induced change, who determined inner change was no longer a university concern, but a matter for public policy.

Presidential speeches across ten years and three full presidential meetings of the International Association of Universities revealed a desperate rearguard action to preserve what may be termed 'the humanist paradigm' of the university. It was, however, far more than an obdurate defence of classical languages, literature and history. This outward rhetoric – and rhetoric is the art of persuasion – hid two issues of great sensitivity, namely, the de facto internal control universities exercised over the valuation of knowledge on the one hand and, on the other, their ability ultimately to control the pace of change. Both of these functions were crucial in determining the boundaries and strength of academia's 'private life'. Without this 'domain of discretion', Accommodation and Adjustment which today's jargon, riddled as it is with managerialist terminology, would reduce to 'institutional micro-steering' risked extinction. No less important, such a disappearance would have a long-lasting consequence for the 'private life' of academia and most especially that part of its identity, intimately related to valuating knowledge. Without the continuation of this essential task, the Academic Estate risked reduction to the status of simple producers of knowledge that others prescribed, a phenomenon associated in German with a broader process known as the '*Verschuelung*' of the university (Heldrich, 1966, p. 35). In effect, the debate university presidents sought to engage focused on a crucial issue – one that, over the ensuing decades, was itself to take on an abiding quality. Could the university acting on its own, without external intervention, meet the pressure of external demands for knowledge? Could the university on its own uphold order over innovation and creativity? Could it show there was sufficient will and capacity to accommodate external demands without external intervention.

The demise of one vision of the university

Self-evidently, these were strategically important questions. While they have to do with the changing concept of change, they also mark the closing of another abiding construct and an equally abiding view of both the university and the perception of the knowledge it conveyed. The 1970s marked the consolidation of the mass university. This, however, is the more obvious aspect. There is another dimension involved. That second dimension casts the university as an historical institution, the university as 'the product of the past' and thus a notion of change as a departure from that past, a vision the Forces of Constancy fought might and main across the 1970s to defend.

Their rearguard action did not succeed. Not because their arguments were weak or flaccid. But precisely because of an unpredictable series of events neither they – nor for that matter anyone else without prescience and second sight – could possibly have foreseen: the economic downturn in the late 1970s and subsequent industrial reconstruction of the 1980s that ushered in the Computer Age, the Communications Society, the Knowledge Economy, post-modernism and Mrs Thatcher! The Voices of Constancy faded away, to be replaced with a counter vision that put a very different interpretation on the university's responsibility to society. Other features of that historical construct also went the way of all flesh. Prime among them was that covert 'hold over' which had survived well beyond the first modernization of the European University in the 19th century, namely, the quasi-religious status of knowledge, of knowledge as a 'mystery', to use a very old term indeed. And with it the notion of knowledge as 'sacred', God-given and for that reason to be dispensed as far as was possible *gratis et pro Deo*, a feature the welfare state had willingly taken on, finally expired (Neave, 2006a, pp. 61–76).

Change as distance travelled

Clearly, higher education has moved an immense distance when we set today's agenda against the views, values and arguments that fed debate in the 1970s. Indeed, as with treason, so with change. The extent of the latter, like the depth of the former, as Charles Maurice de Talleyrand-Périgord, regicide and many times France's foreign minister under both Napoleon and the Bourbons, pointed out, 'is simply a matter of dates' (Neave, 2006b). This, however, is not the only issue involved. There is another and it involves direction. What I have termed 'the Voices of Constancy' viewed change as distance already covered, not as distance that has yet to be covered. Their construction of change, though there were notable exceptions, had them looking backwards from the present. Nowadays, I would suggest, the perspective is very different. Change has us – and others – looking forward from the situation as it is at present to what *ought* to be when the change agenda has been implemented. Voices of Change have replaced the Voices of Constancy. With them has come a new eschatology which is no less risky if only because change itself is now associated with urgency (Kosselleck, 2008, pp. 113–134).

This is no less interesting on its own account. It reverses that essential element which earlier served as key to the valuation of knowledge, namely time or, to use a fashionable expression, sustainability as a pointer to worth or appropriateness. If the notion of change as an exercise in *retro*spection rested on the 'test of time' and durability to validate knowledge and the practices to which it gave rise, change as an exercise in *pro*spection rests on precisely the opposite – namely, the shortage of time available or the possibly hideous consequences if too much time is allowed to elapse before the resolute decision is taken. Indeed, it is very precisely the notion of policy as speed and speed as efficiency that underlines the rise of managerialism on the grounds that democratic participation is apparently incompatible with either speed or efficiency. It lies at the heart of the Evaluative State (Neave, 2012), which, through its regular reviews and assessments, is a powerful device to *impose* conditions, standards and productive rhythms on the Academic Estate. Expedition is a generic feature of contemporary policy-making, which itself is but one phase in the heavier, more complex and more protracted process of bringing change about and which extends to 'take-up' and 'embedding' as the subsequent stages through which policy is translated into established practice. These latter are no less part of the overall process of change though rather less attention is paid to them, except when they result in evident and manifest failure – or threat of failure.

Thus, the drive to precipitation stands out as a feature that unites and permeates all the social constructs with which the imagination of the learned and the insightful has supplied us these three decades past, whether dressed up in the guise of globalization, the Knowledge Economy or the Network Society (Kosseleck, 2008). It is also present – how could it not be? – in higher education as a justification in the rhetoric employed to gain acceptability for the 'reform agenda' just as it is also to be seen in the acceleration of what may be described as the estimated time for implementation (ETI) (Neave & Amaral, 2011, p. 10).

Change in pace

There are many examples to illustrate the change in ETI that has taken place over the past three decades or more. In the 1960s, when the drive to mass higher education began, time for reforms envisaged to work their way into the institutional fabric and become 'embedded' – that is, they become routine practice – was in the region of 20 years. A remarkable instance of ETI foreshortened is, of course, the Bologna Process itself which, despite being geographically the most extensive reform ever to have been attempted in the history of the European university, was originally scheduled for completion by 2010, ten years after its signing (Veiga, 2010). And, doubtless many will point out that at national level, ETI tends to be even shorter, often bringing it – or, more to the point, seeking to bring it – into the limits of a single legislature (Neave, 2007, pp. 109–192), so success may be shown to an admiring citizenry.

Haste to implement, the wish instantly to 'embed' what are held up as 'good practices' are, not surprisingly, further evidence of the very curious situation which higher education finds itself engaged in. Certainly, this is change of a very extensive order. But it is also change of a very different nature from the 'organic change' that characterized the elite university. There is some evidence that the best descriptor to apply to it is that of 'enforced change' in which the determination of '*le pays politique*' allied to the instrumentality of control *a posteriori*, whether through funding incentives or through retrospective monitoring, leaves very little latitude to '*le pays réel*' other than a grudging compliance (Santiago et al., 2006). Compliance, however, is very far indeed from wholehearted acceptance, which in turn raises the question of exactly how far in the culture of Academia and its different disciplinary sub-cultures, which among them can be counted upon as trusty servants to the Prince's wish?

ENVOI

This chapter has taken a very broad brush to the 'problematic' of change in higher education. It set out to examine how higher education has, in the words of the venture that brings us together, 'managed change'. Change in these latter days is most certainly all-pervasive, not just in the institution we all study, but also in the various disciplinary perspectives and canons through which we study it. In a curious way, both the institution we study and the ways we do so are shaped by public policy – and public policy, as I have suggested, is itself subject to a speeding up in the pace at which it advances or, to be more circumspect, in the pace at which it hopes advance will be secured. Indeed, if we take a very abstract view of the essential thrust that emerges from the past three decades in our different lands and systems, it is clear as the day is long that one purpose behind the multiplication of what some scholars have termed

'Agencies of Public Purpose' (Henkel, 2007b, p. 1) – whether they deal with accreditation, quality or cash and whether they dwell in the nation state or above it at a European level – is to make sure that the speed of institutional responsiveness is set – where it is not determined – by forces external to the university.

What is evident in this account is change in the 'cadence of change'. This is obvious in the drive towards mass higher education, which in its earlier phases prior to the mid-1980s saw that cadence take the form of an oscillation from steady state to the instability of reform back to steady state. Reform was thus followed by a period of relative quiescence when the university digested and assimilated it before resuming 'the even tenor of its ways' as the impulse of reform settled down and new practices, hopefully good, were rooted in the usual quotidian tasks the university fulfilled. From the early 1990s onwards and at the macro level, this 'stop/go' rhythm mutated into a reiterative cycle of continuous adjustment, occasionally amplified by new initiatives from government, often to correct what earlier national strategy had enacted and which, in the meantime, had revealed unwelcome and perverse effects. The recent British report 'Securing a Sustainable Future for Higher Education: An Independent Review of Higher Education Funding and Student Finance', which appeared in October 2010, had in part the purpose to correct policy introduced four years earlier, though it too had its perverse effects which were more immediate and certainly more lively.

Yet, acceleration in higher education policy-making at the macro level is easily illustrated in concrete terms. It involves plotting at successive five-year intervals the number of official reports dealing with higher education reform at system level brought out by official Commissions, Review Bodies and Enquiries especially and specifically entrusted by government to come up with recommendations. My guess, on the basis of British and Portuguese experience, is that speeding up in the policy process will clearly emerge in the multiplication of such documents, particularly in the period from 2000 onwards.

Having examined change from a long-term perspective, it is not misplaced to conclude that the prospect which arises from both change, and its management – now conceived as continual, reiterative and intertwined processes – is redoubtable. Indeed, it is far from exaggerated to compare the lot of the individual university with the fate that the prophet Isaiah set aside for the Ungodly: 'There is no peace, sayeth The Lord, unto the Wicked' (Isaiah 48: 22) – and precious little for the rest of us.

Notes

1. I shall not go into the discussion about why university presidents are a good compromise between documentary sources and oral history as representatives of their university and their time.
2. An echo of this earlier construct of the university, wholly based on the valuation of the universal in terms of the humanism, which had driven the university from the mid-16th century, is to be found in a presidential speech at the 1960 International Association of Universities' Mexican Conference. For Marcel Bouchard, Rector of the University of Dijon (France):

> The true Humanities demand that journey through space and time that teaches us to recognize in men of another century, another country, another tongue, the eternal basis of human nature and to feel an identity of condition, a spiritual kinship and brotherhood of the soul which unites us to them across the boundaries of States and beyond the tomb.
>
> (Marcel Bouchard [1960] 'The Iinterplay of scientific and cultural values in higher education today', in Neave [2000, pp. 157–169])

Clark Kerr made a similar point in his famous Godkin Lecture of 1964 'The Uses of the University'. But while Bouchard's argument worked in favour of reinforcing the power of the university to determine what was transmissible knowledge, Kerr's reference to the three institutions of the Western world which had endured in recognizable form from medieval times to the present – the Tynewald of the Isle of Man, the Catholic Church and the university – had another purpose. That purpose was to use the previous vision as a measure of precisely how urgent change was.

References

Andrew, C. (2009) *The Defence of the Realm: The Authorized History of MI5*, London: Allen Lane.

Becher, T. and M. Kogan (1991) *Process and Structure in Higher Education*, London: Heinemann.

Ben David, J. (1978) *Centers of Learning: Britain, France, Germany, USA*, New York: McGraw-Hill for the Carnegie Foundation.

Gibbons, M., M. Trow, C. Limoges, H. Nowotny & P. Scott (1994) *The Production of Knowledge: The Dynamics of Science and Research in Contemporary Societies*, London: Sage.

Heldrich, A. (1996) 'Die Universitaet Muenchen an der Schwelle eines neuen Jahrhunderts: Redeanlaesslich eines Rektoratsubergabe', in R. Böttcher, W. Odersky, G. Hueck & B. Jähnke (eds) *Festschrift fuer Walter Odensky zum 65 Geburtstag am 17 Juli 1995*, New York/Berlin: Walter de Gruyter.

Henkel, M. (1991) 'The new Evaluative State', *Public Administration*, 69 (1), Spring. pp. 121–136.

Henkel, M. (2007a) 'Can academic autonomy survive in the knowledge society? A perspective from Britain', *Higher Education Research and Development*, 26 (1), March. pp. 87–99.

Henkel, M. (2007b) 'Changing conceptions of university autonomy in 21st century knowledge economies: the case of Britain', http://www.fup.pt/old/cipes/docs/eventos/pdf_docs/Henkel_11Maio.pdf

Kogan, M. (2004) 'Management and evaluation in higher education', *UNESCO Forum Occasional Paper series, Paper No. 7*, Paris: UNESCO.

Kogan, M. & D. Kogan (1983) *The Attack on Higher Education*, London: Kogan Page.

Kosselleck, R. (2008) 'Is there an acceleration of history?', in H. Rosa & W. E. Scheuerman (eds) *High Speed Society: Social Acceleration, Power and Modernity*, Pennsylvania: Penn State University Press.

Maassen, P. (1987) 'Quality control in Dutch higher education: internal vs. external evaluation', *European Journal of Education*, 22 (2). pp. 161–171.

Metzger, W. (1987) 'The United States', in B. R. Clark (ed.) *The Academic Profession: Institutional, National and International Settings*, Berkeley/Los Angeles/London: University of California Press.

Ministerie van Wetenschappen en Ondwerijis (1983) *Beleidsnota Schaalvergroting, Taakverdeling en Concentratie Wetenschappilijk Onderwiijs*, Zoetemeer: Ministerie van O & W.

Ministerie van Wetenschappen en Onderwijs (1985) *Nota: Hoger Onderwijs, Autonomie en Kwaliteit*, Zoetemeer: Ministerie van O & W.

Neave, G. (1989) 'From the other end of the telescope', in R. Abel & P. S. C. Lewis (eds) *Lawyers In Society vol. iii, Comparative Theories*, Berkeley/Los Angeles/London: University of California Press.

Neave, G. (1998) 'The Evaluative State reconsidered', *European Journal of Education*, 33 (3), September. pp. 265–284.

Neave, G. (2000) 'Voices of Constancy, Voices of Change: higher education discussed across a turbulent half-century', in Guy Neave (ed.) *Abiding Issues, Changing Perspectives: Visions of the University across a Half-century*, Paris: IAU Press.

Neave, G. (2002) 'The stakeholder perspective historically explored', in J. Enders & O. Fulton (eds) *Higher Education in a Globalising World: International Trends and Mutual Observations*, Dordrecht: Kluwer Academic Publishers.

Neave, G. (2006a) 'On Time and Fragmentation: sundry observations on research, the university and politics from a waveringly historical perspective', in G. Neave, T. Nybom & K. Blueckert (eds) *The European Research University: A Historical Parenthesis?* New York: Palgrave Academic Publications. pp. 63–76.

Neave. G. (2006b) 'On Monsieur de Tallyrand Périgord's Qualities', *Higher Education Policy*, 19 (4), December 2006. pp. 401–409.

Neave, G. (2007) 'A privatização da Educação Superior e a Dinâmica do Estado Avaliador', in *ANAIS Educação Superior: Questão de Estado prioridade social*, São Paulo, Brazil: FNESP.

Neave, G. (2010) 'Burton R. Clark 1921–2009: the Man. His saga and his times', *London Review of Education*, 8 (3), November. pp. 209–216.

Neave, G. & A. Amaral (2011) 'Introduction', in G. Neave and A. Amaral (eds) *The Nation, a Generation and Higher Education. Portugal 1974–2009*, Matosinhos: CIPES Dordrecht/Heidelberg/London: Springer Books.

Neave, G. (2011) 'The changing "Vision Thing": Academia and the changing mission of higher education' *Educação, Sociedade, Cultura*, 31, 16–35.

Neave, G. (2012) *The Prince and His Pleasure: Institutional Autonomy, the Evaluative State and Re-engineering Higher Education in Western Europe*, Basingstoke/New York: Palgrave Macmillan.

Nybom, T. (2003) 'The Humboldtian legacy: reflections on the past, present and future of the European University', *Higher Education Policy* 16 (2), 141–169.

Olsen, J. (2008) 'Institutional autonomy and democratic government', *ARENA Working Paper No. 20*, Oslo, Centre for European Studies, 2–7.

Premfors, R. (1981) *National Policy Styles and Higher Education: France, Sweden and the United Kingdom,* Stockholm: Group for the Study of Higher Education and Research.

Pollitt, C. & G. Bouckaert (2004) *Public Management Reform: A Comparative Analysis*, 2nd edition, New York: Oxford University Press.

Rothblatt, S. (1998) *The Modern University and Its Discontents: the Fate of Newman's Legacies in Britain and America*, Cambridge: Cambridge University Press.

Rothblatt, S. (2007) *Education's Abiding Moral Dilemma: Merit and Worth in the Cross-Atlantic Democracies, 1800-2006*, Oxford: Clarendon Press.

Ruegg, W. (1992) 'Mythology and historiography of the beginnings', in W. Ruegg (ed.), *History of the Universities in Europe, vol. 1 The Middle Ages*, Cambridge, England: Cambridge University Press.

Santiago, R., T. Carvalho, A. Amaral & V.L. Meek (2006) 'Changing patterns in the middle management of higher education institutions: the case of Portugal', *Higher Education*, 52, pp. 215–250.

Shils, E. & H. Daalder (1981) *Universities, Politicians and Bureaucrats: Europe and the United States*, Cambridge, England: Cambridge University Press.

Trow, M. (1970) 'Reflections on the transition from mass to universal education', *Daedalus*, 99 (1), Winter. pp. 1–42.

Trow, M. (1976) 'The public and private lives of higher education', *Daedalus*, 104 (1), November. pp. 113–127.

van Vught, F. (1989) *Governmental Strategies and Innovation in Higher Education*, London: Jessica Kingsley Publishers.

van Vught, F. & P. Maassen (1989) *Dutch Higher Education in Transition. Policy Issues in Higher Education in the Netherlands*, Culemborg: LEMMA.

Veiga, A. (2010) *Bologna and the Institutionalisation of the European Higher Education Area* (unpublished doctoral thesis, University of Porto).

3
Change as an Intellectual Device and as an Object of Research

Taina Saarinen & Jussi Välimaa

Introduction

Change is normally taken for granted in higher education research and policy-making – and in everyday life. It is a matter of fact that we can see change everywhere but there are only very few people who have defined the nature of change as a problematic matter as such (e.g. see Halonen & Häyry, 1990).

As far as we know, change in itself has not been the object of critical comparative analysis in the field of higher education research even though philosophically it has been on the agenda from the time of Aristotle. According to Aristotle, change was defined as a process which has a beginning and an end, and one may see a difference between the beginning and the end. This philosophical starting point provides an intellectual perspective to change as a process which may have different directions. It can be lead to improvements (evolution or progress) or it may result in decay (decline or deterioration).

It has been noted that in the arena of policy-making, change can be seen as intrinsic to policy-making, where the one who has the advantage in discursively stating the problem (the need for change) also has the advantage in constructing the solution (the direction of change) (see Bacchi, 2000). Consequently, change should be understood not just as a policy goal in itself or as an intellectual device used by researchers to analyse a number of different kinds of processes of alterations taking place in higher education. Change is also a political crutch, used to advocate various different goals and for construing different political approaches.

Bearing this policy dimension in mind, in this chapter we will analyse change as it is represented in higher education policy studies. In other words, this chapter problematizes the thematic and concept of change itself in higher education policy research.

Three main categories of higher education research can be recognized in Europe (see Välimaa, 2008). These include, first, policy implementation studies which aim to analyse empirically what has happened or is happening in higher education in relation to policy reforms. The second main category of research focuses attention on higher education as a part of society, where the interest of knowledge focuses on analysing how societal values and policy principles (such as educational opportunities) are implemented in the systems and institutions of higher education. The third tradition of research consists of theoretical studies which have analysed higher education as a social entity – whether an organization, cultural entity or a system of higher education – with the aim of developing a theoretical understanding on and of higher education. The first and the last categories of research are most useful for the purposes of our study because we aim to analyse how change has been defined in theoretical higher education studies and how different understandings of change have been used in policy implementation studies. While higher education reforms are conducted explicitly to cause change, the justification of those reforms is based on unexamined notions of change. Consequently, it seems that higher education reforms are research topics, where the thematic of change presents a central focus of study, although change is rarely problematized. While we realize that change is also a culturally rooted concept, influenced by national, institutional and disciplinary factors (see Stensaker et al. in this book), in this chapter we focus on the concept of change as an intellectual device rather than going into the culturally and ideologically loaded underlying assumptions.

Our aim is, however, not to run through all higher education studies but to focus on the most cited empirical and theoretical studies as illuminative examples of different approaches to change. However, in order to make our point more comprehensive we will use the Bologna Process as an example of different perspectives on change.

We first take a short look into conceptualizations of change in grand social theories (see Mills, 1959/2000; Skinner, 1985) to contextualize the main approaches to social changes. Second, the chapter focuses on the problematic of change in higher education policy implementation research and theoretical studies as examples of mid-range research theories. We examine some higher education policy theories from the point of view of their standing on change.

In the conclusion we draw together the discussion of policy change in relation to the current higher education policies and related research.

Social theories of change

The social historian Peter Burke (1980; 1992) has examined the characteristics of history and social sciences, and in that context he discusses their stand on social change. Burke (1980, pp. 80–81; 1992, p. 131) sees two main traditions in explaining change: theories of modernization and theories of crisis and conflict. In theories of modernization, the central conceptualization is social evolution (as opposed to revolution), where society develops gradually and cumulatively. Internal (as opposed to external) factors steer the development of the society in the direction of structural differentiation. Change takes place from the simple, unspecialized and informal, towards complex, specialized and formal. In this theoretical tradition, reasons for change are often mostly seen as internal to the activity taking place and, consequently, change is an internal process. Thus, the external world offers impulses which stimulate the individual system into adapting into a new equilibrium. In emphasizing the internal nature of change, models of modernization may give an impression of unproblematic unilinearity, as if change were an automatic sequence of stages (Burke, 1992, pp. 132–139).

Burke (1992) gives Spencer, but also Durkheim and Weber as examples of modernization theorists, even if the concepts and interpretations by and of these sociologists differ from each other significantly. He claims that Durkheim uses basically evolutionary terms in describing the gradual replacement of 'mechanical solidarities' with the more complex 'organic solidarities' (1992, p. 132) as the division of labour in society increased. Weber, according to Burke (1992, p. 132), had a tendency to view history as a gradual development towards more complex and impersonal forms of organization (such as bureaucracy and capitalism). Parsons also belongs to the tradition of modernization in Burke's (1980, pp. 82–83) classification, as he saw social development as a progression from primitive to developed and from archaic to modern society (see also Ursin, 2006).

An alternative to the theories of modernization and its ideas of internal development is provided by theories of conflict or coercion, where society is, in historical perspective, seen as a series of societies, following each other discontinuously. Societies and their development are defined by economic systems or 'modes of production', which contain internal contradictions, which in turn lead to conflict, crisis and discontinuous change (Burke, 1980, pp. 89–94; 1992, p. 141). Change is, in other words, dialectic. It is natural that Burke should place Marx, Engels, Lucács and Gramsci into this tradition.

However, rather than concentrating on placing social theorists in the continuum between traditions of modernization or conflict, we should think of the implications of these traditions for social research. Consequently, the existence of society is thought to be based either on order and balance (as is the case within modernization theories) or on a sequential series of conflicts and crises (Burke, 1992; Burrell & Morgan, 2000). In the modernization theories, the focus is on forces and processes that keep the society together; that is, on forces which produce integration, differentiation and balance (hence also 'equilibrium theories'; Paulston, 1977). Society is viewed as a developing organ, a constant structure or a combination of structures, where each component participates in sustaining the whole. Change does take place also in these systems, but it occurs in its different incremental, evolutionary and cumulative aspects. The conflict tradition is represented by the idea of societal change taking place suddenly, in the forms of crisis and conflict (see Paulston, 1977),[1] where both can be thought to include internal and external pressures.[2]

Analysis of five mid-range theories of change in higher education policy research

By changing the perspective from grand social theories into analysing one part of society – that of higher education – we acknowledge that there is also a change in the scale of analysis. It is also true that higher education institutions are characterized by continuity, which in itself is not a typical element in societies, creating a need to create grand social theories to explain how they change. However, it is exactly for this reason that it is interesting to see how change has been defined in the field of higher education studies. This change of perspective also gives us an opportunity to reflect on how categories and dimensions developed to understand and categorize how grand social theories can be utilized in higher education research.

Higher education research is by nature multidisciplinary, where policy issues and problems can be studied from a variety of disciplinary viewpoints and where research problems are often theme-based (Teichler, 2005). Consequently, one of the main trends in European higher education research is policy implementation studies which aim to examine what has happened – or is happening – in higher education in relation to, or as a consequence of, local, national or regional policies (Välimaa, 2008; to name just a few, e.g. see Lane, 1990; articles in Henkel, 1991; Neave & van Vught, 1991; Goedegebuure, 1992; Kogan & Hanney, 2000). As these studies show, even in reform implementation studies, where the thematic of change presents a central focus of study, the concept of change is rarely problematized.

We will move now to discuss five works which have been extensively used and cited in studies dealing with policy change in higher education: Burton Clark's *The Higher Education System* (1983), Ladislav Cerych and Paul Sabatier's *Great Expectations and Mixed Performance: The Implementation of Higher Education Reforms in Europe* (1986), Paul J. DiMaggio and Walter W. Powell's *Institutional Isomorphism and Collective Rationality in Organizational Fields* (1983),Tony Becher and Maurice Kogan's *Process and Structure in Higher Education* (1992) and Maurice Kogan, Marianne Bauer, Ivar Bleiklie and Mary Henkel's *Transforming Higher Education* (2000). The analysis is not meant as a comprehensive review of the use of the concept of change in higher education research, but rather as a problematization of the thematic of change, by treating these extensively used studies as examples of the different views.

The works that we discuss take a distinct standpoint on change and its origin in higher education policy. They also represent different viewpoints with regard to the thematic of change. Clark's (1983) work looks at higher education as a social system and discusses the nature of change in the functioning of the higher education system. Becher and Kogan (1992) also take a theoretical look into the working dynamics of higher education as a system, by using British higher education as an example. They, like Clark, have a need to understand theoretically the causes and nature of the change in that system. Cerych and Sabatier (1986), in turn, represent typical implementation theories common in the 1970s, where the focus is on the rational steering of policy processes. Kogan and others (2000) present an example of the new reform theoretical thinking of the 2000s. They have opened new views both into the character as well as analyses of reforms by using theories of new institutionalism and Bourdieu's field theories. We will also take a critical look at the foundations of new institutional theory by DiMaggio and Powell (1983) because this intellectual tradition has been and is especially influential in European higher education research and is also represented in this book.

We have now discussed the modernization versus conflict theories as grand social theories needed to problematize change and move our focus next to mid-range social theories, as explained in the introduction.

Burton Clark: The Higher Education System

Clark (1983) deals in his classic work on higher education systems also with questions of higher education organization and steering. He approaches the functioning and dynamics of the higher education system from the internal tensions of that system. From the point of view of the dynamics of the system, the struggle between different interest groups is essential (Clark, 1983, pp. 7–8). Clark defines change both widely (the birth of educational system in the society) and narrowly (the changes within that educational system once it has been born). For Clark, change is a continuum which includes 'alterations that vary from simple reproduction to radical transformation' (Clark, 1983, p. 182). Both the need for change as well as its obstacles are integrated within the system (Clark, 1983, pp. 182–183) Change becomes possible when the educational system has first been born and its internal mechanisms start to steer the cumulative change in the system driven by the increase of knowledge.

In Clark's view, the bottom heaviness of the higher education system also defines change. Clark does not believe that externally initiated reforms succeed except when they extend into grassroots innovations. The bottom-heavy academic organization can, according to Clark, change only gradually and change is for the most part invisible. A precondition for horizontal change is, in turn, that those holding boundary roles in information gate-keeping – academic leaders, professors and so forth – link and coordinate the small flows of information between the inside and the outside (Clark, 1983, pp. 234–237).

Clark's view on change is, in other words, modern or equilibrium theoretical. The reference (almost a dedication) to Durkheim's *The Evolution of Educational Thought* in the introduction, as well as discussions about the development and social division of labour of academic institutions, link Clark with the Durkheimian evolutionary tradition. Studying change is possible only in the context of studying historical structures and traditions. Clark is Durkheimian also in the respect that he finds the division of labour to be the driving force in the development and change of the higher education system; that is, a constant increase in knowledge and the consequent need to establish new chairs and fields of study force the field to change. Clark calls this the differentiation of the system, where the opposing forces of integration are, in turn, produced by the academic communities, market logic, and the bureaucratic and normative steering of the state.

Ladislav Cerych and Paul Sabatier: Great Expectations and Mixed Performance. The Implementation of Higher Education Reforms in Europe

Our next example (Cerych & Sabatier, 1986) paints a different picture from Clark (1983). Their study was widely cited in the 1980s and therefore deserves our attention because of its popularity even though academically it is now outdated. In higher education policy of the 1970s and 1980s, and also in the research of the time, change was mostly perceived as top-down implementations. Political goals for change were formulated as plans or 'policies', which were implemented as top-down, rational processes, as a consequence of which policies were evaluated and possibly reshaped. Policy, in other words, changes as it is implemented and reformed. Cerych and Sabatier's (1986) work concentrated on nine higher education policy reforms since the 1960s. In their work, the success and failure of policy is analysed from the point of view of the success of implementations.

Policy change, or reform in the Cerych and Sabatier view, is initiated by discontent with the status quo. Different possible solutions for the problem in question are produced and one of these is selected in the decision-making process. After this, the change is implemented, still following a top-down decision-making process. The implementation of change is followed up with evaluation, after which the reform is continued, reshaped or rejected. Evaluations pay special attention to the goals of the reform and how they are attained. Cerych and Sabatier also stressed the importance of showing the causal connections between the reform and its implementation (Cerych & Sabatier, 1986, pp. 10, 15–16).

Cerych and Sabatier, in fact, neither define reform nor discuss its relationship with change. Instead, they have combined reform and change by using 'scope of change' as an explanatory concept (Välimaa, 2005, p. 265). To be able to describe the changes caused by reforms more accurately, they developed a three-level description. 'Depth of change' refers to how much the change is thought to depart from prevalent values and norms. 'Functional breadth of change' describes those spheres of action where the reform is thought to have an impact. 'Level of change' refers to the target of reform (policy level, institutional level and so forth) (Cerych & Sabatier, 1986, p. 244).

When analysing reforms with the help of the above frame, Cerych and Sabatier (1986, p. 248) draw the following conclusions.

(1) Policies with a wide functional breadth and extensive depth of change face enormous opposition.

(2) Policies with narrow functional breadth and small depth of change are choked, as they do not create enough energy to overcome inertia in the system.
(3) Consequently, reforms aiming at a moderate scope of change are most likely to succeed.

Analysing reforms, Cerych and Sabatier had to conclude that it is difficult enough to discover common goals and that even the most precise goals do not lead to a trouble-free implementation of a reform. They conclude by stating that for implementation, an 'acceptable mix of outcomes' should be compiled (Cerych & Sabatier, 1986, p. 243). Looking specifically at reforms has steered their attention towards externally initiated change, but as the success of reforms is analysed, they also relate externally initiated reforms with the internal logics of the higher education system.

Cerych and Sabatier's reform-based view of higher education policy change represents the implementation analysis typical of the 1970s and 1980s. Simultaneously, their extensive project demonstrated problems with this kind of comparative approach. Assuming that policy implementation follows a rational process, the different realities of national situations remain unaccounted for. In 2003 the Consortium of Higher Education Researchers (CHER) organized a conference concentrating on critically scrutinizing the influential work of Cerych and Sabatier. This depicts both the strong position of top-down implementation analysis in higher education policy research since the 1980s, but also the need to develop new approaches to the analysis of reforms and their implementations, successes and failures (see Gornitzka et al., 2005).

Tony Becher and Maurice Kogan: Process and Structure in Higher Education

Becher and Kogan (1992) analyse the higher education system in a matrix consisting of the structural components of the system (individual, basic unit, institutional and national) and modes (normative and operational). The normative mode consists of values and norms which originate from inside the universities as well as from outside society. The operational mode consists of different actions and operations. Their context is the British system which faced strong political pressures for change in the 1980s.

Right at the beginning of their work, Becher and Kogan (1992, p. 16) explicitly place their work within equilibrium theories, while not citing

Clark (1983), for instance, at this stage. When presenting the normative and operational modes, they state that the system stays in a state of dynamic equilibrium when the normative and operational modes are in balance. And when these modes, which are characterized by values and actions, are off balance, changes in the system are needed before the return to equilibrium and 'normal' operation becomes possible. Another starting point for Becher and Kogan is that at each level of the system values may – and do – differ from each other. On the national level, the needs of the legislators and political decision makers are emphasized. At universities, the organizational goals of efficiency and productivity are emphasized, while the hopes and demands of the state, society and the academic community have to be observed. In Becher and Kogan's model, the central position is held by the basic unit – the unit with the administrative structure and resources to take care of the basic tasks of teaching and research. In basic units the values of different fields of study, influenced by different cultures, are emphasized.

In basic units, the needs, hopes and actions of the whole system meet. It is interesting that in Becher and Kogan's view, the systemic equilibrium can be attained with the measures taken at basic unit level, and often, study programmes. In the basic units, the cultural expectations of different fields, the researchers' demands and the expectations and demands of the universities and the state are operationalized into action. At the individual level, on the other hand, the same pressures between research, teaching and administration meet as in basic units and at universities.

Becher and Kogan find the normative mode (values and norms) the primary defining factors of the systemic balance, as they assume that values guide actions and not vice versa. This may be true when the internal changes within the system are observed. However, when transnational pressures for change are analysed, the situation may appear different. National organizations, such as the Organisation for Economic Co-operation and Development (OECD), tend to work from the built-in idea that they have an effect on the international arena – they are expected to cause change. When Papadopoulos (1994) describes the OECD's education policy role from the point of view of national policies as catalytic, it includes an expectation of intended change, caused by some intervention. In this case it may be possible that the values of international policies may be made into actions, which clash with the values of the academic community or with national values (see Vidovich, 2001) At this stage, however, we aim to problematize how international policy influences affect higher education and we do not explore how they find their way into national policy action or what kinds of effects this might have on national values.

Becher and Kogan define higher education policy change as a tension between organic growth and radical change (1992, pp. 133–135). For them, change is often gradual and incremental, and takes place bottom up. The concept of organic change is not, according to them, in conflict with the concept of equilibrium in their model. In fact, they find the idea of gradual, internal change to be an indication that the equilibrium is, by nature, more dynamic than static.

Maurice Kogan, Marianne Bauer, Ivar Bleiklie and Mary Henkel: Transforming Higher Education

In our next case, Kogan et al. (2000), in turn, look at policy change, on the one hand, as a structural question (through historical institutionalism) and, on the other hand, as a question of human action. With the help of their actor-context model and Bourdieuan concept of social fields, they analyse higher education reforms in three countries (Great Britain, Norway and Sweden) as a field of social action, where 'field' is defined as an institutionalized area of activity in which actors struggle with something that is of importance to them. What is essential in their thinking is that reforms are not a result of top-down implementation processes, but as processes where each level interprets the general policy goals in their own way, since in each field of social action, different struggles take place. The relationships between fields are not necessarily hierarchic, but rather communicative, where actors in different fields make their own interpretations during the struggles in their fields.

Kogan et al. build on Becher and Kogan (1992) and analyse courses of change as a question between natural growth and radical change. Some changes may, for instance, follow OECD country reports, which ease the spreading of international influences through imitation (Rinne, 2006). Massification of higher education is, on the other hand, an example of natural development, which is difficult to locate in an individual actor or country (Kogan & Bauer, 2000, pp. 48–51).

The actor-context model leads Kogan et al. into the central conclusion that the success of policy change cannot be explained by its internal or external origins. Regardless of how changes originate, they will lead into very different kinds of reactions and strategies at the level of, for example, university central administration, departments and individuals. Kogan et al. approach Clark (1983) when they note that changes in formal structures do not necessarily lead into changes in the actions and behaviour of academic individuals. Relations of power and autonomy do not automatically change by reform (Kogan et al., 2000, pp. 212–213).

Change is also dictated by national and local contexts. Higher education phenomena (such as emphasis on quality assurance, the promotion of market logic and demands for accountability) seem to be spreading by international influence. While governments demand change, which spreads with the help of international examples, it is also the case that similar demands may cause different outcomes and be implemented as different kinds of changes in different contexts. For Kogan et al., this is not just a question of national idiosyncrasies having an impact on higher education policy. Their analysis of higher education as a field of social actors also leads them into the conclusion (which is quite essential for higher education research) that higher education policy reforms are nationally only partly coordinated. Different social forces are at play on different fields of change (Kogan et al., 2000, pp. 213–214).

Paul J. DiMaggio and Walter W. Powell: The iron cage revisited: institutional isomorphism and collective rationality in organizational fields

While there exists a fine line between contributions labelled as 'historical institutionalism', represented by Kogan et al. above, and those of 'neo-institutionalists' (DiMaggio & Powell, 1983), we find it necessary to discuss conceptualizations of neo-institutionalism or new institutionalism in this context separately, since it belongs to the influential intellectual approaches in the European higher education research when analysing and explaining institutional changes in higher education (e.g. see Stensaker, 2004; Papadimitriou, 2011). In higher education research, organization is normally understood as a higher education institution. Without going deeper into the differences between an institution and an organization, we would like to remind the reader that they are different things, even though this difference is rarely problematized (see Witte, 2006).

We will focus on an article which has been recognized as one of the starting points for new institutionalism. In their widely cited article, DiMaggio and Powell (1983) aim to explain why organizations in a given organizational field tend to become more homogenous over time instead of remaining different from each other. In other words, they begin their argument with the implicit assumption that organizations should naturally become more heterogeneous in a competitive environment, in order to become more efficient. According to DiMaggio and

Powell, 'the concept that best describes the process of homogenization is *isomorphism*'. This concept originates in population ecology and, following the definition of Hawley (1968), the article describes 'a constraining process that forces one unit in a population to resemble other units that face the same set of environmental conditions'.

The most seminal part of this article is based on the recognition of three different mechanisms of institutional isomorphic change. These are *coercive, mimetic* and *normative isomorphism*. Coercive isomorphism stems from political influence and the problem of legitimacy. These pressures may be both formally and informally exerted on an organization by other organizations or by society's cultural expectations. They 'may be felt as force, as persuasion, or as invitation to join in collusion'. These pressures also may result in ceremonial changes, which does not mean they would be inconsequential (1983, p. 150). According to DiMaggio and Powell, mimetic isomorphism results from standard responses to uncertainty, which is a powerful force that encourages imitation. Organizations may also model themselves after other organizations to reduce uncertainty. Normative isomorphism is, in turn, associated mainly with professionalism which is 'the collective struggle of members of an occupation to define the conditions and methods of their work' (DiMaggio & Powell, 1983, p. 152). According to DiMaggio and Powell, this social force rests, on the one hand, with formal education and legitimation of a cognitive base produced by university professionals and, on the other hand, with the growth and elaboration of professional networks (DiMaggio & Powell, 1983, p. 152).

The authors refer to changes in organizations several times but they do not define what the nature of change is. For them, change is something that happens inside an organization as a result of external pressures (coercive, mimetic or normative). Furthermore, DiMaggio and Powell focus on the ways organizations try to adapt to external pressures and try to change their internal organization in a competitive environment. The driving forces for change seem to be an organization's aim to be successful in its respective organizational fields and the aim to secure their organizational existence. In other words, the source of change is external. The authors also assume that the nature of change is incremental, in other words, it is continuous change. They recognize that 'some organizations respond to external pressures quickly; others change only after a long period of resistance' (1983, p. 154). They do not, however, reflect on the sources and nature of this internal resistance. According to Stensaker (2004), change is indeed one of the most problematic matters in different variations of new institutionalism.

Theories and dynamics of change and different types of higher education policy change

Figure 3.1 depicts different views on change, as found in current higher education policy research. It consists of four fields defined by external versus internal characteristics of change juxtaposed with the tendency towards conflict versus continuous change. At this point, after our analysis of the mid-range research theories presented in the five cases, we approach the grand theories of (balanced) modernization versus conflict as continuums rather than distinct approaches.

We have formed four metaphors on change, based on their constellation on these two axes. External change coupled with continuous change refers to reform; views of change as reform are particularly well represented in Cerych & Sabatier (1986).

External and discontinuous change, in turn, leads to a metaphor of intervention in the system; none of our four cases fit specifically in this group, but examples of lesser used and cited works can be found (e.g. see Rinne, 2006). Change as internal and continuous refers to a gradual evolution in the system. Clark (1983), Becher and Kogan (1992) and DiMaggio and Powell (1983) from our five cases fit most comfortably within this section. And finally, change as internal and discontinuous would mean revolution in the system. Revolutionary, conflict-theoretical views do not seem to be very common in the

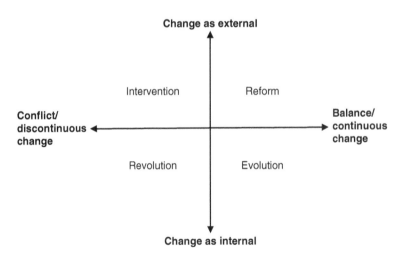

Figure 3.1 Theories and dynamics of change and different types of higher education policy change

canon of higher education policy research, even though Pierre Bourdieu (1988)[3] could be included in this category.

Monolithic versus discursive change: the case of the Bologna Process

Researching change has, particularly in European higher education research, a strong tradition, which can at least partly be explained by the central position of reform in policy. Change is sought after as a positive phenomenon of reform and progress, which is opposite to defining change as something with more negative connotations – crisis or decay (Birnbaum & Shushok, 2001). Politicians who have taken an active interest in policy change have been focused on following up the impacts of policy change, which has possibly lead towards short-term project funding of higher education policy research. The consequence has been that in higher education policy research, reforms have often been observed as a policy implementation process (Cerych & Sabatier, 1986; Kyvik, 2005). Structures of research funding may have contributed to this. There again, the interdisciplinary and theme-based nature of higher education research has also allowed for the application of a wide range of social theories and views (DiMaggio & Powell, 1983; Clark, 1983; Becher & Kogan, 1992; Kogan et al., 2000; Vabo, 2002; Saarinen, 2007).

Recent comparative research has strengthened the view that policy change is the result of international influences and national processes (Bleiklie & Kogan, 2000, p. 11). Transnational influences can, in turn, find their ways into national policies in different and even surprising ways. For instance, Lehikoinen (2005) has described quite deliciously, from the point of view of a ministry official participating in the Bologna meeting in 1999, the first, rather confused stages of the process, as the various actors participated in a situation where it was extremely difficult to see how the process would take shape. The way in which the Bologna Process has taken shape internationally can well be described with Kogan et al.'s (2000) actor-context model, which allows for a more multi-dimensional view of this phenomenon than, for instance, the reform theoretical views of Cerych and Sabatier (1986) or the new institutional theory of DiMaggio and Powell (1983).

Change as discursive power play

Viewing processes of change as internal or external, continuous or discontinuous treats change as monolithic and absolutely definable.

However, recent research also points to other directions in explaining and conceptualizing change in higher education. Policy change can also be seen as a discursive power play or a struggle for meanings and the right to define them (Vidovich & Porter, 1999; Henry et al., 2001, p. 128). Critical and conflict theoretical higher education policy research is only emerging in European higher education policy discussions as we speak (e.g. see Henry et al., 2001; Vidovich, 2001; Nóvoa & Lawn, 2002; Saarinen, 2007), even if it has a longer tradition in the United States (see Paulston, 1977; Slaughter, 2001).

The Bologna Process is explicitly designed to induce change in the higher education systems of the participating countries (e.g. see Bologna, 1999; Prague, 2001). Thus, we decided to use the Bologna Process as an example of a phenomenon which has been interpreted from various viewpoints within recent higher education research (see Westerheijden, 2001; Huisman & van der Wende, 2004; Amaral & Magalhães, 2004; Keeling, 2006; Tomusk, 2006; Witte, 2006).

Figure 3.2 goes back to Figure 3.1 which presented four metaphors for the external versus internal and balance versus conflict-seeking nature of change. This time, however, the figure is used to depict the different discursive formations of a policy, using the Bologna Process as an example. The purpose of the figure is to use the metaphors of intervention, reform, evolution and revolution to illustrate how 'one' process can in fact be seen as many processes. What we see, in fact,

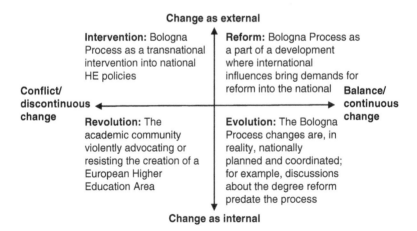

Figure 3.2 The Bologna Process in higher education policy discussions: different metaphors of change

are different possible discursive constructs of a policy. When change is seen in different ways, these constructs are not only intellectual devices used by academics, but they have their effects on policy actions. A particular construct promotes a particular policy; consequently, there is no 'Bologna Process' per se, but several, depending on the viewpoint (Saarinen, 2008).

First, it may be argued that the Bologna Process is a transnational intervention (upper left corner of Figure 3.2) into the traditional monopoly of nation states as definers and steerers of national educational systems. In this view, emphasis is placed on the role of the European Union as a supporter of the process, as well as the creation of a European higher education area as an opposing power to American and Asian higher education in the globally competitive market (e.g. see Keeling, 2006; see also Neave in this book). There is, in fact, ample literature that views the Bologna Process as a neo-liberal takeover of state higher education and other policy arenas (e.g. see Rinne, 2006). It seems that precisely because change is seen as a self-evident goal of policy (see the Introduction), it also makes authoritarian interventions possible.

Second, from a reform (upper right corner) point of view, the Bologna Process can be construed as a situation where a transnational process brings demands for change in the national system and consequently causes some reform(s) to be initiated (e.g. see Westerheijden, 2001).

Third, the Bologna Process can also be interpreted as a natural development or evolution (lower right corner) in Europe. It is a continuation of earlier processes of student and staff mobility and university cooperation. In a similar vein, the process can be seen as being nationally steered, answering to national demands, which existed before the process (see Ahola & Mesikämmen, 2003; Välimaa, 2006).

Fourth, constructing the Bologna Process as a revolution (lower left corner) is something we still have not seen, if we understand revolution as a violent bottom-up development of advocating or resisting a policy. It is obvious that the discourses of revolution (or intervention, for that matter) are not present in the official, ministry-driven data used in this study. This conflict theoretical metaphor of revolution is not easy to fit into higher education policy research. There is no documentation of the academic community rushing to erect barricades in order to cause change by resisting the developments of the Bologna Process or advocating the creation of quality assurance systems or comparable and transparent degree systems. However, conflict theoretical perspectives can be helpful when analysing the uses and users of power in educational reforms. According to Paulston (1977) *qui bono?* or 'Who benefits?' is a typical question presented by those academics who see that society consists of contradictory social actors (or classes).

These metaphors illustrate the fact that an education policy field always consists of various actors, with conflicting needs. Policies are shaped as they are depending on the field of action. This becomes not a question of the success or failure of a particular policy, but of the collisions and frictions of the policies of different actors, which produce and make visible different policies (see our analysis of Kogan et al., 2000, earlier in this chapter; Saarinen, 2008). Consequently, the concern of the implementation theorists such as Cerych and Sabatier (1986) regarding the success or failure of the reform becomes irrelevant, as reforms appear differently in different situations.

Regardless of whether we see change as continuity or conflict, it would seem that the need for change is built into national and international decision-making. Higher education policy is legitimated with a continuous need for change – but the question is, whose view of change becomes the dominant one? Policy discourses are instances of policy-making, as battles for meaning necessarily become battles for policy dominance and this meaning-making is, in turn, fought over using politically, socially and culturally motivated arguments. Policy as discourse inevitably includes different and competing views of policy change (Ball, 1994). In other words, change is a political concept as much as a self-evident policy goal in higher education policy.

Notes

1. Paulston (1977) analyses the theories of social and educational change with the help of two main categories: equilibrium versus conflict theories. Equilibrium theories consist of evolutionary, neo-evolutionary, structural-functionists and systems theories. Conflict theories include Marxist, neo-Marxist, cultural revitalization and anarchistic utopian theories. As can be seen, both the main categories are rather extensive.
2. Some problems, however, remain, such as where to place, for instance, Bourdieu's theoretical aspirations to avoid the traditional dichotomies between structure and individual, or meaning and societal function (see Sulkunen, 2006). For the same reason, theoreticians of rational choice (Collins, 1994) are excluded from our discussion.
3. In *Homo Academicus*, Bourdieu (1988) analyses the crisis of the French university institution in the end of the 1960s. His study is, however, not so much research of higher education change or reform, but a field theoretical analysis of the society from the point of view of higher education (see Välimaa, 2006).

References

Ahola, S. & J. Mesikämmen (2003) 'Finnish Higher Education Policy and the Ongoing Bologna Process', *Higher Education in Europe* 28 (2), 217–227.

Amaral, A. & A. Magalhães (2004) 'Epidemiology and the Bologna Saga', *Higher Education* 48, 79–100.

Bacchi, C. (2000) 'Policy as Discourse: What Does It Mean? Where Does It Get Us?', *Discourse: Studies in the Cultural Politics of Education* 21 (1), 45–57.

Ball, S. (1994) *Education Reform. A Critical and Post-Structural Approach*, Buckingham: Open University Press.

Becher, T. & Kogan, M. (1992) *Process and Structure in Higher Education*, 2nd edition, London: Routledge.

Birnbaum, R. & S. Shushok, Jr (2001) 'The "Crisis" Crisis in Higher Education: Is That a Wolf or a Pussycat at the Academy's Door?', in P. Altbach, P. Gumport & B. Johnstone (eds) *In Defense of American Higher Education*, Baltimore: Johns Hopkins University Press.

Bleiklie, I. & M. Kogan (2000) 'Comparison and Theories', in M. Kogan, M. Bauer, I. Bleiklie & M. Henkel (eds) *Transforming Higher Education. A Comparative Study*. Higher Education Policy Series 57, London: Jessica Kingsley.

Bologna (1999) The European Higher Education Area. Joint declaration of the European ministers of education. Convened in Bologna on the 19 June 1999.

Bourdieu, P. (1988) *Homo Academicus*. Translated by P. Collier, Stanford University Press.

Burke, P. (1980) *Sociology and History*. Controversies in sociology 10, London: George Allen & Unwin.

Burke, P. (1992) *History and Social Theory*, Cambridge: Polity Press.

Burrell, G. & G. Morgan (2000) *Sociological Paradigms and Organizational Analysis: Elements of the Sociology of Corporate Life*, Aldershot: Ashgate.

Cerych, L. & P. Sabatier (1986) *Great Expectations and Mixed Performance: The Implementation of Higher Education Reforms in Europe*, Straffordshire: Trentham Books.

Clark, B. (1983) *The Higher Education System. Academic Organization in Cross-national Perspective*, Berkeley: University of California Press.

Collins, R. (1994) *Four Sociological Traditions*, New York: Oxford University Press.

DiMaggio, P. J. & W. W. Powell (1983) 'The Iron Cage Revisited: Institutional Isomorphism and Collective Rationality in Organizational Fields', *American Sociological Review* 48 (2), 147–160.

Goedegebuure, L. (1992) *Mergers in Higher Education*, Utrecht: LEMMA.

Gornitzka, Å., M. Kogan, & A. Amaral (eds) (2005) *Reform and Change in Higher Education – Analyzing Policy Implementation*, Dordrecht: Springer.

Halonen, I. & H. Häyry (1990) *Muutos* (Change), Helsinki: Suomen filosofinen yhdistys.

Hawley, A. (1968) 'Human Ecology', in D. L. Sills (ed.) *International Encyclopedia of the Social Sciences*, New York: Macmillan.

Henkel, M. (1991) *Government, Evaluation and Change*, London: Jessica Kingsley.

Henry, M., B. Lingard, F. Rizvi, & S. Taylor (2001) *The OECD, Globalisation and Education Policy*, Oxford: Pergamon.

Huisman, J. & M. van der Wende (2004) 'The EU and Bologna: Are Supra- and International Initiatives Threatening Domestic Agendas?', *European Journal of Education* 39, 349–357.

Keeling, R. (2006) 'The Bologna Process and the Lisbon Research Agenda: The European Commission's Expanding Role in Higher Education Discourse', *European Journal of Education* 41 (2), 203–223.

Kogan, M. & M. Bauer (2000) 'Higher Education Policies: Historical Overview', in M. Kogan, M. Bauer, I. Bleiklie, & M. Henkel (eds) *Transforming Higher Education*, London: Jessica Kingsley.

Kogan, M., M. Bauer, I. Bleiklie, & M. Henkel (2000) *Transforming Higher Education*, London: Jessica Kingsley.

Kogan, M. & S. Hanney (2000) *Reforming Higher Education*, London: Jessica Kingsley.

Kyvik, S. (2005) 'The Implementation of the Norwegian College Reform', in Å. Gornitzka, M. Kogan & A. Amaral (eds) *Reform and Change in Higher Education*, Dordrecht: Springer.

Lane, J. (1990) *Institutional Reform. A Public Policy Perspective*, Aldershot: Dartmouth.

Lehikoinen, A. (2005) 'Eurooppalaiset koulutusmarkkinat akateemisen koulutuksen haasteena' [European Educational Markets as Challenges for Academic Education], in R. Jakku-Sihvonen (ed.) *Uudenlaisia maistereita. Kasvatusalan koulutuksen kehittämislinjoja*. Opetus 2000, Jyväskylä: PS-kustannus.

Mills, C. W. (1959/2000) *The Sociological Imagination*, The 40th anniversary edition, New York: Oxford University Press.

Neave, G. & F. A. van Vught (eds) (1991) *Prometheus Bound. The Changing Relationship between Government and Higher Education in Western Europe*, Oxford: Pergamon.

Nóvoa, A. & M. Lawn (eds) (2002) *Fabricating Europe: The Formation of an Education Space*, Dordrecht: Kluwer Academic Publishers.

Papadopoulos, G. (1994) *Education 1960–1990 The OECD Perspective*, Paris: OECD.

Papadimitriou, A. (2011) *The Enigma of Quality in Greek Higher Education. A Mixed Methods Study of Introducing Quality Management into Greek Higher Education*. Dissertation, Twente: University of Twente.

Paulston, R. G. (1977) 'Social and Educational Change: Conceptual Frame Works', *Comparative Education Review* 21 (2–3), 370–395.

Prague (2001) *Towards the European Higher Education Area*. Communique of the meeting of European ministers in charge of Higher Education in Prague on 19 May 2001.

Rinne, R. (2006) 'Like a Model Pupil? Globalisation, Finnish Educational Policies and Pressure from Supranational Organizations', in J. Kallo & R. Rinne (eds) *Supranational Regimes and National Education Policies – Encountering Challenge*, Turku: FERA.

Saarinen, T. (2007) *Quality on the Move. Discursive Construction of Higher Education Policy from the Perspective of Quality*. Dissertation, Jyväskylä: University of Jyväskylä.

Saarinen, T. (2008) 'Social Actors in the Interface of Transnational and National Higher Education Policy', *Discourse: Studies in the Cultural Politics of Education* 29 (2), 179–193.

Skinner, Q. (1985) 'Introduction: The Return of Grand Theory', in Q. Skinner (ed.) *The Return of Grand Theory in the Human Sciences*, Cambridge: Cambridge University Press.

Slaughter, S. (2001) 'Problems in Comparative Education: Political Economy, Political Sociology and Postmodernism', *Higher Education* 41, 389–412.

Stensaker, B. (2004) *The Transformation of Organisational Identities. Intepretations of Policies Concernng the Quality of Teaching and Learning in Norwegian Higher Education.* Dissertation, Twente: University of Twente.

Sulkunen, P. (2006) 'Mikä ihmeen talous? Sosiaalisen synty ja hiipuminen Smithin ja Bourdieun yhteiskuntateorioissa' [What Economy? The Birth and Dying Down of the Social in Social Theories of Smith and Bourdieu], in S. Purhonen & J.P. Roos (eds) *Bourdieu ja minä. Näkökulmia Pierre Bourdieun sosiologiaan,* Tampere: Vastapaino.

Teichler, U. (2005) 'Research on Higher Education in Europe', *European Journal of Education* 40 (4), 447–469.

Tomusk, V. (2006) (ed.) *Creating the European Area of Higher Education. Voices from the Periphery.* Higher Education Dynamics 12, Dordrecht: Springer.

Ursin, J. (2006) 'Korkeakoulutus sosiaalisena järjestelmänä' [Higher Education as a Social System], in J. Ursin & J. Välimaa (eds) *Korkeakoulutus teoriassa – näkökulmia ja keskustelua,* Jyväskylä: Jyväskylän yliopisto.

Vabo, A. (2002) *Mytedannelse i endringsprosesser I akademiske institusjoner.* Dissertation, Bergen: Universitet i Bergen.

Välimaa, J. (2005) 'Social Dynamics of Higher Education Reforms', in Å. Gornitzka, M. Kogan & A. Amaral (eds) *Reform and Change in Higher Education. Analysing Policy Implementation,* Dordrecht: Springer.

Välimaa, J. (2008) 'Reflections on Research Questions, Topics and Themes Identified During the HELF Project', in J. Brennan, J. Enders, C. Musselin, U. Teichler & J. Välimaa (eds) *Higher Education Looking Forward: An Agenda for Future Research,* Strasbourg: European Science Foundation.

Välimaa, J., D. Hoffman & M. Huusko (2006) 'The Bologna Process from the Perspective of Basic Units', in V. Tomusk (ed.) *Creating a European Area of Higher Education – Voices from the Periphery,* Dordrecht: Springer.

Vidovich, L. (2001) 'That Chameleon "Quality": The Multiple and Contradictory Discourses of "Quality" Policy in Australian Higher Education', *Discourse: Studies in the Cultural Politics of Education* 22 (2), 249–261.

Vidovich, L. & P. Porter (1999) 'Quality Policy in Australian Higher Education of the 1990s: University Perspectives', *Journal of Education Policy* 14 (6), 567–586.

Westerheijden, D. (2001) 'Ex Oriente Lux?: National and Multiple Accreditation in Europe After the Fall of the Wall and After Bologna', *Quality in Higher Education* 7 (1), 65–75.

Witte, J. (2006) *Change of Degrees and Degrees of Change: Comparing Adaptations of European Education Systems in the Context of the Bologna Process.* Dissertation, Twente: University of Twente.

Part II

The Dynamics Between Reform and Culture

4
University Strategizing: The Role of Evaluation as a Sensemaking Tool

Nicoline Frølich & Bjørn Stensaker

Introduction

Higher education institutions (hereafter HEI) are increasingly adopting practices from the private sector. One such practice is strategy formulation and strategic development processes. To study such practices and processes is important as we need to strengthen our knowledge of how new practices may influence and change the HEI on the inside, while also recognizing that strategy formulation is about how the HEI interprets its relationship to the environment.

In principle, strategy formulation is about organizing the link between the organization and its environment. Strategy formulation involves making sense of the relationship between the HEI and the external environment and of the HEI's particular state of affairs. Thus, as a point of departure, one can argue that strategic processes are socially constructed – they are enacted, interpreted and explained (Pye, 1995, p. 453). It follows from this that culture is seen as an important factor influencing strategy formulation, although such cultural influence is embedded in the often taken for granted practices associated with strategic processes. This is evident in the prescriptions of the strategy literature itself. For example, in the classical view, a strategy is about where and how to compete (Chandler, 1962) and involves formulating a strategy that directs attention towards the markets in which the organization competes for resources and customers, and identifies the means and tactics to be implemented. Here, the cultural reference is 'business' and a strategy is seen as a specific instrument to be used to survive in a market situation with a strong focus on customers and competition.

Institutional theorists have consistently pointed out that the embed-dedness of an organization in a given cultural context can have a significant effect on how the organization interprets and acts on the cues provided by the environment. Within institutional theory different explanations exist as to what type of mechanisms (scripts or logics) are the carriers of such influence, in other words, cultural-cognitive scripts, normative standards or regulatory rules (Scott, 2008). While such expla-nations have been supported by empirical research, they still cannot explain why many research findings also deviate from the environmen-tal determinism which so often is associated with institutional theory (Denis et al., 2007, p. 182). Denis et al. (2007, p. 182) suggest that this is because research within the institutionalist tradition has tended to 'assume away pluralism' and alternative explanatory models. This is an important point, perhaps especially valid for universities where plural-ism can almost be said to be an essential characteristic (Weick, 1995). Typically such organizations are defined by multiple objectives, diffuse power and complex knowledge-based work processes.

In this chapter we address the challenge of trying to explain variation within institutional theory by focusing on how the internal processes of strategy formation can produce different ideas about the status and the future direction of a HEI depending on how the strategy process is orga-nized. To be more precise, we look explicitly at the role of evaluation as knowledge input to strategic processes and how evaluation may affect the outcome of such processes as a tool that can either disclose or limit pluralism. As such, the study is guided by the following research ques-tion: What is the role of evaluation in framing discussions and decisions in the strategizing process?

We argue that the current study is important in three ways. First, while almost all modern universities have adopted strategic practices and have developed extensive strategic plans – often as a result of external reform demands – there is still little research that shows significant impact of such processes on HEI performance (see Jarzabkowski, 2005). Hence, there is a need for empirical research identifying what happens when universities adopt strategic planning.

Second, and related to the first issue, there is also a need to uncover some of the underlying processes and interactions that form the basis of a strategy – assessing whether it is the conditions surrounding strategic planning that may be inadequate rather than the strategic planning in itself. To assist us in this analysis, we draw on the strategy-as-practice perspective which we see as an invitation to explore the internal processes associated with trying to interpret and make sense of the HEI–environment relation. This approach directs attention towards 'how the practitioners of strategy really act and interact' (Whittington, 1996, p. 731). Strategy-as-practice research looks with interest at a wide range of individuals as potential strategic actors. Hence, this approach allows us to identify some key 'strategists' in the process and how the strategy process evolves in the organization (top-down or bottom-up) (Wooldridge et al., 2008). For example, top management is often portrayed as having a key formal role in strategy formulation, while middle managers are thought to have a more dominant role in strategy implementation, although recent research has started to question such assumptions (Whittington, 2006, p. 619). However, less is known about the linkages between the strategists, characteristics of the organization and environment (Wooldridge et al., 2008).

Third, an important contribution of our study is the critical examining of the assumptions that strategy formulation is a future-oriented and rational process. As noted by the strategy-as-practice approach, strategies can be seen as the outcome of complex and social processes, a finding questioning the rationality surrounding strategy formulation (Jarzabkowski, 2005). Empirically, this approach gives considerable attention to social events such as strategy workshops, dinners, seminars and meetings as important factors in the strategy formation process (Jarzabkowski & Seidl, 2008; Sturdy et al., 2006). We would like to draw attention to another social event – evaluation – which as a starting point may be described as a more technical and fact-finding process involved in strategizing. We explore whether evaluations can also be seen as 'pieces of sense' that are communicated in the strategy process and contribute to the construction of the organizational identity within which a strategy is based.

Strategy formulation as a sensemaking process

Strategy – conditioned by path-dependency and existing practice

Within the academic field of strategy analysis one can identify a growing interest in exploring strategy formation as a social practice (Jarzabkowski, 2005; Jarzabkowski et al., 2007; Jarzabkowski & Whittington, 2008; Whittington, 1996; Whittington, 2006). This interest is in turn influenced by the recent linguistic turn in organization studies (Deetz, 2003; Gabriel, 2000). Pye (1995, pp. 460–461) points out that managing is about reading, writing and relating – the 'interplay between dialogue and doing'. Her point is that managers practise managing through dialogue and doing. Hence, one could argue that a strategy can be seen as a blueprint for organizing and communicating the current and future organizational identity of a given HEI.

The interesting issue is, of course, what sort of sensemaking can create such an identity? Weick (1995) has convincingly argued that sensemaking is predominantly path-dependent. This means that the knowledge base for strategy designation is constructed on existing norms and values, past events and practices. One could criticize this view by arguing that – in the same way as institutional theory – strong path-dependency provides little room for innovation and differentiation. However, Weick (1995) can be said to have added a dynamic element into his perspective by emphasizing that although sensemaking is path-dependent it is also influenced by enactment processes by which members of the organization interact to create an understanding of the organizational environment and critical factors in which the strategy in question is being developed. It is through the combination of these two dimensions that the sensemaking process takes place. In this process, the actors not only develop a common understanding, they also agree upon a response selected from several alternatives. Over time the most beneficial choices are retained in terms of developing routines and rules.

In line with Weick's perspective, strategizing may be understood as an analysis of how the organizational actors construct sensible events, why they do so and to what effect. Reality is seen as an on-going accomplishment that takes form when individuals make retrospective sense of the situations in which they find themselves and their creations (Weick, 1995, p. 61). Furthermore, sense is not something that may be extracted solely from external events; sensemaking and identity are strongly related (Gioia et al., 2000, p. 67). Meaning is not attached to one experience that is singled out; on the contrary, meaning arises from the attention directed towards the experience (Weick, 1995, p. 26). Moreover, sensemaking is based on the actors' values and priorities because actors need values, priorities and clarity about preferences to help them to determine what matters (Gioia and Chittipeddi, 1991, p. 446). Sensemaking may be said to be enactive of sensible environments, as enactment involves individuals producing parts of the environment they are facing (Labianca et al., 2001, p. 325). In addition, the social context binds individuals to actions that they must justify, affecting the saliency of information and providing norms and expectations that constrain explanations (Schultz et al., 2000, p. 1). Hence, the process of sensemaking is an interactive process that takes place between actors and their environment (Weick, 1995, p. 49).

Strategy formation – more complex than often imagined?

Strategizing in universities is undertaken in an organizationally complex setting. The multi-dimensionality of a HEI's objectives hinders the implementation of clear strategies with well-articulated goals and suitable measures. The argument that strategizing is mainly window dressing, myth and ceremony (Meyer & Rowan, 1977) may be related in part to the complexity of the organizations involved. Moreover, the loosely coupled character of the organizations permits the formal structure to be detached from the actual organizational behaviour, which is presumed to be only slightly affected by strategizing. Based on this reasoning, strategizing in universities is heavily influenced by the demands of the environment to which the organization must (formally) conform in order to warrant its legitimacy (DiMaggio & Powell, 1991). However, the March and Olsen version of institutionalism (March & Olsen, 1996) posits that the normative foundation of the organization (Selznick, 1957) has an equally weighty impact on its goals and objectives – this is not a case of anything goes. Accordingly, strategizing involves acknowledging the claims of the environment, the normative basis and the identity of the organization concordantly.

This complex view of strategizing fits nicely with the strategy-as-practice perspective. The perspective is easily distinguished from the top-down rational and instrumental view of strategy (Jarzabkowski, 2005, p. 2). According to the former, strategy is something that is done, a kind of work. According to the latter, strategy is something that an organization possesses (Jarzabkowski & Whittington, 2008, p. 101). In the strategy-as-practice approach, practice refers both to the micro-level (in other words, the actions of actors) and to the macro-level (in other words, different socially defined practices on which the actors draw when 'doing strategy') (Jarzabkowski et al., 2007, p. 7). Strategic activity is activity, related or unrelated to the formal, intended strategy and it impacts 'the strategic outcomes, directions, survival and competitive advantage' of the organization (Jarzabkowski et al., 2007, p. 8). Strategizing is a complex process in which 'the nitty-gritty local routines of strategy are not easily understood' (Whittington, 1996, p. 732).

The strategy-as-practice perspective permits renewed attention to communicative processes. Strategy formulation and implementation encompass 'inspiration – coming up with ideas, identifying opportunities and grasping situations – as well as perspiration – budgeting and planning, the work of the strategic committees and the writing of formal documents' (Whittington, 1996, p. 732; see also Dunford & Jones,

2000). Based on this, the enactment and communication of strategy may be said to involve a relationship with the functioning of the organization, the ordering of tasks and the aim of the strategy given the environment in which the organization is operating. In this process communication becomes a crucial aspect of strategizing. As pointed out by Jarzabkowski (Jarzabkowski, 2005, p. 3), strategy-as-practice is concerned with the

> detailed aspects of strategizing; how strategists think, talk, reflect, act, interact, emote, embellish and politicize, what tools and technologies they use and the implications of different forms of strategizing for organisational activity.

To understand how agreements are reached and actions coordinated, one can argue that the central leadership is not the only actor relevant to the study and that, in general, one should be open as to how other actors are also involved in making 'sense of sensemaking' (Brown et al., 2008). For example, several studies have shown how middle managers are key actors in telling stories about their organization that make sense to different audiences (Sims, 2003; see also Hoon, 2007). This insight is perhaps especially relevant for universities that typically have considerable autonomy located in various faculties, departments and other units. Although we do know that certain actors within an organization can play an important role in the strategic formation process, the key challenge is still that we have more limited knowledge of how organizing affects enactment and sensemaking.

The institutionalization of evaluation in strategy formation

In the classical view, the strategy of an organization is intrinsically linked to the organizational environment in which the organization is operating. In the prevailing rational and instrumental perspective, strategy formulation involves defining the goals of organizational activity and implementing adequate measures. Strategy is the determination of an organization's basic long-term goals and objectives, the adoption of courses of action and the allocation of resources necessary for achieving these goals (Chandler, 1962, p. 13). Ideally, a strategy describes the choices an organization makes about which markets or clients to serve, the distinct way it seeks to provide its outputs, the tactics it employs and the output goals it sets for itself (Scott & Davis, 2007, p. 21). Thus, evaluation should be organized in ways that enable an assessment of whether goals and objectives have been met. Evaluation is mainly retrospective and seen as a more technical process, as a check on whether a strategy has been realized. In this perspective, evaluation is seen as an 'add-on' to other processes.

However, this view of evaluation can be questioned. Not least, one could argue that evaluation today can be considered as an institutionalized practice in universities – in teaching, research and administration. The uses of evaluation are widespread and evaluation is becoming an autonomous activity. An example is the establishment of quality assurance systems within universities and colleges around the world, which in essence is a series of evaluations conducted in a systematic way within the organization and with separate organizational units responsible for running the system. Some authors have, as a consequence, argued that perhaps evaluation is the key organizational process in knowledge institutions such as the HEI (Power, 1997). It follows from this that various forms of evaluation can also affect strategy processes during the formation of such strategies.

How evaluation and strategy formation interact and how evaluation influences strategic processes is nevertheless a little studied phenomenon. In principle, one could distinguish between three different institutional mechanisms (scripts and logics) through which evaluation may affect strategy processes: the instrumental logic (as a regulative mechanism), the logic of appropriateness (as a normative mechanism) and the logic of orthodoxy (as a cultural-cognitive mechanism) (Scott, 2008, p. 52). Some possible expectations of how evaluation may function with regards to strategizing according to the three different logics are outlined below.

According to the instrumental logic, evaluation is conceived as a consequence of rules, laws and sanctions. The fact that in Norway universities and colleges are mandated to have internal quality assurance systems and that student evaluation is an activity that is specified in the Act for Higher Education are specific examples of the relevance of this mechanism. Perceived as an instrument, evaluation could be related to strategic processes by providing evidence of the concrete functioning of a given HEI or college and of how it performs in the areas of quality assurance and with respect to how students perceive their teaching and learning experience.

However, if we consider evaluation within a logic of appropriateness, the role of evaluation might change. The concept of appropriateness points to the need for universities and colleges to follow social obligations within higher education. These might relate to the more historical role and functioning of universities and colleges, and to the values and norms that prevailed in these organizations. As such evaluation could be related to strategic processes by emphasizing the ideational aspects of universities and colleges – the meaning they have for those working there and for the environment. Possible ideational elements that could be highlighted by evaluation are the norms of a close interaction between teaching and research, the collegial nature of higher education or the independence of research from vested interests.

Finally, evaluation could also be linked to a logic of orthodoxy, being part of cultural-cognitive scripts and templates that are seen as popular or dominant in contemporary society. For universities and colleges examples of such popular templates are ideas of universities becoming 'entrepreneurial', 'market-oriented' or even 'competitive' (e.g. see Gioia & Chittipeddi, 1991). For evaluation to fit with this logic, one would expect an emphasis on activities that signal an appreciation of such labels or that symbolize that such ideas have already been implemented in the organization. Possible links between evaluation and strategic processes would enable such logic, if evaluations were designed to focus on popular concepts and provide results that consequently are difficult to ignore when developing new strategies.

Although we are well aware that our three institutional logics may not comprehensively cover the many possible links between evaluation and strategy formation in universities, a structure is set out, in a rather minimalist way, for the many complex interactions that are involved in strategizing, emphasizing both the possibility for strategic formation as a confirmation of status quo and the possibility that strategy formation can also bring about more radical change. Since the three institutional logics are just analysing the role of evaluation in the strategy formation process, it goes without saying that many other factors can also influence the strategic process.

Empirical setting, data and methodology

The empirical basis for the current study is student recruitment strategies at 14 Norwegian universities and colleges, comprising six universities, a specialized HEI and seven university colleges. The empirical basis of the study consists of several qualitative data sets compiled from these HEIs over a number of years. We explore the role of evaluations in strategizing based on case studies of the formulation of student recruitment strategies. Student recruitment strategies have become more important in Norwegian higher education as a consequence of a number of reforms of Norwegian higher education in the past decades, mainly with the aim of improving the quality, effectiveness and efficiency of the sector (Norges Offentlige Utredninger (NOU), 1984, p. 23; 1988, p. 28; 2000, p. 14). In general, the reforms have resulted in greater autonomy for the HEIs, including the possibility for university colleges to apply for university status and thus potentially improve their status and reputation as producers of knowledge. Furthermore, the reforms have created more competition for (better) students, as funding is becoming increasingly dependent on students' ability to progress in, and complete, their studies. Third, a national evaluation system has been created to control whether research and teaching at these now more autonomous institutions is of sufficient quality and relevance.

The first data set consists of semi-structured interviews with two groups of actors at the HEIs. This first series of interviews was conducted in 2004 and 2005 at seven of the institutions and includes a total of 76 semi-structured, in-depth, focus group interviews with key administrators and senior faculty members.

The second data set consists of 21 semi-structured (group) interviews of senior staff members in (study-related) administrative departments and information departments at seven others institutions. These interviews were conducted in 2006, 2007 and 2008. In 2009, five similar interviews were undertaken to update the material.

The third data set consists of various written documents, first and foremost the formal strategies, the documentation underpinning the strategies, the data and statistics used as input for the strategizing process and evaluations conducted during the strategizing process. For this paper, particular emphasis was placed on searching for empirical findings that may have relevance for the institutional logics identified in the theoretical part of the paper.

Findings

In general, the empirical findings show support for all three institutional logics although evaluation does seem to be linked to some logics more than others.

Evaluation as a rule-governed process

The most dominant institutional logic associated with evaluation in our findings is that this process appears to be matched with strategy formation in the student recruitment area in a relatively standardized and uniform way. Hence, in most institutions, the strategy process can be characterized as a rather rule-governed process and is usually started a year ahead of the application deadline. At most of the institutions, the routine incorporates three common elements: a review and an evaluation of the strategy process and instruments from the previous process; a student satisfaction survey targeting the students who started their studies the previous year; and an assessment of the need to change the strategy based on the perceived position of the institution in the student market.

While evaluation in this way is very much linked to the strategy formation process, one might also argue that this strong link between evaluation and strategy development creates a very institutionalized way of organizing the whole process. Perhaps this result indicates an increasing professionalization of the whole strategizing process where evaluation and strategizing together are forming a new template for how such processes should be organized.

However, there might also be a price to be paid for this strong link. An evaluation routine focusing solely on the students already enrolled at the institutions (in other words, student satisfaction surveys) may limit how those in charge of formulating student recruitment strategy perceive their students and thus their environment. At many of the institutions, this often results in a strategy which is less open for new types of input, with evaluation serving as the prime tool for maintaining the status quo. This overall finding suggests that evaluation seems to play a vital role in limiting the creative potential of a strategy formation process and is a strong indication that the ways such processes are organized may in fact limit strategic planning as a tool for developing more dynamic universities.

However, although more rarely, we also found illustrations of the possible dynamic role that evaluation might play in strategy formation processes. We were able to identify individual institutions that were capable of altering their strategic approach and where evaluation has a more pro-active role. Some of these institutions managed to change in response to a need to be repositioned in the student market. Others did so by chance as a result of incidents, of which they only later realized the significance. Three such examples are given below.

Evaluation as a reminder of normative ideals

While almost all the institutions carried out student satisfaction surveys, some institutions combined these with other regular evaluation exercises. One such exercise was internally initiated academic (peer review) evaluations of study programmes, departments and faculties within the institution. In most cases these evaluations were not intended to be used as input to student recruitment strategies. They were sometimes initiated by a particular department or faculty, or they were performed as self-evaluation exercises as part of a broader national evaluation of specific disciplines.

Although implemented for academic purposes, these evaluations exerted significant influence in the strategic thinking in some of the institutions. A close reading of the evaluation reports indicates that they often directed the institutions towards their societal purpose and responsibility, and how they could best serve society. For example, these reports contained recommendations that often emphasized the importance of attracting full-time students (to emphasize and stimulate quality) or of promoting diversity in the student body by attracting both male and female students, and students from a variety of ethnic backgrounds.

These recommendations seem to have functioned as an 'institutionalized reminder' of how Norwegian HEIs should carry out their recruitment strategies. They highlighted the social and academic dimensions of the institutions in question, which seem to have been difficult to ignore when developing student recruitment strategies. In the words of one of our informants:

> By emphasising gender issues and ethnicity, we also feel that we are doing the right thing when developing our student recruitment strategy. It provides an ethical dimension we like. After all, we are not selling soap – we are higher education providers.

In this way the evaluations contributed to an evocation of the normative foundations of the institutions, which sometimes can be overlooked when the focus is directed towards student satisfaction surveys.

Although the empirical data relates to exactly how institutions were 'reminded' about their normative role, anecdotal evidence does suggest that middle managers sometimes played a very important role as translators and mediators between these different processes. This is perhaps not surprising as middle managers are among those who would have very good access to information, both about academic reviews and strategy processes in general. While access to information is undoubtedly important, it seems that the role of being a middle manager may be interpreted as one of trying to establish a sense of cohesion and integration between different sets of expectations. One informant underlined the point in the following way:

We have always worked in line with the social dimension which is expressed in the Bologna declaration. Maybe it is because we are based in an urban area. We have always had the type of educational professional programmes we have, and an explicit commitment to recruiting a diverse group of students.

In this way, some middle managers can truly be central strategic actors in their mediation between the organizational identity and self-understanding, and the externally generated expectations of how HEIs should behave in the student market.

Evaluation as modernization and myth

As mentioned above, Norwegian HEIs have faced increasing competition for students during the past decade. The statistical winners in this game have generally been institutions located in urban areas. Certain institutions in rural areas have experienced trouble in recruiting both an adequate number of students and students with the desired characteristics.

These institutions have attempted to reposition themselves in the higher education market, often choosing the strategy of entering into the market for lifelong learning. Evaluation reports have played a significant role in this reorientation and we have identified two different uses of evaluation in such processes. First, forms of evaluation have changed, opening up new ways of determining what information to collect and how to collect it – a way of modernizing the institution. It is interesting to note that while institutions have sought out information that could help them to create a better fit with their environment, the results of the evaluations have actually influenced and 'reshaped' the environment as well. Second, evaluation has been employed as a means to legitimize changes in the student recruitment strategy by reinterpreting the results of evaluations to portray the institution as flexible and technology-savvy, thereby highlighting students' possibilities for studying when and where they like. The realities behind this use of evaluation can still be questioned, leading to an interpretation that evaluation has been used more for window-dressing purposes.

At one of the institutions studied, the need to reorient its position led to the development of evaluation tools intended to disclose how people in the region perceived the role of the institution in a regional development perspective. This evaluation generated substantial interest and led to the establishment of a new regional institutional network for examining possibilities for creating new study programmes and courses aimed at the regional market. One of the initiators of this form of evaluation underlined how it has changed the way the institution thinks about student recruitment:

> In the past, we used to sit around the table with our traditional perceptions and prejudices of what sort of study programmes the students wanted. These days we use evaluation as a correction of our within-the-box thinking. We are probably not outside-the-box yet, but the box is certainly becoming larger.

Interestingly, in this context the evaluation process has been transformed from a summative to a formative instrument linked to the student recruitment strategy by inviting outside stakeholders to join in interpreting the data – a process that some informants also say has changed the way key stakeholders perceive the institution. The example illustrates that in the face of a crisis (lack of students) rule-bounded or normative logics may be challenged by alternative (external) recipes for determining the most appropriate (networking with outside stakeholders) way to proceed.

Being faced with a potential crisis, in the form of few applicants, may also lead to a stronger formalization and tougher forms of evaluation inside the organization. An informant at another institution that has experienced the need to reposition itself in the student market due to lack of young applicants explains how external evaluations influence the institution's knowledge of its own position:

> A few years ago there were a lot of applicants and enough students. Then we saw a downturn. We established a group to look into student recruitment. One of the faculty members, a scholar in marketing, wrote a report to the board. The report became the foundation of our recruitment strategy [...] Recently, in the wake of the establishment of an external evaluation system, a formally established quality commission at the institution consisting of academic and administrative leaders sits down, evaluates and reports on student recruitment [...] using preset terms like 'input quality' and 'programme quality'.

In this way, evaluation has contributed to a more 'evidence-based' and formalized approach creating new types of practice at the institution and breaking away from the routine which characterizes the strategy formation process at so many other institutions. However, both the establishment of external evaluative networks and tougher evaluation bodies inside the institutions are initiatives that fit well with current external templates for how HEIs should respond to strategic challenges in the environment. The institutions are 'modernized', but the modernization is well within the scope of popular ideas in the environment.

Among our case institutions one could also identify one institution in which evaluation can be said to have taken on a myth-building function. While many Norwegian HEIs worry that the increasing marketization of higher education will lead to a development where the student is perceived (and start to act) just like a customer, one of our case institutions seemed to be less concerned about this. On the contrary, the institution convincingly used evaluation as a tool to brand itself in the student market. This institution wanted to signal that it was a modern and international institution, and therefore actively sought an international accreditation label as part of the student recruitment process. According to one informant, the objective of gaining this accreditation was mainly reputational:

> Our institution is relatively young and our academic specialisation also makes us quite vulnerable. We needed this international accreditation to stand out from similar providers in Norway, and at the same time profile ourselves as a global player in higher education.

Of course, an interesting twist is that while the institution did obtain accreditation, the evaluation (accreditation process) revealed certain mismatches between the identity of the institution and environmental expectations. One of these was the gap between the institution's distinct local profile in certain study programmes and the image it sought to project of being an international player. While the institution externally presented its strategy as a response to increasing competition for students 'internationally', in reality the primary recruitment measures of the institution continued to focus on the national and regional level, addressing young people interested in higher education in arenas dedicated to this purpose.

Evaluation in strategy formulation

Strategy formulation – like managing (Pye, 1995) – involves an attempt to handle and organize the environment–organization relationship. Much influenced by information stemming from various forms of evaluations, members of universities and colleges interact to create a picture of the organizational environment in which the strategy is being developed.

Hence, although our study does not allow us to draw too strong conclusions, the findings do indicate how important the organization of strategy formation processes is and how important middle management can be both as organizers of evaluations and as interpreters of the information stemming from the evaluations conducted. In this way, our study does support findings emphasizing the role of 'strategy practitioners' as a potential critical connection between intra-organizational strategy practice (in other words, strategy work) and the extra-organizational practices that rely on this work (Whittington, 2006, p. 620).

An important finding in our study is the flexible ways in which evaluation can be linked to the strategizing process. Evaluation can be an element of both stability and change in the strategizing process. Our study has revealed that evaluation may play a variety of roles.

- Evaluation can structure mindsets by creating rule-like and standardized practices.
- Evaluation can be a carrier of norms and important values.
- Evaluation can be part of modernization processes and can also be used more symbolically in relation to the environment.

In most of the institutions studied evaluation seems to have caused more standardization and rule-like behaviour, in the sense that it determines what information to look for and how it should be analysed. Hence, evaluation – which is often considered as a tool for critically examining past behaviour and challenging the performance of organizations – is in practice a tool that may contribute to conservatism and conformity. In more theoretical terms, we are tempted to argue that evaluation and strategizing together have formed a distinct institutional practice that seem to strengthen each other.

Contrary to this, the more dynamic and distinct strategizing processes seem to occur when evaluation and strategizing processes operate in a more disintegrated way, as institutional practices that challenge each other, create tensions and contestations. Depending on the specific situation and context, such tensions and contestations may lead to different outcomes for the strategy development process. An example is when organizational self-understanding converges with strong norms in the academic field and where the result is that evaluation functions as a carrier of norms (March & Olsen, 1996; Scott, 2008). In this case, strategizing as a form of modernizing the institutions is rejected and the institutions can use the strategy process as a way of strengthening their organizational identity ('After all, we are not selling soap ... ').

However, the role of evaluation can also be part of modernization processes, for example, if there is a misalignment between organizational performance and organizational survival. In a situation characterized more by crisis than stability, evaluation seems to be forced out of the role of standardizing tool – creating a different understanding of the environment by bringing in new stakeholders into the process. The result was that the whole strategizing process became more creative leading to unplanned alliances with other HEIs and external stakeholders with the objective of cooperating on enrolment strategies. In the case where the organizational capacity for establishing such links is poorer while ambitions may still be high, evaluation is also flexible enough to be used as a purely symbolic tool leading to the well-acknowledged finding that some organizational practices are nothing but myths and ceremony (Brunsson & Olsen, 1997; Meyer & Rowan, 1991). An illustration of this is the institution's attempt to brand itself as international while at the same time offering, and being very dependent on, a number of regionally based courses for lifelong learning.

Our small study has several possible implications for theorizing about the relationship between sensemaking, organizing and strategy. First, our findings suggest that there is a close relationship between organizing (evaluation) and sensemaking. While the process of sensemaking is often associated with cultural features of the organization such as identity, the lived experience and other social-psychological dimensions, our data suggest that organizing shapes the lens through which sense is made. However, in most institutions the lenses created seem to lead to conformity more than creativity.

A second finding showed that organization of the strategizing process, not least the tensions that may arise from a decoupling between evaluation and strategizing, could also be used in a more instrumental fashion. While traditional views of organizing strategic processes tend to emphasize a more systemic approach, our findings suggest that more dynamic processes may in fact arise from a more anarchic organizational approach in which competing sensemaking processes are confronted, creating new ideas and ways to think forward, and leading to more dynamic translations of ideas and possible practices to undertake (see Czarniawska & Joerges, 1996). In a more theoretical perspective, this may also imply that sensemaking activities can be 'tailored' through organizing and are more subject to instrumental processes than assumed by established concepts of sensemaking. This is a potentially important insight as evaluations – in addition to providing recommendations for future action or at least a statement about the current situation – also entail a strong element of negotiation between the organization and the environment.

References

Brown, A. D., P. Stacey, and J. Nandhakumar (2008) 'Making sense of sensemaking narratives', *Human Relations*, 61, 1035–1062.

Brunsson, N., and J. P. Olsen (1997) *The reforming organization*, Bergen: Fagbokforlaget.

Chandler, A. D. J. (1962) *Strategy and structure: Chapters in the history of the American industrial enterprise*, Cambridge: MIT Press.

Czarniawska, B., and G. Sevón (1996) *Translating organizational change*, Berlin: Walter de Gruyter.

Deetz, S. (2003) 'Reclaiming the legacy of the linguistic turn', *Organization*, 10, 421–429.

Denis, J.-L., A. Langley, and L. Rouleau (2007) 'Strategizing in pluralistic contexts: rethinking theoretical frames', *Human Relations*, 60, 179–215.

DiMaggio, P. J., and W. W. Powell (1991) 'The iron cage revisited: institutional isomorphism and collective rationality in organizational fields', in W. W. Powell and P. J. DiMaggio (eds) *The new institutionalism in organizational analysis*, Chicago: The University of Chicago Press.

Dunford, R., and D. Jones (2000) 'Narrative in strategic change', *Human Relations*, 53, 1207–1226.

Gabriel, Y. (2000) *Storytelling in organizations: facts, fictions and fantasies*, Oxford: Oxford University Press.

Gioia, D. A., and K. Chittipeddi (1991) 'Sensemaking and sensegiving in strategic change initiation', *Strategic Management Journal*, 12(6), 433–448.

Gioia, D. A., M. Schulz, and K. G. Corley (2000) 'Organisational identity, image and adaptive instability', *Academy of Management Review*, 25, 63–81.

Hoon, C. (2007) 'Committees as strategic practice: the role of strategic conversation in a public administration', *Human Relations*, 60, 921–952.

Jarzabkowski, P. (2005) *Strategy as practice: an activity-based approach*, London: Sage.

Jarzabkowski, P. (2008) 'Shaping strategy as a structuration process', *The Academy of Management Journal*, 51, 621–650.

Jarzabkowski, P., J. Balogun, and D. Seidl (2007) 'Strategizing: the challenges of a practice perspective', *Human Relations*, 60, 5–27.

Jarzabkowski, P., and D. Seidl (2008) 'The role of meetings in the social practice of strategy', *Organization Studies*, 29, 1391–1426.

Jarzabkowski, P., and R. Whittington (2008) 'Hard to disagree, mostly', *Strategic Organization*, 61, 101–106.

Labianca, G., J. F. Fairbank, J. B. Thomas, and D. A. Gioia (2001) 'Emulation in Academia: balancing structure and identity', *Organization Science*, 12, 312–330.

March, J. G., and J. P. Olsen (1996) 'Institutional perspectives on political institutions', *Governance*, 9, 247–264.

Meyer, J. W., and B. Rowan (1977) 'Institutional organizations: formal structures as myth and ceremony', *American Journal of Sociology*, 83, 340–363.

Meyer, J. W., and B. Rowan (1991) 'Institutionalized organizations: formal structure as myth and ceremony', in W. W. Powell and P. J. DiMaggio (eds) *The new institutionalism in organizational analysis*, Chicago: The University of Chicago Press.

Norges Offentlige Utredninger (1984) Produktivitetsfremmende reformer i statens budsjettsystem (Haga-utvalgets innstilling) *Norwegian official report on productivity reforms of the state budget system*, Oslo: Statens Trykksaktjeneste.

Norges Offentlige Utredninger (1988) Med viten og vilje (Hernes-utvalgets innstilling). *Norwegian official report (The Hernes commitee's report) on higher education in Norway*, Oslo: Statens Trykksakstjeneste.

Norges Offentlige Utredninger (2000) Frihet med ansvar. Om høgre utdanning og forskning i Norge (Mjøs-utvalgets innstilling). *Norwegian official report on the quality reform*, Oslo: Statens Trykksaktjeneste.

Power, M. (1997) *The audit society: rituals of verification*, Oxford: Oxford University Press.

Pye, A. (1995) 'Strategy through dialogue and doing. A game of "Mornington Crescent?" ', *Management Learning*, 26, 445–462.

Schultz, M., M. J. Hatch, and M. Holten Larsen (2000) *The expressive organization: linking identity, reputation and the corporate brand*, Oxford: Oxford University Press.

Scott, W. R. (2008) *Institutions and organisations: ideas and interests*, 3rd edition, Thousand Oaks: Sage.

Scott, W. R., and G. F. Davis (2007) *Organizations and organizing: rational, natural and open system perspectives*, Upper Saddle River: Pearsons.

Selznick, P. (1957) *Leadership in administration*, New York: Harper & Row.

Sims, D. (2003) 'Between the milestones: a narrative account of the vulnerability of middle managers storying', *Human Relations*, 56, 1195–2111.

Sturdy, A., M. Schwarz, and A. Spicer (2006) 'Guess who's coming to dinner? Structures and uses of liminality in strategic management consultancy', *Human Relations*, 59, 929–960.

Weick, K. E. (1995) *Sensemaking in organizations*, Thousand Oaks: Sage.

Whittington, R. (1996) 'Strategy as practice', *Long Range Planning*, 29, 731–735.

Whittington, R. (2006) 'Completing the practice turn in strategy', *Organization Studies*, 27, 613–634.

Wooldridge, B., T. Schmid, and S. W. Floyd (2008) 'The middle management perspective on strategy process: contributions, synthesis and future research', *Journal of Management*, 34, 1190–1221.

5
Let the Devil Choose: Frustration or Anxiety in the Wake of Performance Measurement in Universities

Cláudia S. Sarrico & Ana I. Melo

Introduction

The purpose of this chapter is to discuss changes and challenges in the management of universities by using two archetypes – the ivory tower and the mass university – as an intellectual device to illustrate the nature of changes from traditional to contemporary universities.

The university is a complex organization, which may consist of many sub-cultures and disciplinary cultures. When we use the term 'university' we refer to one of the dominant sub-cultures in universities, namely the management, which likes to be identified as 'the university'. This sub-culture is, indeed, becoming increasingly important in our time of global university rankings, with international competition among higher education institutions resulting in the current focus on performance measurement and management activities.

Performance objectives should provide the means by which a university's strategy is translated into courses of action, setting out the priorities for teaching and learning, research and scholarship and the third mission. Together with the university mission they specify the tasks to be undertaken. Pressures for increased performance in relation to financial and resource allocation issues, teaching and research quality, student and other dimensions of stakeholder satisfaction, will be ever more prevalent, given increased market competition and state regulation in times of financial constraints and heightened consumer assertiveness.

Universities, as with other professional services, have, in the past, been accused of complacency – the ivory tower archetype: professors might have known better, but they were often perceived as arrogant or self-important by students and funding agencies, being detached from society. In the last decade, universities were pushed into the mass university archetype, more focused on standardized procedures and on the introduction of performance and accountability assessment mechanisms. In fact, these institutions are, currently, competing for resources, these being financial, material or human, and face an increased pressure for accountability to their funders, students and society at large. However, lately, they started to feel the need to differentiate in order to be at the top of the league tables, which became increasingly important. They have perceived that excellent universities will not only have to be good in their academic or research standards, but also in the experience they provide to students and to staff.

Dealing with increased, often contradictory, pressures is not easy. How can the experience of students and staff be improved without increasing cost? How can efficiency in terms of progression, retention and graduation rates be improved without compromising academic standards and values, and widening access policies? Performance objectives are the basis for the development of performance measurement systems and a key way of linking performance measures to strategy. However, control systems are part of a cultural web, with trade-offs between efficiency and flexibility, corresponding to either compliant or adaptive cultures. Often, universities experience a schizophrenic situation whereby they are increasingly required to be both, which generates frustration and anxiety.

Additionally, organizational control systems often lag behind what is desired to reinforce new behaviours. The phrase 'what gets measured gets managed, but what gets rewarded gets done' illustrates the current situation with teaching quality in many institutions: it gets measured and thus gets managed, but it does not get rewarded, so it does not get done. It also exemplifies how the core culture of an organization changes extremely slowly.

In this chapter, we will explore how universities are coping with the pressures to be both ivory tower and mass university.

Pressure for increased performance in universities

Many universities around the world have been operating in an environment where the public sector has been reinventing itself in the form of what became known as 'managerialism' (Aucoin, 1990; Pollitt, 1993; Peters, 1996), 'New Public Management' (Hood, 1991), 'market-based public administration' (Lan & Rosenbloom, 1992), the 'post-bureaucratic paradigm' (Barzelay, 1992) or 'entrepreneurial government' (Osborne & Gaebler, 1992). The key features of this reinvention have been 'a focus on management, not policy, and on performance appraisal and efficiency; [...] the use of quasi-markets and contracting out to foster competition; cost cutting; and a style of management which emphasizes, amongst other things, output targets, limited-term contracts, monetary incentives and freedom to manage' (Rhodes, 1991).

Thus, universities have been subjected to several exogenous forces that reflect the changing context. Among others, there have been pressures to democratize access to higher education, to contain costs, to be accountable for the money spent, to increase productivity, to improve the quality of teaching and research, and to develop the third mission and show its impact on society. These external pressures have, in turn, led to internal ones as a reactionary consequence.

In order to address the environmental change, many universities started to rethink their traditional forms of organization, governance and management, and implemented new strategies that put an emphasis on the introduction of effective coordination and control systems, needed to improve organizational performance (Clark, 1998; Vilalta, 2001; De Boer, 2003). As a result, the university culture has increasingly moved towards a market-driven enterprise culture, largely reflecting the new management models that have spread through the public sector (Ackroyd & Ackroyd, 1999).

However, the implementation of these new strategies is far from straightforward. For example, in terms of the introduction of performance management systems, which comprise the collection, reporting and use of performance data that may be used to influence staff behaviour and to drive improvement, there is evidence that many universities spend a large amount of time and resources in measuring performance, not using the data collected and thus getting only limited value from those efforts (Melo et al., 2010; Sarrico et al., 2010).

Even though almost every management manual assumes that by having a clear strategy managers will know what initiatives to approve and to reject, customers will know what to expect, employees will know what to provide and operations will know how they have to deliver the service thus naturally leading to organizational success, in practice, that seldom happens (Jarzabkowski & Wilson, 2002; Jarzabkowski, 2003). Strategy formulation means change and that change is constrained by both the external and internal environments. That is why it is so important to understand the endogenous and exogenous forces that are driving universities to change their missions, structures and processes and analyse how these institutions are responding to these new challenges.

From the ivory tower to the mass university and back

Throughout organizational history, a tension has been observed between quality and productivity, effectiveness and efficiency, adaptability and compliance, giving rise to what some call the classical and neo-classical organizations, the mechanistic and organic archetypes. The pressure to change from one archetype to another can lead institutions to either frustration or anxiety, depending on the change of direction (Johnston & Clark, 2008). Figure 5.1 attempts to show how those tensions occur in higher education representing two archetypes, the ivory tower and the mass university, and the often existing gap between what is promised (marketing) and aspired to, and the reality (operations) of what universities can offer.

The ivory tower

The ivory tower archetype is characterized by small numbers of students and low student-staff ratios, where students feel they are treated as

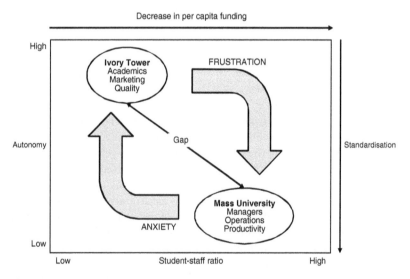

Figure 5.1   Frustration and anxiety in universities
Note: Inspired by Johnston and Clark (2008).

individuals and there is a large autonomy for academics and flexibility in the way things are done. In this type of institution, academics have high degrees of creative discretion both in teaching and research. There is often a high dependence on key professors' skills and knowledge. There is resistance to the generation of standard processes, leading to inconsistent approaches. There is an emphasis on innovation and on personal development. The management style here is likely to be collegial, focusing on getting the best out of every individual. Few processes are documented, partly because there is no consistency in the types of activity performed and partly because academics may resist what appears to be an attempt to impose controls on their autonomy.

Although for many centuries universities were ivory towers, standing aside from society, they started to feel the pressure to move towards a more commoditized type of institution, as student numbers increased and pleas for increased quality and accountability arose.

The move from the ivory tower archetype to the mass university is well documented in the higher education literature. In fact, there is a widely shared opinion among scholars that the changes that have occurred in higher education from the late 20th century onwards forced universities towards a shift in their identity. Bauer et al. (1999), for example, talk about 'transforming universities' and Amaral et al. (2003) discuss the existence of a 'managerial' revolution. As Mora (2001) puts it, '[universities] have gone from training a selected elite [the ivory tower], to educating a large proportion of the population, under what has come to be called the mass system of higher education' (see Trow [1973] for a seminal essay on the issue).

However, the transition from the ivory tower to the mass university (the lower right corner in Figure 5.1) will lead to frustration and, possibly, to some academics leaving the university.

The frustrated university

The most significant aspect of this type of transition is the impact on individual academics. Many of them will argue that they have joined academia for the professional autonomy they had and that they enjoy the creativity associated with their role. However, as Olssen and Peters (2005) argue, by being defined from outside the academic role, targets and performance criteria are increasingly diminishing the sense in which academics are autonomous, challenging the concept of 'academic freedom'. Thus, the traditional notions of professional academic autonomy and freedom start to compete with a new set of pressures, with academics feeling that managers are imposing procedures on them, which do not comply with self-improvement and self- and collegial accountability, the core values of the academic culture (Laughton, 2003). Moreover, academics often complain about the high level of bureaucratic work demanded from them, often deviating their attention from teaching and research (Newton, 2002; Harvey, 2006).

Therefore, as the university grows and moves towards the mass university corner, academics do not seem motivated to turn their creativity into developing consistent and, arguably, more efficient processes. In fact, they will resist the implementation of standardized processes, often imposed on them, claiming that the system prevents them from operating in the most effective way.

In this 'frustrating situation', academics often perceive that they still have high degrees of discretion, despite the standard processes being implemented. They sometimes feel they are 'above' the system, which does not apply to them, and that they can circumvent its requirements in order to get on with the job in the way they think best.

Managers at this type of university may want to restrict the degree of discretion of some or all of their academics. A common reason for this would be that, as a consequence of actual or desired growth, as a result for instance of widening access policies, systems and standardized processes, thus reducing the opportunity for individuals to develop their own way of doing things. This is particularly relevant in universities trying to comply with evaluation and accreditation processes.

The problem with academics that have become used to high levels of perceived discretion is that they find it particularly difficult to work in an environment where they feel that their freedom is restricted. They may comply with the system if the alternative is to lose pay or status in the university, but they find the system difficult to accept and are likely to become disaffected as a result.

It is important to recognize the concerns of these academics because they frequently possess the skills and knowledge that are essential to retain. This may be achieved in some cases by providing them with opportunities for development through involvement in activities that do not conflict with the objectives of the more standardized processes being implemented; this is often the case with a research-teaching divide. The university may grant more freedom in research in exchange for more compliance in teaching, which has become more regulated.

The transition will also put an increasing onus on managers, as they will be expected to offer a clearer direction for the university as a whole, and for its employees, in the form of strategic and action plans, and staff appraisal and developmental procedures.

In this rather organic style of organization type, the challenge will be to ensure a reasonably consistent approach, as great variability often brings in inefficiency. However, academics will resist the transition, which will probably be better accommodated if they can own the processes and be creative, rather than act as labourers that do not own up to their job.

The mass university

The mass university archetype is characterized by large volumes of students in an increasingly standardized environment. It represents higher education as a commodity service. Its focus is increasingly on a consistent service provision, prodded on by a multiplicity of regulatory agencies that regulate access and minimum quality standards, assured by evaluation and accreditation agencies. Power (1997) called this the 'audit society', submerged by rituals of verification and based on the intensive use of standardization procedures. Increasingly, members of academic staff receive formal standardized training before being allowed into the classroom. High volumes of students and consistent teaching procedures lend themselves to the use of information technology and distance or part-distance learning in an attempt to reduce costs.

Barnett (2000) uses the concept of 'performativity' to argue that marketization has become a new universal theme, commodifying teaching and learning and the various ways in which higher education must meet the new performative criteria with an emphasis on measurable outputs. As a consequence of this marketization, there has been an increased emphasis on performance and accountability assessment, with the accompanying use of performance indicators and individual appraisal systems. This has led to a shift from 'bureaucratic-professional' forms of accountability to 'consumer-managerial' accountability models, where academics need to demonstrate their utility to society and increasingly compete for students, who provide a considerable percentage of core funding through tuition fees (Olssen & Peters, 2005). This focus on accountability encompassed efforts to promote standardization, transparency, quality and efficiency by increasing surveillance and centralizing authority.

The management style of the mass university is frequently directive. The procedures have usually been designed by the centre, without consultation, which then carries out periodic audits to ensure compliance with what has been predetermined.

To avoid the trap of being a commodity service, mass universities may feel the need to differentiate from the rest and join the elite, by extending the range of their service provision. The need to be different in order to be at the top has been enhanced by the introduction of league tables, from which *The Times* Higher Education World University Rankings and the Academic Ranking of World Universities (ARWU), published by the Centre for World-Class Universities and the Institute of Higher Education of Shanghai Jiao Tong University (China), are good examples.

Even though mostly used in the Anglo-Saxon world, the usage of league tables will most likely be extended to other countries. In fact, recent developments at the European level indicate the will to increase accountability, through the development of rankings and other classification tools.

The signing of the Bologna Declaration in 1999 has put more pressure on states to establish national quality frameworks and on higher education institutions to introduce quality assurance mechanisms. New decisions have been made at the follow-up meetings that happen every two years to analyse the implementation of the Bologna Process. In Bergen in 2005, the ministers of education agreed to the Standards and Guidelines for Quality Assurance in the European Higher Education Area (ENQA, 2005), drafted by the European Association for Quality Assurance in Higher Education (ENQA), in cooperation with the European University Association (EUA), the European Association of Institutions of Higher Education (EURASHE) and the European Students' Union (ESU, formerly ESIB). At the London meeting in 2007, the ministers of education established the European Quality Assurance Register for Higher Education (EQAR), based on a proposal drafted by ENQA, EUA, EURASHE and ESU (ENQA, 2007). While in 2009, the ministers of education held another meeting in Leuven, opening the way to the implementation of a ranking system, in a section entitled 'Multidimensional Transparency Tools':

> We note that there are several current initiatives designed to develop mechanisms for providing more detailed information about higher education institutions across the EHEA [European Higher Education Area] to make their diversity more transparent. We believe that any such mechanisms, including those helping higher education systems and institutions to identify and compare their respective strengths, should be developed in close consultation with the key stakeholders.
> (Leuven Communiqué, 2009)

Within this trend, the European Commission commissioned a report on the possibility of establishing a classification of European universities (van Vught, 2009) and funded two projects to analyse the implementation of a multi-dimensional ranking system: U-Map and U-Multirank. Kaiser and Jongbloed (2010) describe these projects, '[While] the U-Map project provides a mapping of institutions, the U-Multirank project aims at a ranking of institutions'. These recent developments will most likely lead to a ranking of European universities and to the implementation of a stratified European Area of Higher Education.

By enabling comparisons, the introduction of these classification tools will most certainly drive universities into pursuing the quality that will enable them to reach the top of the rankings, thus allowing a few of them to be considered part of the elite group – back to the ivory tower.

However, the move from the lower right corner of Figure 5.1 towards the upper left corner will arguably raise anxiety.

The anxious university

The problem with commoditized higher education is that universities might seek to differentiate themselves in an increasingly competitive market and thus feel the need to move in the commodity-capability continuum. In this vein, they may wish to increase the amount of autonomy given to academics, namely to pursue research and/or third mission projects. They may also want to increase the range of their educational offering. In this case, academics may be asked to take more decisions and to carry out a greater proportion of the tasks needed.

This change may well be planned and executed, typically involving investment in training and support systems and including the recruitment of support staff (Sarrico, 2010). In these circumstances, academics may believe they are being moved from what might feel like a reasonably safe environment, where they are provided with a clear structure and procedures to follow, to one where individual decision-making is required.

The academics involved in this process may want to engage in this challenge, but feel either unsure of their own ability to do it or uncertain about how much real discretion the university is willing to give them. In this process of change, some academics may not perform immediately to the desired level and may be dismissed as not being up to the challenge.

The role of managers here changes from being the owner and 'enforcer' of procedures to ensuring that academics and support staff are developed. It is more likely that staff will be able to deal with the transition with support and training.

A schizophrenic situation for universities

Many universities will be under pressure to change, not choosing a particular corner, but positioning themselves in the capability-commodity continuum. On the one hand, the ivory tower university may be under pressure to increase the number of students it takes in and drive down the high per capita cost of operating. On the other hand, the mass university, dealing primarily with high numbers of undergraduate students, may be under pressure to become more flexible, offer customized education, become increasingly involved in third mission projects, all as a way to diversify funding sources and be more research directed, in an attempt to distinguish itself in a competitive environment.

If, at first, the move might have been in the direction of capability towards commodity, following a massification trend, pressures in the opposite direction can clearly be observed. Being requested to be both ivory tower and mass university, universities are put in a schizophrenic situation, suffering, at the same time, from frustration and anxiety. But how are universities dealing with this dilemma?

Coping strategies

Similar to other institutions, universities have been able to find ways of coping with conflict throughout history. Two types of coping strategies will be discussed here: loosely coupling and decoupling strategies, and translation strategies.

Loosely coupling and decoupling strategies

Scholars have used 'loose coupling' and 'decoupling' to account for the relatively weak influence of government policy on this type of institution.

The idea of 'coupling', in general, and 'loose coupling', in particular, came to prominence in the writings of Glassman (1973), in the context of Biology, and then of March and Olsen (1975), cited by Weick (1976), and Weick (1974, 1976), with regard to institutions in general and educational institutions in particular. These authors originally introduced the concept of 'coupling' to challenge functional notions about how organizations operate and argue for attention to their institutional environment. This term, usually defined as the 'relationship among elements or variables' (Beekun & Glick, 2001), captures how organizations are made up of interdependent elements that are more or less responsive to, and more or less distinctive from, each other (Hallett & Ventresca, 2006).

Orton and Weick (1990) introduce the dimensions of distinctiveness and responsiveness to differentiate four types of coupling. If there is neither distinctiveness nor responsiveness, the system is not really a system. They call it a 'non-coupled' system. If there is distinctiveness, but no responsiveness, the system is 'decoupled'. If there is responsiveness without distinctiveness, the system is 'tightly coupled'. If there is both distinctiveness and responsiveness, the system is 'loosely coupled'.

Weick (1976) defines 'loose coupling' as a situation in which elements are responsive, but retain evidence of separateness and identity. Orton and Weick (1990) argue that 'loose coupling allows theorists to posit that any system, in any organizational location, can act on both a technical level, which is closed to outside forces (coupling produces stability), and an institutional level, which is open to outside forces (looseness produces flexibility)'.

This concept challenged the assumption that organizations operated with clear means to an end goals, responsiveness and coordination. Moreover, it considered the existence of broader environments that interpenetrated organizations, further challenging the integrity of a unit-level organization (Hallett & Ventresca, 2006). The concept of 'loose coupling' was analytically powerful because it helped scholars to understand why many organizations, including educational institutions such as universities, continued to operate using familiar routines and practices despite waves of policy reforms and environmental pressures to change.

In many cases, these organizations avoid conflict by buffering 'their formal structures from the uncertainties of technical activities by becoming loosely coupled, building gaps between their formal structures and actual work activities' (Meyer & Rowan, 1977).

The concepts of 'decoupling' and 'loose coupling', that is, practices that enable organizations to sustain formal structures while unit activities vary, represent a break with the assumption that structure controls actions.

This perspective is particularly relevant in universities, given their high degree of autonomy and their integration into the state hierarchy. On the one hand, universities must adapt themselves to the various strains of public authority. By contrast, the norms of academic freedom and autonomy dominate internally. The result of state control on the one hand and autonomy on the other implies that we are dealing with complex organizations where the formal and the informal are partly opposed to each other. Problems that arise where different 'logics' meet are solved with apparent adjustments. 'Loosely coupling' and 'decoupling' strategies have thus been used in these institutions as coping strategies to resolve the tension between formal structures and informal practices. There are also institutions simultaneously aligning with and decoupling from multiple external pressures and influences in order to cope with and survive the multiple underlying logic that motivates them. These are hybrid institutions (Parker, 2011).

Going back to our model, several examples of coping strategies for dealing with anxiety and frustration are presented.

The ivory tower within the mass university

One possible strategy would be to have two universities emerging within each university, with one set of academics feeling they are working for the mass university and another for the ivory tower. The first group will most likely be on teaching contracts only, mainly teaching undergraduates, or will be moving from one research assistant position to the next, mainly on temporary contracts; the second group will be in tenure-tracked positions with time and resources to do research, low teaching loads, the possibility of sabbaticals and will be teaching mainly postgraduate, fee-paying students. In this case, different strategies to accommodate the ivory tower within the mass university can be observed.

Modular organization as a form of customization

More and more often the teaching offered by the university takes the form of modules. This allows for the appearance of customization in a, for all purposes, mass education format, whereby students may choose from different teaching modules, thus 'customizing' their syllabus and thus having the experience of 'personal service'.

Differentiation between teaching and research

The university will benefit from standardization at the level of undergraduate provision, becoming more customized at the postgraduate level. Increasing separation of teaching and learning from research and scholarship, with dual career paths formally acknowledged or emerging in practice will occur as a result of promotion policies. Another emergent phenomenon might be the actual creation of separate organizations within the university, such as 'centres of excellence', where people are shielded from the perils of the mass university by way of increased resources for postgraduate supervision and research, and scholarship activities, in a very autonomous environment.

The accommodation of the two archetypes might be better accomplished in university systems that operate as a network, such as the California state system (Douglass, 2000) or some other multi-campus universities with different units, which cater for different missions.

Translation strategies

The translation view highlights the significance of the local context and local actors as they confront ideas and practices from around the world (Czarniawska & Joerges, 1996; Czarniawska, 2005). The translation process takes different trajectories depending upon the context in which the translators are able and willing to reframe or transform existing institutional settings in ways that fit the current demands.

Czarniawska provides the shortest definition of the translational approach to fashion. 'Fashion creates as it is followed. It is the subsequent translations that simultaneously produce and reproduce variations in fashion: repetition creates and re-creates difference. [...] Fashion stands for change. But as fashion is also repetitive, in long-range perspective it stands for tradition' (Czarniawska, 2005). While previous views of fashion limited it to certain processes to avoid paradoxes, the translation view, according to Czarniawska (2005), better enhances our understanding in exactly those paradoxical terms:

> Fashion, then transpires as a highly paradoxical process. Its constitutive paradoxes are invention and imitation, variation and uniformity, distance and interest, novelty and conservatism, unity and segregation, conformity and deviation, change and status quo, revolution and evolution. And it is indeed translation, side by side with negotiation that is used to resolve these paradoxes in each practical action.

However, if fashion setters are not pushing fashions on fashion consumers, why do specific ideas, objects and techniques travel widely while others do not? In their chapter, 'Translation Is a Vehicle, Imitation Its Motor, and Fashion Sits at the Wheel', Czarniawska and Sevón (2005) talk about a market in which management fashion producers sell the same management innovation to similar buyers and the notion that innovations diffuse because fashion setters push them onto passive adopters, like marionettes. It is the act of imitation by many translators that marks them as fashion followers. These imitators in turn create the reputation, as successful fashion setters, of those they imitate or presumably they would go out of business.

What drives fashion is a shared desire to arrive at the same result. Each fashion, and the travelling imitative translation it animates, must be understood in the historical and special context of the previous fashion it displaced and the next fashion that will replace it.

Going back to our model, some universities might attempt to be fashion followers, while others will be fashion producers. Fashion followers might try to implement certain procedures, processes or structures in order to imitate those they see as natural leaders (the best universities in the rankings). These 'imitation' behaviours can be seen when comparing the mission statements of several universities. Indeed, as Parker (2011) argues, 'the missions that universities formally publish are increasingly convergent and homogenised'. The obsession with published rankings often leads universities to try to be at least as good as the 'fashion setters'. That means setting the same demanding objectives, which will enable them to move from mass university to ivory tower, where in this respect, of course, the local context plays an important role. In the process of reframing or transforming existing institutional settings, some universities will get there and build a reputation for themselves. Others will not succeed and remain at the lower corner of Figure 5.1, as undistinguished mass universities.

Conclusions

A problem with the existence of the ivory tower and the mass university archetypes is the possibility of a divergence between what is 'promised' or 'aspired to', typically the ivory tower concept of university, and what 'exists' or 'needs to exist', typically the mass university. The perceived gap between the two concepts may affect academic satisfaction, but also student satisfaction, since what is expected by both is beyond what is experienced. In our discussion, it seems that the university is destined to permanence in a state of tension, be it frustration or anxiety, as there are forces pushing it in the direction of the mass university, such as policies to widen access, and forces pushing it in the direction of the ivory tower, such as 'excellency' policies trying to position national systems in an increased global and competitive environment of higher education.

The management of universities is finding strategies to cope with these tensions, trying to accommodate the ivory tower and mass university types within them, if not explicitly choosing a firm position in the capability–commodity continuum.

References

Ackroyd, P. and S. Ackroyd (1999) 'Problems of University Governance in Britain: Is more Accountability the Solution?', *The International Journal of Public Sector Management*, 12, 171–185.

Amaral, A., O. Fulton and I. M. Larsen (2003) 'A Managerial Revolution?', in A. Amaral, V. L. Meek and I. M. Larsen (eds) *The Higher Education Managerial Revolution?* (Dordrecht: Kluwer Academic Publishers), 275–296.

Aucoin, P. (1990) 'Administrative Reform in Public Management: Paradigms, Principles, Paradoxes and Pendulums', *Governance*, 3, 115–137.

Barnett, R. (2000) *Realising the University in an Age of Supercomplexity* (Buckingham: The Society for Research into Higher Education and Open University Press).

Barzelay, M. (1992) *Breaking Through Bureaucracy: A New Vision for Managing in Government* (Berkeley: University of California Press).

Bauer, M., B. Askling, S. G. Marton and F. Marton (1999) *Transforming Universities: Changing Patterns of Governance, Structure and Learning in Swedish Higher Education* (London: Jessica Kingsley Publishers).

Beekun, R. I. and W. H. Glick (2001) 'Organization Structure from a Loose Coupling Perspective: A Multidimensional Approach', *Decision Sciences*, 32, 227–250.

Clark, R. B. (1998) *Creating Entrepreneurial Universities: Organizational Pathways of Transformation* (Oxford: Pergamon).

Czarniawska, B. (2005) 'Fashion in Organizing', in B. Czarniawska and G. Sevón (eds) *Global Ideas: How Ideas, Objects and Practices Travel in the Global Economy* (Malmö: Liber & Copenhagen Business School Press), 129–146.

Czarniawska, B. and B. Joerges (1996) 'Travels of Ideas', in B. Czarniawska and G. Sevón (eds) *Translating Organizational Change* (Berlin: de Gruyter) 13–48.

Czarniawska, B. and G. Sevón (2005) 'Translation Is a Vehicle, Imitation its Motor, and Fashion Sits at the Wheel', in B. Czarniawska and G. Sevón (eds) *Global Ideas: How ideas, Objects and Practices Travel in the Global Economy* (Malmö: Liber & Copenhagen Business School Press), 7–12.

De Boer, H. (2003) 'Who's Afraid of Red, Yellow and Blue?', in A. Amaral, V. L. Meek and I. M. Larsen (eds) *The Higher Education Managerial Revolution?* (Dordrecht: Kluwer Academic Publishers), 89–108.

Douglass, J. A. (2000) *The California Idea and American Higher Education: 1850 to the 1960 Master Plan* (Stanford: Stanford University Press).

ENQA (2005) *Standards and Guidelines for Quality Assurance in the European Higher Education Area* (Helsinki: ENQA).

ENQA (2007) *Report to the London Conference of Ministers on a European Register of Quality Assurance Agencies* (Helsinki: ENQA).

Glassman, R. B. (1973) 'Persistence and Loose Coupling in Living Systems', *Behavioral Science*, 18, 83–98.

Hallett, T. and M. J. Ventresca (2006) 'How Institutions Form: Loose Coupling as Mechanism in Gouldner's Patterns of Industrial Bureaucracy', *American Behavioral Scientist*, 49, 908–924.

Harvey, L. (2006) 'Impact of Quality Assurance: Overview of a Discussion between Representatives of External Quality Assurance Agencies', *Quality in Higher Education*, 12, 287–290.

Hood, C. (1991) 'A Public Management for All Seasons', *Public Administration*, 69, 3–19.

Jarzabkowski, P. (2003) 'Strategic Practices: An Activity Theory Perspective on Continuity and Change', *Journal of Management Studies*, 40, 23–55.

Jarzabkowski, P. and D. C. Wilson (2002) 'Top Teams and Strategy in a UK University', *Journal of Management Studies*, 39, 357–383.

Johnston, R. and G. Clark (2008) *Service Operations Management* (Harlow: FT Prentice Hall).

Kaiser, F. and B. Jongbloed (2010) 'New Transparency Instruments for European Higher Education: The U-Map and the U-Multirank Projects'. *2010 European Network for Indicator Designers (ENID) Conference*. Leiden.

Lan, Z. and D. H. Rosenbloom (1992) 'Editorial', *Public Administration Review*, 52, 535–537.

Laughton, D. (2003) 'Why Was the QAA Approach to Teaching Quality Assessment Rejected by Academics in UK HE?', *Assessment and Evaluation in Higher Education*, 28, 309–321.

Leuven Communiqué (2009) *Leuven Communiqué*, http://www.ond.vlaanderen. be/hogeronderwijs/bologna/conference/documents/Leuven_Louvain-la-Neuve_Communiqué_April_2009.pdf

March, J. G. and J. P. Olsen (1975) *Choice Situations in Loosely Coupled Worlds*, unpublished manuscript (Stanford University).

Melo, A. I., C. S. Sarrico and Z. Radnor (2010) 'The Influence of Performance Management Systems on Key Actors in Universities: The Case of an English University', *Public Management Review*, 12, 233–254.

Meyer, J. W. and B. Rowan (1977) 'Institutionalized Organizations: Formal Structure as Myth and Ceremony', *The American Journal of Sociology*, 83, 340–363.

Mora, J.-G. (2001) 'Governance and Management in the New University', *Tertiary Education and Management*, 7, 95–110.

Newton, J. (2002) 'Views from Below: Academics Coping with Quality', *Quality in Higher Education*, 8, 39–61.

Olssen, M. and M. A. Peters (2005) 'Neoliberalism, Higher Education and the Knowledge Economy: From the Free Market to Knowledge Capitalism', *Journal of Education Policy*, 20, 313–345.

Orton, J. D. and K. E. Weick (1990) 'Loosely Coupled. Systems: A Reconceptualization', *Academy of Management Review*, 15, 203–223.

Osborne, D. and T. Gaebler (1992) *Reinventing Government: How the Entrepreneurial Spirit is Transforming the Public Sector* (Reading: Addison-Wesley).

Parker, L. (2011) 'University Corporatisation: Driving Redefinition', *Critical Perspectives on Accounting*, 22(4), 434–450.

Peters, B. G. (1996) *The Future of Governing: Four Emerging Models* (Lawrence, KS: University of Kansas).

Pollitt, C. (1993) *Managerialism and the Public Services* (Oxford: Blackwell).

Power, M. (1997) *The Audit Society: Rituals of Verification* (Oxford: Oxford University Press).

Rhodes, R. A. W. (1991) 'Introduction', *Public Administration Review*, 69, 1–2.

Sarrico, C. S. (2010) 'On Performance in Higher Education: Towards Performance Governance?', *Tertiary Education and Management*, 16, 145–158.

Sarrico, C. S., M. J. Rosa, P. N. Teixeira and M. F. Cardoso (2010) 'Assessing Quality and Evaluating Performance in Higher Education: Worlds Apart or Complementary Views?', *Minerva*, 48(1), 35–54.

Trow, M. (1973) *Problems in the Transition from Elite to Mass Higher Education* (Berkeley: Carnegie Commission on Higher Education).

van Vught, F. (2009) *Mapping the Higher Education Landscape* (Dordrecht: Springer).

Vilalta, J. (2001) 'University Policy and Coordination Systems between Governments and Universities: The Experience of the Catalan University System', *Tertiary Education and Management*, 7, 9–22.

Weick, K. E. (1974) 'Middle Range Theories of Social Systems', *Behavioral Science*, 19, 357–367.

Weick, K. E. (1976) 'Educational Organizations as Loosely Coupled Systems', *Administrative Science Quarterly*, 21, 1–19.

6
The Changing Culture of Academic Research: From Organizations to Networks

Amy Scott Metcalfe

Introduction

At the start of the 21st century, higher education became more fully understood as an integral component of national and regional economic competitiveness. With this changing socio-economic role, governments have placed more emphasis on expanding the research capacities of colleges, universities and institutes. Even with tight budgets due to the global economic crisis of 2008–2010, allocations for academic research have continued to rise in many countries, although the nature of the relationship between funding agencies and higher education institutions has changed. In addition, the spread of New Public Management's principles into the higher education sector, which some see as reforms, promoted an increasing attention to research evaluation and accountability. These changes have been understood as necessary to measure the outcomes of research while ensuring responsible and adequate public spending on innovation. Once in place, some believe that these accountability measures have the potential to be linked to performance-based funding schemes that may affect academic science and knowledge production, for better or for worse (OECD, 2010; Polster, 2003; Savoie, 1995).

From a management perspective, both structural and cultural perspectives might be considered as levers to increase research performance. In addition, incentives for research output and penalties for declining research performance have implications for academics at the individual level. Both the UK's Research Assessment Exercise and Australia's Research Quality Framework contain mechanisms for managerial oversight at various institutional levels, with implications for individual academic researchers. These quality frameworks have helped solidify output-oriented and comparative assessment criteria for research and have simultaneously contributed to a move away from researcher-centric evaluation norms, such as those closely associated with the academic sciences.

The guiding question for this chapter is: 'To understand changes in academic research, should we focus on cultural or structural aspects?' The Canadian research context serves as an example, preceded by a discussion of academic science and its relationship to notions of academic culture. Next, trends in academic research structure are presented, with an eye to how these changes have been discussed in the literature. Then, the Canada Foundation for Innovation (CFI) is introduced as an example of an organization that has contributed to a growing 'postacademic' (Ziman, 1996) research culture in Canada through its funding formula and eligibility expectations. This is followed by a discussion of the Canada Research Chairs (CRC) programme, which is presented as an example of individual-level research reforms. Next, a commercialization agreement between the Associations for Colleges and Universities of Canada (AUCC) and the federal government is presented in relation to publically supported, private market incentives for academic research and the effect on research culture. Finally, theoretical implications are discussed.

Academic science and research culture

Academic science has long had an interdependent relationship with government and thus an eye towards external validation and rewards in the form of research grants and their structural effects. Yet, academic science has also developed a strong culture, articulated as the Mertonian norms of communalism, universalism, disinterestedness and organized scepticism. As Hackett (1990) noted two decades ago, science is shifting away from Mertonian norms towards other value systems, many of which are influenced by changing governmental relations with the scientific community, and increasing private investment in academic research. These changes have been described as being part of the entrepreneurial university (Clark, 1998) and exhibiting the characteristics known as academic capitalism (Slaughter & Leslie, 1997; Slaughter & Rhoades, 2004). The culture of academic science moves towards that of industrial science and vice versa as these externally focused (market) value systems and their reward structures take hold.

In Chapter 1, Henkel, Välimaa, Sarrico and Stensaker noted the tensions between endogenous and exogenous influences on academics and hence discrepancies in the literature regarding the most effective standpoint for asking empirical questions about 'culture', including which evidence points are pertinent to this phenomenon. With regard to the overall academic environment, Hackett (1990) described culture as 'a set of guiding values, beliefs, principles, rules, and material objects that shape human behavior' (pp. 242–243). However, he stated that the culture of academic science

> is a blend of the cultures of science and academe, and the resulting cultural mix is further shaped through interaction with and accommodation to its clients, competitors, and patrons. Finally, and most importantly, academic science is undertaken within organizations, and organizations have unique properties, dynamics, and goals which endure across sectors, communities, cultures, and societies. (p. 245)

Because academic science happens within higher education institutions and campus affiliates (such as research hospitals), there is an exchange between the various research communities within university boundaries. Research culture can be understood as the overarching research milieu, as the characteristics Hackett describes apply not only to science, but also other fields where research is conducted.

To return to Henkel et al.'s Introduction to this volume, we might consider the following passage in the context of the research functions of higher education institutions:

> Hence, in principle, one can argue that the classical divide between these two conceptions [normative and structural perspectives] is rooted in their views about how changes occur and to what extent culture is open for manipulation – whether culture is 'manageable'. Is it 'deep' and inseparable from the organization in question or is it an 'attachment' to the organization, an element that can be changed in a more instrumental way? (p. 7)

These questions are integral to current debates in the literature on academic research. In particular, 'deep' aspects of research culture might be dependent upon infrastructure investments caused by organizational 'attachments' to missions, strategies and niche competencies. Exogenous and endogenous effects might be inseparable, both empirically and phenomenologically. Yet, managers will continue to ask, which is more important for growth: a strong research culture or strong research infrastructure? Should governments invest in researchers or in facilities? Observations of researcher mobility show that people can be influenced to move towards better environments, but the clustering of people is in itself also a type of infrastructure that may supersede material aspects. Perhaps the key is the purpose for study: for whom and for what purpose is research on research conducted? We may find that studies *of* change are different from studies *for* change, regardless of a focus on normative or structural aspects, or both.

Changes in research structure

With new protocols for measuring the fruits of academic labour, change in the field of research is often reported in the material terms of an annual yield; the 'products' of research are either up or down from the previous year. These descriptive statistics lend themselves well to institutional reports, state or provincial planning documents, or country-level comparisons.

While research culture has been largely understood in terms of disciplinary norms or in the context of institutional sub-units such as departments, the organizational frame that is often brought to bear on these discussions does not adequately fit research infrastructure, as the conduct of research extends beyond organizational boundaries. For example, when we consider research activity, inter-organizational relationships are common, such as university–industry relations (Etzkowitz & Leydesdorff, 1997; Fisher & Atkinson-Grosjean, 2002; Tuunainen, 2005). Yet, at times these inter-organizational analyses are so focused on structures and optimal outputs, that they forgo recognition of research culture – with the exception of studies that compare industrial norms with academic norms and the resulting effect on knowledge.

For the usual purpose and audience – that is, policy-making and government – the question of what has changed in academic research over the past two decades has already been answered. In the report *Higher Education to 2030, Volume 2: Globalization* (OECD, 2009), Chapter 5 is titled, 'What is changing in academic research? Trends and prospects' (Vincent-Lancrin, 2009). With statistics drawn from the Organisation for Economic Co-operation and Development (OECD) and other sources, the author discusses trends in academic research across several countries. Academic research is defined as 'research and development (R&D) undertaken in the higher education sector, including universities, polytechnics, etc., and research centres that have close links with higher education institutions' (p. 146). In general the report shows that 'academic research is growing in scale, becoming more international, more collaborative, both between sectors and with lay people, and also more competitive' (p. 167). Central themes of the report include the 'massification' of academic research, the role of basic research in contemporary science, the relationship between academic research and New Public Management, the rise of private funding and internationalization, the creation of a new social contract for research and the role of information and communication technology.

In terms of massification, it is reported that over the 1980s and 1990s, the number of researchers in the higher education sector increased about 130 per cent (Vincent-Lancrin, 2009). Within OECD countries, the share of R&D conducted by the higher education sector also increased. The OECD report tied this growth in personnel and expenditures with increased output in the form of academic publishing (both articles and books), of which article publication rose 52 per cent from 1988 to 2005. Citing the US example, the report notes that the number of books published by American university presses increased 32 per cent from 1993 to 2007.

Vincent-Lancrin's chapter goes on to say that because higher education performs a greater percentage of basic research compared to other R&D sectors, this forms a 'special feature' of academic research. The assessment is that by watching the trends of basic research, such as the relative share and absolute funding compared with other R&D sectors (such as government, industry and non-profit organizations), the 'competitive advantage' (p. 153) of higher education can be understood. That basic research has been increasing in industry and private non-profit organizations over the last 20 years, albeit still performing basic research to a lesser extent than higher education and government, may indicate that higher education institutions and national research centres will no longer be seen as the obvious site for this type of work. The trend towards greater private share of basic research (in both profit-making and non-profit organizations) may have implications for the employment of researchers and cross-sector collaboration.

Another trend that has come to define academic research is the rise of 'competition and quasi-market forces' (Vincent-Lancrin, 2009, p. 156) in the process of awarding research funding, leading to a concentration of academic research in fewer institutions per system and potentially in fewer fields that are populated by more specialized researchers. Vincent-Lancrin links these developments with New Public Management, seeing a connection between efforts to increase efficiency and accountability in the public sector with the concentrated ways in which research is funded and managed.

Related to this trend is the rise in commercialization of academic research, and private sector cooperation in funding research that is located in higher education. Vincent-Lancrin sees that public-private collaboration 'might reflect the willingness of many countries to see higher education institutions play a role in regional development' (p. 158) in an effort to replicate the successes of well-known innovative cities and regions. This is likely to be closely related to the balance of basic and applied research as these are distributed among sectors within a given region. In some places a university's strength in basic research becomes an industrial asset; in others, it might be the willingness of a university to participate more fully in applied research. As such, the indicators of commercialization that are tied to academic research do not describe this relational, and perhaps regionally specific, balance.

While regionalism emerged as a characteristic of academic research, so has internationalization. Indeed, the OECD report referenced above was dedicated to the topic of globalization, of which the chapter on changes in academic research was just one element. Vincent-Lancrin notes a growth in researcher mobility, as well as international collaboration. In addition, funding from foreign sources was also on the rise in the period between the 1980s and 2000s. Although Vincent-Lancrin links some of these increases to policy efforts to promote greater international trade and mobility, it is also likely that the increase in competition that he noted is creating a globally stratified academic research system. There may be concern with local development, as described in the previous paragraph, but the research conducted and those involved to achieve those ends may be increasingly internationalized, providing a new dimension to the 'productivity paradox' for the 21st century.[1] In other words, funders at the local level might expect R&D to contribute to regional or national competitiveness, but to do so a world-wide network of researchers must be engaged, either as a talent pool or as arbiters of quality. This opens the door for unintended spillovers into 'free-riding' jurisdictions, the threat of 'brain drain' and a tendency to shift the focus of research away from local needs towards that which is more widely applicable. Thus, research investments made in the name of regional development cannot be guaranteed to lead to a localized net gain given the concomitant ratcheting effects of international competition.

Finally, Vincent-Lancrin ends his chapter with the idea that academic research has been let out of the ivory tower so to speak and is now part of the social realm in such a way as to cause a redefinition of the social contract for research. As the increase of private donations and student tuition as a percentage of overall funding in some systems led to questions about who steers institutions, so too is academic research potentially subject to trends in public opinion. The discourse around 'student-as-consumer' tuition models and marketization may soon be familiar in the research function, as 'philanthropist-as-consumer' research funding becomes more prevalent.

The above method of reporting trends in quantifiable national-level data and considering their implications for policy is entrenched in higher education research. As stated at the beginning of this summary of *Higher Education to 2030, Volume 2: Globalization* (OECD, 2009), for many the question of 'what is changing in academic research?' is answered by Vincent-Lancrin's chapter therein, following its title. However, another reading of the report and the research chapter is that rather than merely a descriptive and thoughtful accounting, the work itself and the data on which it is based are contributing factors to changes in academic research. Thinking reflexively we might notice that research on research has a tendency to reinforce particular assumptions about purpose, evidence, method and dissemination. Expectations about which data are useful for policy-making and how these data should be best analysed and presented may influence the tenor of the ensuing conversation. To state this another way, will we know what *matters* when we only know what *counts*? We also might consider that international comparisons beget international comparisons, adding fuel to the fire of an already competitive and nationalistic research climate. A report such as *Higher Education to 2030* may influence change in higher education while it also serves as a resource for understanding where and how change has occurred to this point.

Therefore, if our aim is to understand academic research culture, we must use national-level and international data with caution, so as not to extrapolate normative shifts from statistical trends. How then might we begin to examine research culture, given the above changes noted in the descriptive data? In the next section I describe examples from one national perspective, to see how research reforms have particular policy effects that may lead towards a greater understanding of shifts in research culture.

Canadian research reforms: normative and structural implications

Recent developments in the Canadian research context can serve as examples of reforms intended to create both normative and structural shifts in the research environment, to increase research performance. These examples help to show that neither a cultural nor a structural viewpoint would be sufficient alone to understand the quantitative and qualitative changes in the Canadian research context. In addition, a combination of the cultural and structural viewpoints may be necessary to perceive the unintended consequences of these political reforms.

In 2002, the federal government of Canada built upon previous prosperity policies (see Prosperity Secretariat, 1991) by initiating a national Innovation Strategy through the publication of two related documents: *Achieving Excellence* (Industry Canada, 2002), and *Knowledge Matters* (HRDC, 2002). The former was concerned with building the nation's R&D through a combination of university, industrial and governmental efforts, while the latter pertained to workforce development and skills training (Metcalfe & Fenwick, 2009). In the *Achieving Excellence* document, the government listed three key innovation challenges, linked to three corresponding goals. These can be matched with existing and contemporaneous research reforms (see Table 6.1). Each of these reforms was intended to influence Canadian research infrastructure and culture. Menzies and Newson (2008) state that 'these initiatives are likely to further accentuate hierarchical rankings and intense competition among universities and their researchers' (p. 508).

Table 6.1 Canada's Innovation Strategy and research reforms

Innovation Strategy challenges	Innovation Strategy goals	Resulting research reforms
Innovation environment challenge	Work towards a better innovation environment: build an environment of trust and confidence, where the public interest is protected and marketplace policies provide incentives to innovate	Canada Foundation for Innovation (1997)
Skills challenge	Increase the supply of highly qualified people; ensure the supply of people who create and use knowledge	CRCs programme (2000)
Knowledge performance challenge	Create and use knowledge strategically to benefit Canadians; promote the creation, adoption and commercialization of knowledge	AUCC commercialization agreement (2002)

Adapted from Industry Canada (2002, p. 33).

Canada Foundation for Innovation

The CFI describes itself as 'an independent corporation created by the Government of Canada to fund research infrastructure' (http://www.innovation.ca/en/about-the-cfi/cfi-overview). Unlike the three main granting councils in Canada, the CFI is a non-profit organization that mainly funds capital investments rather than projects or individuals. In this way, the recipient institutions of CFI funding are literally building Canadian research infrastructure in concrete ways.

An advantage of this type of funding from a management perspective is that it cannot cross national borders and can serve as a catalyst for future funding in that the need to maintain or expand the facilities in question are visible to provincial governments and potential private sector investors. In addition to these structural effects, the CFI represents a significant culture shift in Canadian research in that it requires awardees to raise 60 per cent in matching funds, from public and/or private sources. Furthermore, as these investments are capital in nature, the institutions are involved in the process of grant-writing, fundraising and oversight in ways that are not part of the normal agency-researcher funding paradigm. New personnel have been hired by colleges and universities to coordinate CFI applications and related efforts to secure and sustain the necessary funding mix.

The CFI, as an infrastructure fund that necessarily fixes investments into particular geographic places, has the potential over time to build 'research castles', which are physical places for the confluence of intense research activity, 'highly qualified personnel', resources and academic rewards; these castles are even more elite than the ivory tower metaphor has previously suggested. In the Canadian context, the concentration of resources and the creation of a nationally stratified university structure run counter to the historic value of equalization among the provinces and populace. As Polster (2003) puts it,

> The initial advantage of larger, research-intensive universities will be reinforced by their greater ability to support and develop state-sponsored strategic research initiatives. Due to their generally larger endowments, richer alumni, greater 'donation appeal,' and/or more valuable stock of intellectual capital, these universities have more resources than smaller, less research-intensive universities to invest in their strategic research initiatives. Their greater resources also put these universities in a better position to recruit and retain excellent researchers, as well as to lure any potential and actual 'research stars' from smaller institutions which cannot afford to offer as generous

packages of resources and rewards. As their relative ability to build and develop research excellence grows, Canada's larger, research intensive universities will attract even larger shares of granting council (and other) funds. This will result in their receiving even greater shares of CRC and CFI funding, producing a benevolent cycle for them and a vicious spiral for the rest, particularly universities in more remote and/or economically disadvantaged parts of the country. (p. 187)

Indeed, the number of Canada Research Chair positions allocated per university is determined by each institution's relative success in obtaining federal research funding in the previous three years. Castles are forming, attracting knights from all realms.

CRC programme

Concerned with recruiting and retaining Canada's 'best and brightest' academic researchers, the Canadian government permanently established the CRC programme in 2000. Two types of chairs, Tier 1 and Tier 2, were established to distinguish more senior 'outstanding researchers' from 'exceptional emerging researchers', with corresponding institutional grants for each level (Tier 1 receives $200,000 annually for seven years and Tier 2 receives $100,000 annually for five years). CRCs must be nominated by an eligible, degree-granting Canadian institution and approved by a 'college of reviewers' comprised of researchers from various Canadian or foreign universities, private sector companies and government agencies. Unlike typical university faculty appointments which are decided at the departmental level, in the CRC nomination and selection process upper-level administrators and deans are extremely involved.

These appointments have been contentious in many universities, for a few reasons. First, although all fields of intellectual activity are meant to be represented, it has been noted that the programme favours the sciences, raising concerns that more structural investments will continue to be concentrated in already well-funded areas. Side and Robbins (2007) state that even though the intent was to give Canada a competitive edge, the CRC programme

has created an élite research community, heavily weighted in favor of science, engineering, and technology, that perpetuates and rewards a narrow concept of excellence, and that flagrantly ignores equity, further institutionalizing inequalities for women and likely also for faculty from all equity groups in Canadian universities. (p. 173)

In addition, questions about the long-range sustainability of these positions (Dufour, 2010) and the insertion of administrative preferences into faculty hiring decisions have surfaced. Furthermore, as study by Grant and Drakich (2010) found, although many CRCs have had positive experiences, some have found that their departmental relationships are strained and the extent of their rewards are misunderstood by their peers, leaving them to feel like 'the rich kid on the block' (p. 33). As departmental colleagues were less involved in the hire, they may rebuff or resent an administrative insertion of a 'star' faculty member into their unit. Not only might this upset the balance of academic autonomy, but may also create a more competitive internal culture and raise concerns about the availability of scarce resources for research.

AUCC commercialization agreement

As there is no formal higher education accreditation agency in Canada, the membership of the AUCC serves a quasi-official body that recognizes and legitimizes universities and four-year colleges. Presidents of the 95 public and non-profit institutional members regularly come together through the work of this intermediating organization (Metcalfe, 2010) and the body acts as a 'lobby' for the higher education sector, albeit informally. The AUCC describes its objectives as 'public policy and advocacy; communications, research and information-sharing; [providing] scholarships and international programs' (http://www.aucc.ca/about_us/index_e.html).

In the same year that the federal Innovation Strategy was written, the Canadian government and the AUCC finalized an agreement titled, *Framework of Agreed Principles on Federally Funded University Research* (AUCC & Government of Canada, 18 November 2002). The document stipulates that all Canadian research universities and most research-active comprehensive universities would double the amount of research they conducted and triple the amount of commercialization of academic research, both by 2010. While an assessment of the progress Canadian institutions have made towards this target by the end of the deadline year has not yet been released, estimates in 2008 were that meeting these goals would be accomplished in time (AUCC, 2008; Rasmussen, 2008).

The commercialization agreement highlights the unbundling of the research function and the creation of 'para-academics' in the area of technology transfer (Macfarlane, 2011). The government's commercialization agenda has not been as widely accepted by university technology transfer staff as might be expected given the discourse about technocrats in the academy. In a study of staff members at Canadian technology transfer offices (TTOs), Bubela and Caulfield (2010) found that these academic employees 'recognized the role of universities as knowledge creation and social good, and their own role as broader than commercialization defined by traditional metrics' (p. 451). In particular, those working within TTOs in Canada were found to value the traditional social contract for research and not necessarily agree with the emphasis on some of the metrics used to define success in their line of work. As one of their respondents noted, 'What we do should benefit society in some way and it doesn't always have to be commercializable' (p. 448). However, as Macfarlane (2011) notes,

> The audit of research activity conducted in the UK and Australia has encouraged a growth in roles related to research and research management and has impacted substantially on teaching through the increased use of graduate students and part-time faculty as teachers, releasing academics to pursue publication and grant-getting targets. (p. 68)

While few in Canada would wish for a nationalized research assessment, the commercialization agreement has institutionalized assessment metrics and mechanisms, which some fear may lead to audit creep. Furthermore, anecdotal evidence in the research universities supports the creation of new 'teaching-only' and 'research-only' tracks for academics, meaning that the nexus of teaching and research will be potentially more difficult to maintain.

Theoretical implications for the study of research reforms

Given the implementation of the above research reforms by the Canadian government, and initial examinations of the resulting effects on research culture and infrastructure, what theoretical frameworks might be useful to study these developments? One of the cross-cutting themes of the three examples above is the way in which these reforms force researchers to extend beyond disciplinary and institutional boundaries in new ways. The CFI requires that researchers enlist support from administrators and support staff, who in turn must cobble together 60 per cent of project funding from other sources. This work links research networks with academic administrative networks in order to leverage the institutions' social capital in the philanthropic and industrial communities. The CRC programme casts a net out into the research community to pull in researchers from around the world, drawing upon interpersonal networks and the ties between faculty, deans and administrators. That the adjunction process for nominated CRCs includes industry representatives as well as academics is a point that deserves further attention. Finally, the AUCC commercialization agreement with the federal government highlights the role of intermediating organizations and presidential networks, and the role of para-academics who liaison with industry on behalf of academic researchers. Thus, while the tenets and data points of organizational culture have been used to examine academic culture (Tierney, 1988), it may be that network approaches to the formation of the values, norms, behaviours *and* structures of research might be more appropriate in the current climate.

However, it is useful to revisit the question of for whom and for what research on research is conducted. It is not likely that only scholars of the academic profession, and the subset of those who study academic scientists, are the only authors and audiences for studies pertaining to both research culture and infrastructure. Yet, an empirical investigation of research culture is not usually included in policy analysis, where preference is more often given to output measures.

In addition, from a structural perspective, academic researchers are too often understood only in the collective sense, as part of the peer review process or another collegial apparatus. This is a curious level of analysis from a profession in which academic freedom is held as central to intellectual development, unless we consider academic freedom to mean freedom from external pressures but not freedom from each other. The lens of academic culture may prevent us from seeing individuals and their material choices, while still assuring us of the explanatory power of normativity, even when interdisciplinarity, commercialization, internationalization and contractual differentiation challenge the notion of an academic collective.

Theoretically speaking, it may require an entirely different framework to study both research culture and infrastructure. Table 6.2 lists some possible theoretical points of entry for this work.

The theories listed above have not been widely applied to the study of research culture, with perhaps some aspects of Castell's network society (such as research milieu) and Latour's actor–network-theory being the

Table 6.2 Network theories for the study of research culture and infrastructure

Theory	Author(s)	Potential benefits for research culture studies
Network society	Castells (2000)	Research is contextualized in ICT networks and a rapidly globalizing world
Rhizomes	Deleuze and Guattari (1987)	Networks are relational and far-reaching; de-emphasis of institutional boundaries
Liquid modernity	Bauman (2000)	Flows are not idealized but personalized; stability of social institutions and careers are questioned
Actor–network-theory	Latour (2005)	Connected to science studies; emphasizes material aspects as well as social

exceptions. Of course, this is not an exhaustive list, but there is potential for providing new insights with these theories or a framework of several of these.

Methodologically speaking, these theories do not require any specific approach and could be utilized with case studies, phenomenological studies, qualitative interviews, narrative inquiry, policy discourse analysis, social semiotics, social network analysis or survey methods. In contrast to theories of organizational culture, these points of entry are not inherently structural, behavioural or functional. In addition, unlike academic capitalism, these theories are not, *prima facie*, critical in the neo-Marxist sense, but they lend themselves to studies of power flows and social stratification. For example, Deleuze and Guattari (1987) state that 'a rhizome ceaselessly establishes connections between semiotic chains, organizations of power, and circumstances relative to the arts, sciences, and social struggles' (p. 7). As we strain to observe forces that are simultaneously disarticulating social bodies like the 'university' while ardently rebuilding or constructing anew 'castles' of research 'excellence', the change that might be most important is which alternative theoretical approach to employ.

Note

1. Vincent-Lancrin's discussion of the continued scepticism about paradigm shifts as a result of wide spread use of information and communication technology (ICT) demonstrates that the old productivity paradox still holds in some areas, although it has led to greater collaboration.

References

AUCC (2008) *Momentum: The 2008 Report on University Research and Knowledge Mobilization*, Ottawa: Association of Universities and Colleges of Canada.

Bauman, Z. (2000) *Liquid Modernity*, Cambridge: Polity.

Bubela, T. M. and T. Caulfield (2010) 'Role and Reality: Technology Transfer at Canadian Universities', *Trends in Biotechnology, 28*, 447–451.

Castells, M. (2000), *The Rise of the Network Society*, Second Edition, Oxford: Blackwell Publishers.

Clark, B. R. (ed.) (1998) *Creating Entrepreneurial Universities: Organizational Pathways of Transformation*, Pergamon: IAU Press.

Deleuze, G. and F. Guattari (1987) *A Thousand Plateaus: Capitalism and Schizophrenia*, Minneapolis, MN: University of Minnesota Press.

Dufour, P. (2010) 'Supplying Demand for Canada's Knowledge Society: A Warmer Future for a Cold Climate?' *American Behavioral Scientist, 53*(7), 983–996.

Etzkowitz, H. and L. Leydesdorff (eds) (1997) *Universities and the Global Knowledge Economy: A Triple-helix of University-Industry-Government Relations*, London: Continuum.

Fisher, D. and J. Atkinson-Grosjean (2002) 'Brokers on the Boundary: Academy-Industry Liaison in Canadian Universities', *Higher Education, 44*(3–4), 449–467.

Grant, K. R. and J. Drakich (2010) 'The Canada Research Chairs Program: The Good, the Bad, and the Ugly', *Higher Education, 59*, 21–42.

Hackett, E. J. (1990) 'Science as a Vocation in the 1990s: The Changing Organizational Culture of Academic Science', *The Journal of Higher Education, 61*(3), 241–279.

HRDC (2002) *Knowledge Matters: Skills and Learning for Canadians: Canada's Innovation Strategy*, Ottawa, ON: Human Resource Development Canada (Document SP-482-02-02).

Industry Canada (2002) *Achieving Excellence: Investing in People, Knowledge and Opportunity*, Ottawa, ON: Industry Canada (Document C2-596/2001E-1N2).

Latour, B. (2005). *Reassembling the Social: An Introduction to Actor-Network Theory*, Oxford and New York: Oxford University Press.

Macfarlane, B. (2011) 'The Morphing of Academic Practice: Unbundling and the Rise of the Para-academic', *Higher Education Quarterly, 65*(1), 59–73.

Menzies, H. and J. Newson (2008) 'Time, Stress and Intellectual Engagement in Academic Work: Exploring Gender Difference', *Gender, Work and Organization, 15*(5), 504–522.

Metcalfe, A. S. (2010) 'Examining the Trilateral Networks of the Triple Helix: Intermediating Organizations and Academy-Industry-Government Relations', *Critical Sociology, 36*(4), 1–17.

Metcalfe, A. S. and T. Fenwick (2009) 'Knowledge for Whose Society? Knowledge Production, Higher Education, and Federal Policy in Canada', *Higher Education, 57*(2), 209–225.

OECD (2009) *Higher Education to 2030: Volume 2, Globalisation*, Paris, France: Centre for Educational Research and Innovation, Organization for Economic Development and Cooperation.

OECD (2010) *Performance-based Funding for Public Research in Tertiary Education Institutions: Workshop Proceedings*, Paris, France: Organization for Economic Development and Cooperation.

Polster, C. (2003) 'Canadian University Research Policy at the Turn of the Century: Continuity and Change in the Social Relations of Academic Research', *Studies in Political Economy, 71/72,* 177–199.

Prosperity Secretariat (1991) *Prosperity Through Competitiveness,* Ottawa: Prosperity Secretariat.

Rasmussen, E. (2008) 'Government Instruments to Support the Commercialization of University Research: Lessons from Canada', *Technovation, 28,* 506–517.

Savoie, D. J. (1995) 'What is Wrong with the New Public Management?', *Canadian Public Administration, 38*(1), 112–121.

Side, K. and W. Robbins (2007) 'Institutionalizing Inequalities in Canadian Universities: The Canada Research Chairs Program', *Feminist Formations, 19*(3), 163–181.

Slaughter, S. and L. Leslie (1997) *Academic Capitalism: Politics, Policies, and the Entrepreneurial University,* Baltimore, MD: Johns Hopkins University Press.

Slaughter, S. and G. Rhoades (2004) *Academic Capitalism in the New Economy: Markets, State, and Higher Education,* Baltimore, MD: Johns Hopkins University Press.

Tierney, W. G. (1988) 'Organizational Culture in Higher Education: Defining the Essentials', *The Journal of Higher Education, 59*(1), 2–21.

Tuunainen, J. (2005) 'Hybrid Practices? Contributions to the Debate on the Mutation of Science and University', *Higher Education, 50*(2), 275–298.

Vincent-Lancrin, S. (2009) 'Chapter 5, What is Changing in Academic Research? Trends and Prospects', in OECD (ed.), *Higher Education to 2030: Volume 2, Globalisation* (pp. 145–178), Paris, France: Centre for Educational Research and Innovation, Organization for Economic Development and Cooperation.

Ziman, J. (1996) ' "Postacademic Science": Constructing Knowledge Networks and Norms', *Science Studies, 9*(1), 67–80.

7

Is There a Bridge Between Quality and Quality Assurance?

Maria J. Rosa & Alberto Amaral

Introduction

Some authors (Harvey & Newton, 2006) argue that quality no longer bears a relation to the core activities of universities. Quality assurance processes are becoming bureaucratic processes and compliance structures, increasingly removed from the academic concerns that lie at the heart of quality in higher education.

Recent developments in quality assurance seem to indicate a movement towards accreditation that corresponds to a change from a cycle of trust and confidence in institutions into a cycle of suspicion. At European level, the communiqué from the Leuven Ministerial Conference (2009) indicates that ministers and the Commission are inclined to develop rankings and classification tools that are quite removed from the academic endeavour.

The Organisation of Economic Co-operation and Development (OECD) is taking a different approach by developing the Assessment of Higher Education Learning Outcomes (AHELO) project. This project aims to assess learning outcomes by evaluating the skills and capabilities students have acquired as they graduate (or shortly after) or the recognition they gain in further competition. Measuring learning outcomes is proposed as a feasible strategy for assessing the quality of the students' learning experiences instead of relying on proxies of quality.

The quality enhancement movement being developed in several countries repatriates the responsibility for promoting quality of education to higher education institutions, the remit of external agencies being limited to quality audits of the internal quality enhancement mechanisms. This movement may be seen as an attempt at re-establishing societal trust in institutions and needs to count on the foreseeable opposition of external agencies. However, it is likely to conquer the preferences of academics.

In this chapter, different hypotheses for the future of quality assurance are analysed and the degree of acceptability by the academic community is foreseen, taking into account the perceptions academics hold of the purposes of quality assurance mechanisms, including those related to the quality improvement of knowledge creation and student learning.

Quality and quality assurance

Although quality assessment and accreditation systems have been in operation for some years, there are no extensive studies of their effects on the quality of teaching or on reactions linked to academic tradition or the norms and values of disciplines, schools and higher education institutions (Westerheijden et al., 2006).

Stensaker et al. (2008, p. 1) state 'although a main function of external quality assurance is to stimulate change and improvement of teaching and learning, there are still few studies focusing on these issues'. Harvey and Newton (2006, p. 237) argue that the preponderant forms of external quality assurance processes 'hijack and mystify quality as a politically motivated, ideological, compliance structure [...] "quality" no longer has anything to do with academic endeavour: knowledge creation and student learning' (Harvey & Newton, 2006, p. 237). And they propose transforming 'quality assurance in the direction of the improvement of the student experience' (Harvey & Newton, 2006, p. 236).

The perspectives, attitudes and positions of academics towards quality assurance are still a relatively underdeveloped research subject (Lomas, 2007; Nasser & Fresko, 2002; Newton, 2000; Westerheijden et al., 2007). Academics tend to see quality assessment and assurance 'as being accountability led as opposed to improvement led (Laughton, 2003; Newton, 2000), and therefore alien to core values of academic culture' such as self- and collegial accountability and self-improvement (Laughton, 2003, p. 317). They seem to be sceptical of both internal and external quality assessments, since these processes tend to 'generate reports but do not engage with the heart of the academic endeavour' (Harvey, 2009, p. 1). Lomas (2007) and Watty (2006) argue that for academics quality is mainly linked to assurance (i.e. fitness for purpose and conformity with external standards) rather than with enhancement and transformation (i.e. dissemination of good practices aiming at improvements, namely at teaching level). And Papadimitriou et al.

(2008, p. 10) put forward the idea that academics see quality assurance 'mostly as a matter of consistency, of compliance with (externally given) requirements' rather than as being linked with excellence. In other words, quality assurance emerges as an instrument much more linked with the establishment of threshold quality in higher education than with enabling institutions and academics to go beyond such a threshold (Papadimitrious et al., 2008).

Academics rail against the high level of bureaucracy involved in quality assessment, the lack of time to deal with its requirements and, consequently, the diversion of their attention away from what really matters, such as teaching, academic issues and so on (Harvey, 2006; Newton, 2002). They see quality processes as consuming time and resources and as an administrative burden (Laughton, 2003; Lomas, 2007; Newton, 2010; Papadimitriou et al., 2008; Stensaker, 2008; Stensaker et al., 2008).

However, academics also see some positive attributes in quality assessment. This is especially true for assessment processes directed more at institutions as a whole, seen as less 'burdensome and intrusive' than those directed at individual academic performance (Laughton, 2003, p. 319). Institutional accreditation is another process that academics tend to favour, being seen as providing the opportunity for institutions to reflect on their mission and purpose and 'to join an elite club' (Bell & Taylor, 2005, p. 248) through compliance with accreditation rules.

Massification, New Public Management and markets

In Europe the development of quality assurance activities started much later than in the USA. The emergence of the 'Evaluative State' (Neave, 1988, p. 7) dates from the late 1980s, with increasing public relevance given to quality. However, the development of quality assurance in Europe was fast. Schwarz and Westerheijden (2004) report that in the early 1990s less than 50 per cent of European countries had initiated quality assessment activities at supra-institutional level, while in 2003 all countries except Greece had entered into some form of supra-institutional assessment.

European quality assurance systems share important procedural elements – internal self-evaluation, visits by an external expert review panel, external evaluation and public reporting (Thune, 2002). However, there were important differences in political discourses (Neave, 1998, 2004) that ranged from a mainly European and political discourse, with universities assumed as a public service (e.g. France and Sweden) to a mainly economic discourse, market-based and inspired in the USA (e.g.

the UK and the Netherlands), the role of the state being regarded as excessive (Neave, 2004). In general, the rhetoric of quality improvement prevailed over the rhetoric of accountability.

There were also differences in the ownership of the system and in the consequences of quality assessment – with or without a direct impact on funding. In some cases, the high level of trust between government and institutions allowed the ownership of the quality agencies to be entrusted to organizations linked to the universities (the Vlaamse Interuniversitaire Raad [VLIR] in Flanders, the Veriniging van Universiteiten [VSNU] in the Netherlands and the Fundação das Universidades Portuguesas [FUP] in Portugal). These agencies were similar to the US accrediting organizations, in that they had a guild character.

Over the last two decades there were changes linked to the increasing use of markets as instruments for public regulation (Dill et al., 2004) and the emergence of New Public Management and related concepts. In Europe, the development of a supra-national governance layer and developments linked to the Bologna Process also had an influence.

The intrusion of the rhetoric and management practices of the private sector into higher education resulted in important changes. This phenomenon, which has been interpreted by several authors using concepts such as 'managerialism' (Amaral et al., 2003; Miller, 1995) 'new managerialism' or 'New Public Management' (Deem, 1998, 2001; Meek, 2002; Reed, 2002) is associated with the emergence of market or quasi-market modes of regulation.

When quasi-markets are implemented, government agencies engaged in passing contracts in the name of consumers face the classical principal-agent dilemma: 'How the principal [government] can best motivate the agent [institutions] to perform as the principal would prefer, taking into account the difficulties [the principal facts] in monitoring the agent's activities' (Sappington, 1991, p. 45, cited in Dill & Soo, 2004, p. 68).

Delegation problems can be analysed using the principal-agent theory (Kassim & Menon, 2002). Delegation problems become more acute when agents have considerable autonomy, as is the case with universities. Indeed, autonomous institutions competing in a market have to decide either to uphold the primacy of public good or promote their own 'private good', in the later case not performing as the principal would prefer.

This may lead to a contradiction in neo-liberal policies. On the one hand, institutions should be allowed to operate freely under the rules of market competition. On the other hand, governments ensure institutions behave as governments want them to by introducing an increasing number of compliance mechanisms, including performance indicators and measures of academic quality, under the guise of quality assessment or accreditation, transforming quality assurance into a compliance tool.

Loss of trust

The implementation of New Public Management has been accompanied by attacks not only against public services but also against professionals. Reed (2002, p. 166) argues the advocates of 'new managerialism' claimed the introduction of market mechanisms in the management of public services 'would provide that imperative drive towards operational efficiency and strategic effectiveness so conspicuously lacking in the sclerotic professional monopolies and corporate bureaucracies that continued to dominate public life'. Thrupp (1998) describes the use of policies of blame in UK and New Zealand as a strategy of government for 'pursuing failing students and incompetent teachers with uncommon vigour' (Thrupp, 1998, p. 196) in an 'attempt to construct school failure as the clear responsibility of schools in order to gain ideological power as agents of accountability' (Thrupp, 1998, p. 195). And Ball (1998) refers ironically to the new instruments of public policy that, by mimicking private sector values and tools, will awake sclerotic public services from their state of comfortably sheltered and slow routines towards the 'fast, adventurous, carefree, gung-ho, open-plan, computerised, individualism of choice, autonomous enterprises and sudden opportunity' (Ball, 1998, p. 124).

The other target of New Public Management policies was the professions and specifically the academic profession. Trow (1996) argues that the British government has developed efforts 'to subject the whole of the system and its members to [...] a kind of mass degradation ceremony, involving the transformation of academic staff - scholars and scientists, lecturers and professors alike - into employees, mere organizational personnel' (Trow, 1996, p. 9). Slaughter and Rhoades (2004) consider that as patent policies in the USA allow institutions to claim the ownership of virtually all intellectual property that its members produce made them 'less like university professionals and more like corporate professionals whose discoveries are considered work-for-hire, the property of the corporation, not the professional' (Slaughter & Rhoades, 2004, p. 225).

The emergence of New Public Management and the use of blame policies resulted in loss of trust in institutions (Trow, 1996) and demands for more accountability. Recent literature shows a decline of trust in public institutions, including higher education institutions, as well as professionals. Comparing state approval versus accreditation schemes, in the years 1998 and 2003, reveals an overwhelming movement from state approval towards accreditation schemes (Schwarz & Westerheijden, 2004). All recently implemented quality systems are based on accreditation rather than on quality assessment (e.g. Germany, Austria, Norway and Portugal). This reflects an increased lack of trust in the ability of higher education institutions to satisfy the government and society of their capacity to ensure adequate standards of quality.

In the Netherlands, a meta-evaluation system run by the Inspectorate for Higher Education was supposed to ensure that the assessment procedures were properly run. In Portugal, a commission was set up to coordinate the quality assessment process and to issue recommendations for the rationalization and improvement of the higher education system, in other words, to meta-evaluate the system. However, this has not been sufficient to protect quality assurance agencies. In Flanders 'policy makers, employers and journalists questioned the vagueness of the visitation reports and the lack of a clear overall conclusion' (Van Damme, 2004, p. 144) and in Portugal 'the Minister has publicly complained [...] that the conclusions of the reports of quality evaluation agencies were quite obscure' (Amaral & Rosa, 2004, pp. 415–416). These three national quality assurance agencies were extinguished by government and replaced with 'independent' accrediting agencies (Amaral, 2007).

The problem is that universities were not able 'to develop and then translate support in the society at large into political support' (Trow, 1996, p. 5) when they came under attack from New Public Management and blame policies (Ball, 1998). Universities have rested on their claims for the specialism of their 'unique' attributes while their environment changed dramatically. For Mala Sing, if universities want to preserve their core attributes then they must do a better job of making their case to society, making the core values matter to more than just themselves, and forging alliances with other social forces to give effect to them (Futures Project, 2001, p. 11).

Universities must convince society that they care for what they do by self-imposing 'measures of quality, commitments to insuring access and greater transparency about financing' (Futures Project, 2001, p. 10). The big question is how far universities will succeed in regaining trust. As Trow (1996, p. 10) reminds us, 'Trust cannot be demanded but must be freely given. In Trollope's novels, a gentleman who demands to be treated as a gentleman is almost certainly no gentleman.'

The future of quality assurance: three hypotheses

Recent trends in European higher education indicate that the accountability component is being reinforced relative to the improvement of the teaching and learning component. The emergence of markets in higher education and the need for their efficient operation increased demands for improved consumer information on the quality of education. This legitimizes the state to provide information to consumers by disclosing the results of quality assessment and using performance indicators. The emergence of New Public Management and the attacks on the efficiency of public services resulted in the loss of trust in higher education institutions and their professionals. The implementation of the Bologna Process and its convergence with the Lisbon strategy are changing the traditional pact between the university and society by shifting the balance towards the economic function of the university. This shift may lead to a stratified European Area of Higher Education (EAHE) and the introduction and/or reinforcement of European accreditation systems.

European Commission, ministers and rankings

The Bologna Process has been a very important tool for change. The ministers of education assembled in Bergen in 2005 gave their blessing to the European Standards and Guidelines for Quality Assurance (ESG), drafted by ENQA (European Association for Quality Assurance in Higher Education) (2005), in cooperation and consultation with its member agencies and the other members of the E4 group (its members are ENQA representing European accreditation agencies, European University Association (EUA) representing universities, European Association of Institutions of Higher Education (EURASHE) representing polytechnics and European Students' Union (ESU) representing European student associations). In 2007, the ministers of education assembled in London established the European Quality Assurance Register for Higher Education (EQAR) based on a proposal drafted by the E4 (ENQA, 2007). More recently (28 and 29 April 2009), the ministers of education held another conference in Belgium. The final communiqué states,

> there are several current initiatives designed to develop mechanisms for providing more detailed information about higher education institutions across the EHEA to make their diversity more transparent. [...] These transparency tools [...] should be based on comparable data and adequate indicators to describe the diverse profiles of higher education institutions and their programmes.
>
> (Leuven Communiqué, 2009)

At Leuven, the student representation saw the danger of the communiqué opening the way to a ranking system and proposed the inclusion of a phrase that would make rankings unacceptable. However, they failed, holding an isolated position against the representatives of higher education organizations such as EUA, EURASHE, the Coimbra group and other partners such as ENQA. The Commission not only commissioned a report on the possibility of establishing a classification of European universities (van Vught, 2009) but it also funded two projects to analyse the implementation of a multi-dimensional ranking system (U-Map and U-Multirank projects). European ministers and the Community are apparently determined to implement a fast and lean system to classify or rank universities, having realized that using quality systems will not produce a timely, clear answer. The Center for Higher Education Policy Studies (CHEPS) provides additional explanation:

> a logical next step for Europe with respect to transparency measures is the development of a classification of higher education institutions. [...] In this phase we will evaluate and fine-tune the dimensions and their indicators and bring them into line with other relevant indicator initiatives; finalise a working on-line classification tool; articulate this with the classification tool operated by the Carnegie Foundation; develop a final organisational model for the implementation of the classification.
>
> (CHEPS, 2011)

The design intends to follow the 'Berlin Principles on the ranking of higher education institutions' which stress the need to take into account 'the linguistic, cultural, economic and historical contexts of the educational systems being ranked'. The approach is to compare only institutions that are similar in terms of their missions and structures. The project is linked to the idea of a European classification ('mapping') of higher education institutions developed by CHEPS. The feasibility study includes focused rankings on particular aspects of higher education at institutional level (for example, internationalization and regional engagement) and two field-based rankings for business and engineering programmes. As Kaiser and Jongbloed (2010) explain, 'the classification is an instrument for mapping the European higher education landscape. [...] In contrast to the U-Map classification project, U-Multirank is a ranking project. [...] U-Multirank pays attention mostly to output (performance) and impact (outcomes)'.

The convergence of the Bologna Process and the Lisbon strategy is giving the European Commission an increasing influence over European higher education (Amaral & Neave, 2009a), despite the weak legal basis for Community intervention as education has always been considered an area of national sensitivity (Gornitzka, 2009). The activities and policies of the European Commission apparently aim at building a stratified EAHE against the traditional view still prevailing in many European countries that national universities are all equal, which is reminiscent of the legal homogeneity principle.

The student experience and the evaluation of learning outcomes

Bennett (2001) considers the only valid approach for assessing the quality of education is based on the value added, meaning what is added to students' capabilities or knowledge as a consequence of their education at a particular college or university, or more simply, the difference a higher education institution makes in their education. However, as Bennett (2001) recognizes, the assessment of value added is difficult for a number of reasons such as its many dimensions, differences between institutions and time for consequences of education to fully unfold, as well as complexity and cost. A workable alternative is assessing outcomes, by evaluating the skills and capabilities students have acquired as they graduate (or shortly after) or the recognition they gain in further competition.

OECD (2008) has produced a report providing an international perspective on current practices in standardized learning outcomes assessment in higher education, drawing on examples from a number of countries. The assessed outcomes include both cognitive outcomes and non-cognitive outcomes. The OECD report tries to answer four questions. What is being assessed? How are these outcomes being assessed? Who each instrument is going to assess? Why is the assessment being applied?

Cognitive learning outcomes 'range from domain-specific knowledge to the most general of reasoning and problem-solving skills' (Shalveson & Hunag, 2003, p. 13). The OECD considers a division of cognitive learning outcomes into knowledge outcomes involving the 'remembering, either by recognition or recall, of ideas, materials or phenomena' (Bloom & Krathwohl, 1956, p. 62) and skills outcomes, both divided into generic and domain-specific.

A non-cognitive learning outcome refers to changes in beliefs or the development of certain values (Ewell, 2005). Studies on non-cognitive outcomes often focus on the presence of certain theorized stages of identity development (Pascarella & Terenzini, 2005) and may be developed both through classroom instruction and out-of-class activities organized by higher education institutions to supplement the curriculum. However, the definition of desirable non-cognitive outcomes is controversial and subject to cultural contexts and not always shared by all stakeholders. Some studies suggest that non-cognitive outcomes are related to social maturation, generational effects (Pascarella & Terenzini, 2005) or 'significant life events' (Glenn, 1980, cited in Pascarella & Terenzini, 2005, p. 272).

The OECD, following discussions at the 2006 OECD Ministerial Conference in Athens, has launched the new AHELO project. In the presentation leaflet, the OECD proposes to develop 'an assessment that compares learning outcomes in an universally sound manner, regardless of culture, language, differing educational systems and university missions' while considering 'current university rankings may do more harm than good because they largely ignore a key measure of quality, namely what goes on in the seminar rooms and lecture theatres'.

For the OECD, AHELO is a ground-breaking initiative to assess learning outcomes on an international scale by creating measures valid for all cultures and languages (OECD, 2009a). The OECD initially proposed that a large number of higher education students in over ten different countries take part in a feasibility study to determine the bounds of this ambitious project, aiming at the possible creation of a full-scale AHELO upon its completion.

The initial plan was that the 'feasibility study' would consist of four 'strands': three assessments to measure learning outcomes in terms of generic skills and discipline-related skills (in Engineering and Economics) and a fourth value-added strand, based on research. The measurement of generic skills (e.g. analytical reasoning, critical thinking, problem-solving, the practical application of theory, ease in written communication, leadership ability, the ability to work in a group) would be based on an adaptation of the Collegiate Learning Assessment (CLA) developed in the USA. For the discipline-based strands the study would concentrate on the approach used in the tuning process for Engineering and Economics. The fourth value-added strand would not be measured, as this would not be compatible with the timeframe of the study. Therefore, 'the feasibility study would only explore different methodologies, concepts and tools to identify promising ways of measuring the value-added component of education' (OECD, 2009a, p. 10).

The OECD considers the importance of context, although recognizing the difficulty of context measurement. The feasibility study aimed at defining the limits of a contextual inquiry, dividing context into four topical areas: physical and organizational characteristics, education-related behaviours and practices, psycho-social and cultural attributes, and behavioural and cultural attributes. In the proposed model student learning outcomes 'are a joint product of input conditions and the environment within which learning takes place' (OECD, 2009b, p. 4). Inputs may include student characteristics related to learning, such as gender and socio-economic status (Pascarella & Terenzini, 1991, 2005) and environment consists of the setting in which learning takes place, curricula and pedagogies and student learning behaviours (Kuh, 2008; Pascarella & Terenzini, 1991, 2005).

It is not yet possible to guess what the outcome of AHELO will be. The OECD has been facing some financial difficulties and the feasibility stage has now a more modest scope than in the initial proposal. It is possible that in the end AHELO will produce positive results, allowing the OECD to assume a virtuous position by claiming that AHELO provides a clear comparison of universities by looking at competencies of graduates in a way that avoids much of the shortcomings of plain ranking systems.

Learning outcomes are also present in the European Standards and Guidelines (ESG). The ESG state that quality assurance programmes and awards for internal quality assurance within higher education institutions are expected to include 'development and publication of explicit intended learning outcomes'. Student assessment procedures should 'be designed to measure the achievement of the intended learning outcomes and other programme objectives' (ENQA, 2005, p. 17).

Regaining trust and the quality enhancement movement

Massification, the emergence of markets as instruments of public regulation and the influence of New Public Management have resulted in a loss of trust in institutions and academics, reinforcing the accountability component over the improvement component in quality processes. Within this context a new movement seems to be emerging – the quality enhancement movement. Quality enhancement may be seen as an attempt by universities to regain trust by restating that quality is their major responsibility and that the role of outside agencies should be limited to quality audits.

In 2005 the Higher Education Funding Council for England (HEFCE) commissioned the Quality Assurance Framework Review Group (QAFRG), a critical analysis of the existing quality audit model for England and Wales. The QAFRG recommended a stronger quality enhancement emphasis of quality audits and a shift in the balance towards quality enhancement in quality audits (Higher Education Academy, 2008, p. 8). QAFRG recommendations have resulted in a political settlement that curtailed the remit of the Quality Assurance Agency for Higher Education (QAA) while the Higher Education Academy (HEA), funded in 2004 from a merger of the Institute for Learning and Teaching in Higher Education (ILTHE), the Learning and Teaching Support Network (LTSN) and the Teaching Quality Enhancement Fund (TQEF) National Coordination Team (NCT), was entrusted with the promotion of quality enhancement by 'supporting institutions in their strategies for improving the student learning experience' (Higher Education Academy, 2011).

A report (Higher Education Academy, 2008) produced by a team composed of staff members from the HEA, HEFCE and the QAA considers the increasing relevance of quality enhancement is promoted 'to an extent, by contextual changes in, for example, the concept of "student", the relationship of the student to the HE provision and the perception of the role of the HE sector in society' (Higher Education Academy, 2008, p. 6).

However, quality enhancement still remains a poorly defined concept. The HEA report, although presenting the QAA's definition as 'the process of taking deliberate steps at institutional level to improve the quality of learning opportunities', recognizes that institutions are still looking for their own definition as that emerged from several institutional replies to the questionnaire used to collect information for the report.

Even without a widely accepted definition of quality enhancement, there are however a number of common patterns to every institutional approach. From the HEA report and the paper by Filippakou and Tapper (2008) some ideas about the characteristics of quality enhancement emerge, taken from replies of diverse higher education institutions. It is accepted that quality enhancement will repatriate the responsibility for the quality of learning process to within the institution and external vigilance will rely on institutional audits rather than on more intrusive forms of quality assessment, such as programme level accreditation. Institutions agree with the idea that they have the main responsibility for the quality of education and quality enhancement can only be successfully implemented 'in the context of a flexible, negotiated evaluative model' (Filippakou & Tapper, 2008, p. 92) and should be 'by definition non-mandatory, and should be shaped by the actual participants in the teaching and learning process' (Filippakou & Tapper, 2008, p. 94).

Filippakou and Tapper (2008) question whether quality enhancement is effectively a new discourse leading to a different interpretation of the higher education quality agenda or if it merely is 'part of the developing discourse of quality assurance with its potential for change threatened' by the way it may be implemented (Filippakou & Tapper, 2008, p. 91).

Filippakou and Tapper (2008, p. 92) argue 'assurance and enhancement are concepts with distinctive meanings, with enhancement promising more than assurance, and although apparently giving greater space to academics, also making more demands of them.'

Institutions show concern that external intervention, namely under the guise of QAA-led audits may damage or destroy quality enhancement and innovation:

> External scrutiny could hinder QE [quality enhancement]. Especially when QE is so rigidly defined.
>
> > (Higher Education Academy, 2008, p. 29)

> quality enhancement has almost nothing to do with quality assurance [...] Quality assurance could even actually damage quality because it can divert people away from quality enhancement [...] If your quality assurance framework is positively draconian [...] I should think [you could] scrap quality enhancement altogether.
>
> > (Filippakou & Tapper, 2008, p. 92)

> you shouldn't have as a stimulus the fear of failing the QAA at audit. [...] Quality enhancement will come about because academics themselves feel that more needs to be done, not because they think they are not going to do well in the league tables.
>
> > (ibid., p. 95)

> I think they [QAA] are going to come in and see what our procedures are like as they always have [...] there is no sign they are really going to focus on things that might encourage us really to make the enhancement side more seriously.
>
> > (ibid., p. 96)

Sursock (2002, p. 2) argues, 'the quality assurance debate [...] is really about power. It is a question of how quality is defined and by whom', which 'can induce distortions that are not necessarily in the best interests of students, graduates, employers or society at large'. And Neave (2004, p. 224) considers 'evaluation systems are not independent of what a government's intentions are, nor from what its policy is'.

Filippakou and Tapper (2008) raise this question when they refer to problems associated with the institutionalization of quality enhancement as having 'the power to determine the meaning of key concepts, how they are put into effect [...] what the policy outcomes should be' (Filippakou & Tapper, 2008, p. 93). For them, the QAA's idea that quality enhancement should be promoted using the model of 'good practice', which is considered 'another function of the New Public Management model of governance' (Filippakou & Tapper, 2008, p. 94), is a reason for concern.

Filippakou and Tapper (2008) argue that QAA is developing a strategy to reassert its own authority using its own definition of what quality enhancement means and how it is to be promoted. Recent developments support this argument. In a recent document (QAA, 2011) containing the operational description of the new QAA institutional review of higher education institutions, which has replaced the former quality audit system, it is stated 'themes will be selected to allow for enhancement as well as for the assurance of quality, and sufficient enquires will be carried out to provide useful and timely good practice guidance for the sector' (QAA, 2011, p. 2). The new process should also allow institutions to know how far they are 'reflecting nationally-agreed good practice in the quality of students' learning opportunities' (QAA, 2011, p. 3).

Bridging quality and quality assurance: is it possible?

Harvey and Newton (2006) argue that traditional quality assurance systems do not address the core elements of academic endeavour, knowledge creation and student learning. Members of the higher education community consider quality assurance has nothing to do with quality enhancement and may even damage quality.

There are presently several developments taking place in different contexts. We have analysed three different developments: multidimensional rankings promoted at European level, the OECD AHELO project and the quality enhancement movement.

What the future will be is just another guess. Options for the future of quality systems are not separate from considerations relating to the type of higher education system the relevant authorities want to foster. Recent developments show there is a trend for replacing quality assessment agencies owned by universities or by organizations representing universities, moving instead to independent accreditation agencies (the Netherlands, Flanders and Portugal), while agencies based on quality audit have been replaced by agencies based on accreditation (e.g. Denmark and Norway). And in England, the QAA, although introducing quality enhancement as a component of quality audits, still maintains an accountability component.

At European level, the objectives of Brussels apparently put more emphasis on competition and the creation of a stratified EAHE than

on cooperation and quality improvement. There is increasing emphasis on market mechanisms, New Public Management and competition,
accompanied by the loss of trust in institutions. This reinforces the
possibility that a highly stratified EAHE will develop, following developments of the Bologna Process and supported by the Commission (which
does not trust academics and their market aloofness) and with the help
of ministers (who see the virtues of cost-saving and easily digestible
information). This will produce a ranking system of European universities, albeit under the more palatable guise of U-Map classifications,
multi-dimensional global university rankings or focused institutional
rankings, or field-based rankings or even using the official nickname
of multi-dimensional transparency tools.

An interesting alternative may develop from the OECD's decision
to move forward with the implementation of a system for measuring
learning outcomes that is much closer to notions of the quality of the
students' learning experience than to ranking or classification systems.
However, it will take some time for the OECD system to produce results,
if it produces results at all. And it is evident that such a system will be
very expensive.

However, the OECD will not give up on the implementation of
AHELO unless the economic crisis leaves no alternative. The AHELO
project has an irresistible strategic value for OECD as it is a very important instrument for reinforcing the influence of the Château de la
Muette over higher education. Indeed much of the OECD's influence
is based on opinion-forming which is a clear expression of 'the capacity of an international organization to initiate and influence national
discourses' (Martens et al., 2004, p. 2). And evidence suggests that
the ability of the OECD to shape and influence opinion on education is at least partly based on the regular publication of cross-national
and comparative educational statistics and indicators, one of the most
important being the performance indicators of school achievement
(PISA) (Amaral & Neave, 2009b).

Lastly, there is the quality enhancement movement. Considered more
palatable by academics, it also corresponds to the restoration of public
trust in higher education institutions, a most challenging objective for
university leaders. Quality enhancement will offer academics an alternative compatible with academic norms and values and creates a bridge
with quality, provided that external interventions under the guise of
rigid audit systems are not implemented.

The answers given by Portuguese academics to a questionnaire on
the purposes of quality assessment (a research project conducted by

the Centre for Higher Education Policy Studies [CIPES]) reveal a strong agreement with the idea that quality systems should promote quality improvement and innovation in higher education (Rosa et al., 2011). Academics strongly favour the idea of improving the quality of teaching and learning processes supported by appropriate strategies, the development of their own skills and strategies, and the implementation of internal quality assurance systems; all the while the Humboldtian ideal of linking teaching to research is clearly valued. Academics also agree with the adoption of policies to promote innovation in teaching and learning practices.

Portuguese academics are also in favour of external accountability and providing information to students (so they can make informed choices) and to institutional governance bodies to facilitate quality management, the promotion of institutional reputation and social image, and the collective identification of institutional strengths and weaknesses. However, academics show a lower level of agreement or even disagreement with other purposes, such as using the results of quality assessment to penalize or reward institutions, for resource allocation or for the control of the higher education network.

Another survey on the perceptions of academics regarding the impacts of internal quality management conducted in the Netherlands (Kleijnen et al., 2011) also found that in general 'academics were positive about the attention paid to the relevant quality aspects within their departments: "teaching and learning", "information and facilities" and "results" [...] academics were positive about the effects of quality management in terms of improvement and negative about its effects in terms of control' (Kleijnen et al., 2011, pp. 148–149). Academics also perceived the improvement effect as being strongly linked to quality management activities within the department.

These findings support the promotion of innovation and flexibility, and reliance on internal quality systems, which is compatible with the quality enhancement movement. These findings also support proposals from the Council of Europe, which has produced two important documents, one on public responsibility for higher education and research (Weber & Bergan, 2005), the other on higher education governance (Kohler et al., 2006). These documents stress two fundamental ideas: that governance should avoid micro-management, leaving reasonable scope for innovation and flexibility, and that quality assessment mechanisms should be built on trust and give due regard to internal quality development processes. No doubt every academic would strongly support these ideas based on elevated and generous principles (Amaral,

2008), although it remains an open question as to how far national quality agencies will favour quality enhancement over accountability.

However, the policies promoted by the European Commission and the ministers in charge of higher education may well lead to developments in a direction contrary to that proposed in the documents produced by the Council of Europe. And research results show this proposed direction will not have full academic support, which may raise questions about its degree of acceptance.

Finally, recent developments in Germany show that some *Länder* are starting to worry about the amount of work and the huge costs associated with a generalized system of programme accreditation (Ziegele & Affeld, 2008). In Lower-Saxony there has already been a movement towards a system of institutional audits. Does this mean that we will be moving back to a system based on the fundamental responsibility of institutions for quality, supported by a less intrusive system of audits? From our analysis it seems that academics could be willing to support such a system if it promotes quality enhancement rather than accountability.

So far, our best guess is that Europe will be moving into a system of simplified classification and ranking while national systems move to less expensive systems than those based on a generalized assessment/accreditation of study programmes.

References

Amaral, A. (2007) 'From Quality Assurance to Accreditation – A Satirical View' in J. Enders and F. van Vught (eds) *Towards a Cartography of Higher Education Policy Change*, Czech Republic: UNITISK, pp. 79–86.

Amaral, A. (2008) 'Quality Assurance: Role, Legitimacy, Responsibilities and Means of Public Authorities' in L. Weber and K. Dolgova-dreyer (eds) *The Legitimacy of Quality Assurance in Higher Education*, Strasbourg: Council of Europe.

Amaral, A. and G. Neave (2009a) 'On Bologna, Weasels and Creeping Competence' in A. Amaral, G. Neave, C. Musselin and P. Maassen (eds) *European Integration and the Governance of Higher Education and Research*, Dordrecht: Springer, pp. 271–289.

Amaral, A. and G. Neave (2009b) 'The OECD and Its Influence in Higher Education: A Critical Revision' in A. Maldonado and R. Bassett (eds) *International Organizations and Higher Education Policy: Thinking Globally, Acting Locally?*, London and New York: Routledge, pp. 82–98.

Amaral, A. and M.J. Rosa (2004) 'Portugal: Professional and Academic Accreditation – The Impossible Marriage?' in S. Schwarz and D. Westerheijden (eds) *Accreditation and Evaluation in the European Higher Education Area*, Dordrecht: Kluwer Academic Press, pp. 127–157.

Amaral, A., A. Magalhães and R. Santiago (2003) 'The Rise of Academic Managerialism in Portugal' in A. Amaral, V.L. Meek and I. Larsen (eds) *The Higher Education Managerial Revolution?*, Dordrecht: KLUWER Academic Press, pp. 131–153.

Ball, S. (1998) 'Big Policies/Small World: An Introduction to International Perspectives in Education Policy', *Comparative Education*, 34(2), 117–130.

Bell, E. and S. Taylor (2005) 'Joining the Club: the Ideology of Quality and Business School Badging', *Studies in Higher Education*, 30(3), 239–255.

Bennett, D. (2001) 'Assessing Quality in Higher Education', *Liberal Education*, 87(2), pp. 1–4.

Bloom, B. and D. Krathwohl (1956) 'Taxonomy of Educational Objectives: The Classification of Educational Goals, by a Committee of College and University Examiners'. *Handbook 1: Cognitive Domain*, New York: Longmans.

CHEPS (2011) Classifying European Institutions for Higher Education (StageII), http://www.utwente.nl/mb/cheps/research/projects/ceihe/

Deem, R. (1998) 'New Managerialism in Higher Education: The Management of Performances and Cultures in Universities', *International Studies in the Sociology of Education*, 8(1), 56–75.

Deem, R. (2001) 'Globalisation, New Managerialism, Academic Capitalism and Entrepreneurialism in Universities: Is the Local Dimension Still Important?', *Comparative Education*, 37(1), 7–20.

Dill, D. and M. Soo (2004) 'Transparency and Quality in Higher Education Markets' in P. Teixeira, B. Jongbloed, D. Dill and A. Amaral (eds) *Markets in Higher Education: Rhetoric or Reality?*, Dordrecht: Kluwer Academic Publishers, pp. 61–85.

Dill, D., P. Teixeira, B. Jongbloed and A. Amaral (2004) 'Conclusion' in P. Teixeira, B. Jongbloed, D. Dill and A. Amaral (eds) *Markets in Higher Education: Rhetoric or Reality?*, Dordrecht: Kluwer Academic Publishers, pp. 327–352.

ENQA (2005) *Standards and Guidelines for Quality Assurance in the European Higher Education Area*, Helsinki: ENQA.

ENQA (2007) 'Report to the London Conference of Ministers on a European Register of Quality Assurance Agencies', *Occasional Paper 13*, Helsinki: ENQA.

Ewell, P.T. (2005) 'Applying Learning Outcomes Concepts to Higher Education: An Overview', prepared for the University Grants Committee, http://www.khu.hk/caut/seminar/download/OBA_1st_report.pdf

Filippakou, O. and T. Tapper (2008) 'Quality Assurance and Quality Enhancement in Higher Education: Contested Territories?', *Higher Education Quarterly*, 62(1/2), pp. 84–100.

Futures Project (2001) 'Privileges Lost, Responsibilities Gained: Reconstructing Higher Education', *A Global Symposium on the Future of Higher Education*, Columbia University Teachers College, 14–15 June 2001.

Glenn, N. (1980) 'Values, Attitudes and Beliefs' in O. Brim and J. Kajan (eds) *Constancy and Change in Human Development*, Cambridge, MA: Harvard University Press.

Gornitzka, A. (2009) 'Networking Administration in Areas of National Sensitivity: The Commission and European Higher Education' in A. Amaral, G. Neave, C. Musselin and P. Maassen (eds) *European Integration and the Governance of Higher Education and Research*, Dordrecht: Springer, pp. 109–131.

Harvey, L. (2006) 'Impact of Quality Assurance: Overview of a Discussion Between Representatives of External Quality Assurance Agencies', *Quality in Higher Education*, 12(3), pp. 287–290.

Harvey, L. (2009) 'A Critical Analysis of Quality Culture', retrieved September 2010, at: http://www.inqaahe.org/admin/files/assets/subsites/1/documenten/1241773373_16-harvey-a-critical-analysis-of-quality-culture.pdf

Harvey, L. and J. Newton (2006) 'Transforming Quality Evaluation: Moving On' in D. Westerheijden, B. Stensaker and M.J. Rosa (eds) *Quality Assurance in Higher Education: Trends in Regulation, Translation and Transformation*, Dordrecht, Springer, pp. 225–245.

Higher Education Academy (2008) *Quality Enhancement and Assurance: a Changing Picture?*, York: Higher Education Academy.

Higher Education Academy (2011) http://www.heacademy.ac.uk/aboutus

Kaiser, F. and B. Jongbloed (2010) 'New Transparency Instruments for European Higher Education: the U-Map and the U-Multirank Projects', *paper presented to the 2010 ENID Conference*, 8–11 September 2010.

Kassim, H. and A. Menon (2002) 'The Principal-Agent Approach and the Study of the European Union: A Provisional Assessment', *Working Paper Series*, Birmingham: European Research Institute, University of Birmingham.

Kleijnen, J., D. Dolmans, J. Willems and H. van Hout (2011) 'Does Internal Quality Management Contribute to More Control or to Improvement of Higher Education? A Survey on Faculty's Perceptions', *Quality Assurance in Education*, 19(2), pp. 141–155.

Kohler, J., J. Huber and S. Bergan (2006) 'Higher Education Governance Between Democratic Culture, Academic Aspirations and Market Forces', *Higher Education Series No. 5*, Strasbourg: Council of Europe.

Kuh, G.D. (2008) *High-Impact Educational Practices: What They Are, Who Has Access to Them, and Why They Matter*, Washington, DC: Association of American Colleges and Universities (AACU).

Laughton, D. (2003) 'Why Was the QAA Approach to Teaching Quality Assessment Rejected by Academics in UK HE?', *Assessment and Evaluation in Higher Education*, 28(3), pp. 309–321.

Leuven Communiqué (2009) http://www.ond.vlaanderen.be/hogeronderwijs/bologna/conference/documents/Leuven_Louvain-la-Neuve_Communiqué_April_2009.pdf

Lomas, L. (2007) 'Zen, Motorcycle Maintenance and Quality in Higher Education', *Quality Assurance in Education*, 15(4), pp. 402–412.

Martens, K., C. Balzer, R. Sackmann, and A. Weymann (2004) 'Comparing Governance of International Organisations – The EU, the OECD and Educational Policy', *TransState Working Papers No. 7, Sfb597*, Bremen: Staatlichkeit im Wandel – (Transformations of the State).

Meek, V.L. (2002) 'On the Road to Mediocrity? Governance and Management of Australian Higher Education in the Market Place' in A. Amaral, G. Jones and B. Karseth (eds) *Governing Higher Education: National Perspectives on Institutional Governance*, Dordrecht: Kluwer Academic Publishers, pp. 235–260.

Miller, H.D.R. (1995) *The Management of Changes in Universities*, Buckingham: SHRE/Open University.

Nasser, F. and B. Fresko (2002) 'Faculty Views of Student Evaluation of College Teaching', *Assessment and Evaluation in Higher Education*, 27(2), pp. 188–198.

Neave, G. (1988) 'On the Cultivation of Quality, Efficiency and Enterprise: An Overview of Recent Trends in Higher Education in Western Europe, 1986–1988', *European Journal of Education*, 23(1/2), pp. 7–23.

Neave, G. (1998) 'The Evaluative State Reconsidered', *European Journal of Education*, 33(3), pp. 265–284.

Neave, G. (2004) 'The Bologna Process and the Evaluative State: A Viticultural Parable' in *Managerialism and Evaluation in Higher Education, UNESCO Forum Occasional Paper Series No. 7*, Paris: ED-2006/WS/47, pp. 11–34.

Newton, J. (2000) 'Feeding the Beast or Improving Quality? Academics' Perceptions of Quality Assurance and Quality Monitoring', *Quality in Higher Education*, 6(2), pp. 153–162.

Newton, J. (2002) 'Views from Below: Academics Coping with Quality', *Quality in Higher Education*, 8(1), pp. 39–61.

Newton, J. (2010) 'A Tale of Two "Qualitys": Reflections on the Quality Revolution in Higher Education', *Quality in Higher Education*, 16(1), pp. 51–53.

OECD (2008) *Assessment of Learning Outcomes in Higher Education: A Comparative Review of Selected Practices*, Paris: OECD.

OECD (2009a) *Assessment of Higher Education Learning Outcomes*, Paris: OECD.

OECD (2009b) *Analytical Framework for the Contextual Dimension of the AHELO Feasibility Study*, Paris: OECD.

Papadimitriou, A., J. Ursin, D. Westerheijden and J. Välimaa (2008) 'Views on Excellence in Finnish and Greek Universities', *paper presented to the 21st Annual Conference of CHER – Consortium of Higher Education Researchers*, Pavia, 11–13 September 2008.

Pascarella, E.T. and P.T. Terenzini (1991) *How College Affects Students*, San Francisco: Jossey-Bass.

Pascarella, E.T. and P.T. Terenzini (2005) *How College Affects Students*, Volume 2, San Francisco: Jossey-Bass.

QAA (2011) *Institutional Review of Higher Education Institutions in England and Northern Ireland: Operational Description*, http://www.qaa.ac.uk/reviews/institutionalreview/IRoperational.pdf

Reed, M. (2002) 'New Managerialism, Professional Power and Organisational Governance in UK Universities: A Review and Assessment' in A. Amaral, G. Jones and B. Karseth (eds) *Governing Higher Education: National Perspectives on Institutional Governance* (Dordrecht: Kluwer Academic Publishers), pp. 163–186.

Rosa, M.J., C.S. Sarrico and A. Amaral (2011) 'The Perceptions of Portuguese Academics on the Purposes of Quality Assessment', *paper presented to the 24th Annual Conference of CHER – Consortium of Higher Education Researchers*, Reykjavík, Iceland, 23–25 June 2011.

Sappington, D.E.M. (1991) 'Incentives in Principal-Agent Relationship', *Journal of Economic Perspectives*, 5(2), pp. 45–66.

Schwarz, S. and D. Westerheijden (2004) *Accreditation and Evaluation in the European Higher Education Area*, Dordrecht: Kluwer Academic Press.

Shalveson, R.J. and L. Huang (2003) 'Responding Responsibility to the Frenzy to Assess Learning in Higher Education', *Change*, 35(1), pp. 11–19.

Slaughter, S. and G. Rhoades (2004) 'Contested Intellectual Property: The Role of the Institution in Unites States Higher Education' in A. Amaral, L.V. Meek and I. Larsen (eds) *The Higher Education Managerial Revolution*, Dordrecht: Kluwer Academic Press, pp. 203–228.

Stensaker, B. (2008) 'Outcomes of Quality Assurance: A Discussion of Knowledge, Methodology and Validity', *Quality in Higher Education*, 14(1), pp. 3–13.

Stensaker, B., L. Langfeldt, L. Harvey, J. Huisman and D. Westerheijden (2008) 'An In-Depth Study on the Impact of External Quality Assurance', *paper presented to the 30th EAIR Forum*, Copenhagen, Denmark, 24–27 August 2008.

Sursock, A. (2002) 'Reflection from the Higher Education Institutions' Point of View: Accreditation and Quality Culture', *paper presented at Working on the European Dimension of Quality: International Conference on Accreditation and Quality Assurance*, Amsterdam, The Netherlands, 12–13 March 2002.

Thrupp, M. (1998) 'Exploring the Policies of Blame: School Inspection and its Contestation in New Zeeland and England', *Comparative Education*, 34(2), pp. 195–208.

Thune, C. (2002) 'Future Relationships and Dilemmas of Quality Assurance and Accreditation', *paper presented at the 24th EAIR Annual Forum*, Prague, Czech Republic.

Trow, M. (1996) 'Trust, Markets and Accountability in Higher Education: A Comparative Perspective', *Higher Education Policy*, 9(4), pp. 309–324.

Van Damme, D. (2004) 'Quality Assurance and Accreditation in the Flemish Community of Belgium' in S. Schwarz and D. Westerheijden (eds) *Accreditation and Evaluation in the European Higher Education Area*, Dordrecht: Kluwer Academic Press, pp. 127–157.

van Vught, F. (2009) *Mapping the Higher Education Landscape*, Dordrecht: Springer.

Watty, K. (2006) 'Want to Know About Quality in Higher Education? Ask an Academic', *Quality in Higher Education*, 12(3), pp. 291–301.

Weber, L. and S. Bergan (2005) 'The Public Responsibility for Higher Education and Research', *Higher Education Series No. 2*, Strasbourg: Council of Europe.

Westerheijden, D., B. Stensaker and M.J. Rosa (2006) *Quality Assurance in Higher Education: Trends in Regulation, Translation and Transformation*, Dordrecht: Springer.

Westerheijden, D., V. Hulpiau and K. Waeytens (2007) 'From Design and Implementation to Impact of Quality Assurance: An Overview of Some Studies Into What Impacts Improvement', *Tertiary Education and Management*, 13(4), pp. 295–312.

Ziegele, F. and C. Affeld (2008) 'Quality and Accreditation in German Higher Education – Models and Recent Trends' in A. Amaral (ed.) *Reforma do Ensino Superior: Quatro Temas em Debate*, Lisboa: Conselho Nacional de Educação, pp. 361–376.

8
Students' Perceptions of Quality Assessment: Is There an Option Besides Treating Them as Consumers?

Sónia Cardoso

Introduction

At the turn of the 21st century, the rise of the knowledge society and economy (Olsen & Peters, 2005; Scott, 1997; Slaughter & Rhoades, 2004; Shattock, 2009) led to the emergence of the entrepreneurial university (Barnett, 2003; Clark, 1998; Etzkowitz, 2003a, 2003b). Effects of this are seen in the education provided by universities and in the way students are being conceptualized.

Framed by a progressive shift from a 'public-good knowledge/learning regime' to an 'academic capitalist knowledge/learning regime' (Slaughter & Rhoades, 2004), educational programmes are increasingly being reshaped by utilitarian logics, oriented more to the training of students for employment in the new knowledge-based economy than to educational growth.

Simultaneously, under the rationale of higher education as a 'good' benefiting primarily students, they are compelled to assume a larger responsibility towards its financing. Increasing students' consumer consciousness about what to expect in terms of educational experience and of returns on the investment in human capital promotes a reshaping of their identity from learners and institutional actors to consumers (Slaughter & Rhoades, 2004).

Conceptualized as such, students are more and more taken into account in the definition of several aspects of their education and in particular the assessment of its quality. The underlying assumption is that students are in pursuit of quality education and that their choices, expectations and perceptions can influence the promotion of educational improvement (Slaughter & Rhoades, 2004).

Within this context, a major question arises, apparently not yet answered by research on quality: whether students, in relation to universities' quality assessment, see themselves as consumers or, on the contrary, as institutional actors. Based on a revision of relevant literature on the subject, this chapter has the purpose of putting forward arguments to answer this question.

This discussion is organized in four parts. The first is focused on the analysis of the context of the emergence of the notion of the student as consumer within higher education and on its use as a background to student participation in quality assessment.

Next, an overview is made of the arguments legitimizing student participation and the modes in which this participation is occurring since the 1990s in European countries, including Portugal.

A third area of focus is based on a limited set of works reporting essentially Portuguese students' perceptions of quality assessment. The chapter reflects upon these perceptions, trying to understand to what extent they reproduce assumptions and beliefs indicting the (self-)concept of students as consumers.

The chapter concludes by emphasizing that, despite the increasing influence of such (self-)conception, this does not constitute the only 'identity' assumed by students in their relation with higher education and universities. Therefore, attention is drawn to the multiplicity of 'identities' or concepts framing this relation, namely regarding one of its specific dimensions – quality assessment.

Students as consumers

Since the 1970s several[1] concepts have emerged to try to define the beneficiaries of public services, as is the case with client, customer, consumer or service user (Clarke, 2007; Jung, 2010; McCulloch, 2009; McLaughlin, 2009; Vidler & Clarke, 2005). This trend is also evident at the level of higher education, through the increasing tendency to conceptualize students as clients or consumers of the products and services provided by universities, in other words, study programmes and support for their pursuit (McCulloch, 2009).

Several interrelated factors contributed to this trend, namely growing market regulation and consumerist logic, and the drive to equate (as in the case of public services) student participation with the suitability of educational services (Clarke et al., 2007; McLaughlin, 2009). This is also influenced by structural changes occurring in modern societies at the level of the relation between the state and the public sphere and of the social understanding of what is 'public' (Clarke et al., 2007; Olsen & Peters, 2005; Slaughter & Rhoades, 2004).

A progressive attempt of the state to transform its role in society by transferring market and private management mechanisms to the public sector is verifiable over the last three decades, driven, among other factors, by increasing financial constraints and the rise of neo-liberalism and its associated discourses, as with, for example, managerialism/New Public Management. This led to a progressive replacement of the traditional public service ethos by a closer relationship with private management. New values and concepts embedded in business culture emerged, such as that of client, customer or consumer, progressively replacing the traditional public administration notion of user or citizen (Cardoso et al., 2011; Clarke, 2007; Clarke et al., 2007; Jung, 2010; Olsen & Peters, 2005; Vidler & Clarke, 2005; Williams, 2009). The main aim of this reconceptualization is to empower individuals, increasing their freedom and capacity to make rational choices in terms of the fulfilment of needs. At the same time, it intends to reduce the state's responsibility towards this fulfilment while increasing public organizations' accountability, responsiveness, cost-efficiency, flexibility and quality (Cardoso et al., 2011; Clarke, 2007; Clarke & Newman, 1997; Clarke et al., 2007; Jung, 2010; McCulloch, 2009; McLaughlin, 2009; Vidler & Clarke, 2005).

This new political and organizational logic has gradually permeated higher education, embodied in the alignment of universities with the changing social understanding of what is 'public' and increasing adoption of market and market-like behaviours as well as a market ethos and ideology (Olsen & Peters, 2005; Slaughter & Rhoades, 2004). This became evident in many aspects of institutional operation, including the mission, goals and response to the demands of society and the labour market (Barnett, 1990, 2003; Menon, 2003; Olsen & Peters, 2005; Shattock, 2009; Slaughter & Rhoades, 2004).

Indeed, the relationship between universities and society has undergone substantial changes over the last three decades. This is due to a proliferation of the perception of universities as institutions playing a central role in the knowledge society, by not only producing and reproducing knowledge and human and cultural capital, but also by solving economic and social problems and providing competent graduates to the rapidly changing knowledge-based labour market (Barnett, 2003; Clark, 1998; Johnstone et al., 2006; Scott, 1997). This constitutes a transformation of the traditional roles of universities since, from active agents attached to and collaborating with society, these institutions subsume to its interests and needs, linked with the market economy (Rothblatt, 1993).

As a way to respond to these new demands, study programmes started to be progressively structured towards developing certain skills and competences in students, perceived as required by the labour market. This ascribed higher education with an increasingly utilitarian and vocational character, focused on training graduates for the fulfilment of specific tasks and functions in the new society and economy (Barnett, 1990; Scott, 1997; Slaughter & Rhoades, 2004; Olsen & Peters, 2005).

In summary, using the arguments of Slaughter and Rhoades (2004), one can argue that during the last 30 years, a significant change occurred within universities, characterized by a move from a 'public-good knowledge/learning regime', valuing knowledge as a public good and the public/private separation in its delivery, to an 'academic capitalist knowledge/learning regime', valuing the privatization of knowledge and the profits resulting from it (Slaughter & Rhoades, 2004).

The 'traditional' university then gave way to the entrepreneurial university (Clark, 1998; Shattock, 2009) or a business-like organization (Little & Williams, 2010; Lomas, 2007; Olsen & Peters, 2005), attempting to reconcile private and managerial values, concepts and practices, including those of the consumerist logic, with traditional or academic ones (Clark, 1998; Slaughter & Rhoades, 2004). In other words, the university is driven by a new 'academic capitalism', embodied in its increasing articulation and response to the new demands of the knowledge society; the effort to create new types of knowledge, providing the knowledge society with its required innovation, intellectual dynamism and knowledge creation and transfer; the expansion of its managerial capacity; and the generation of non-public funding through the development of entrepreneurial academic activity (Clark, 1998; Shattock, 2009; Slaughter & Rhoades, 2004).

These developments, besides imposing a new approach to educational planning and decision-making (Menon, 2003), based on the consumerist logic, were also linked to a relevant change in the way students began to be conceptualized.

The growing conception of higher education as a service or product, along with the increasing role of students in supporting the costs of their education (namely, in some countries, due to the introduction of tuition fees), induced their progressive perception as clients or consumers rather than as citizens benefiting from a public good or, even, as institutional actors (Bergan, 2003; Cardoso et al., 2011; Johnson & Deem, 2003;

Johnstone et al., 2006; Kogan et al., 1994; Lomas, 2007; McLaughlin, 2009; Morley, 2003; Newson, 2004; Pitman, 2000; Robertson, 2000; Sharrock, 2000). The main rationale behind this is the idea of higher education being a good, benefiting primarily individual students (who are enhancing their human capital), so they and their families are expected to bear a larger share of its costs (Clarke, 2007; Johnson & Deem, 2003; Johnstone et al., 2006; Lomas, 2007; McCulloch, 2009; Slaughter & Rhoades, 2004).

Perceived as consumers, students are converted into conscious actors of their educational rights, holding the capability to define strategies and make rational choices supported by informed and improved decision-making processes, aiming to optimize the satisfaction of their needs, motivations and expectations of higher education (McCulloch, 2009; Newson, 2004; Robertson, 2000).

Thus, the student identity is being reconstructed, defined and redefined by universities' market and entrepreneurial behaviours (Barnett, 2003; McLaughlin, 2009; Slaughter & Rhoades, 2004). Examples of this can be found in the development by these institutions of new services and practices to attract students, such as the advertising and marketing of both study programmes and the overall institutional environment and life style; the increasing participation of students in institutional decisions on crucial issues, such as the curricular organization of degrees (centred more and more in the development of professional competences); or the definition of the institutional profile based on students' interests and expectations (Cardoso et al., 2011; McCulloch, 2009; Morley, 2003; Newson, 2004; Olsen & Peters, 2005; Pitman, 2000; Robertson, 2000; Slaughter & Rhoades, 2004).

However, the conceptualization of students as consumers seems to have permeated other spheres of higher education beyond the behaviour of universities. That is the case in the assessment of the quality of higher education.

Over the last three decades, mainly as a consequence of the change of the state's positioning towards higher education, assessment has emerged as a way to regulate the quality of universities (namely as suppliers of a qualified labour force) and to ensure their compliance with government objectives (Amaral & Rosa, 2010; Barnett, 1990; Brennan & Shah, 2000; Lomas, 2007; Neave, 1988, 1998; Neave & van Vught, 1994).

Further, assessment has become a mechanism through which governments try to ensure that universities provide as much information as possible on their performance and quality to various higher education stakeholders (namely students, potential students, students' families or employers) (Lomas, 2007; Little & Williams, 2010; Slaughter & Rhoades, 2004). One of the main aims behind this was to increase institutional accountability by demonstrating quality to society and, especially, students, since they invest their trust and money in their education. Another aim was to help students and prospective students estimate the quality of education and make informed choices on which universities to attend (Barnett, 2000, 2003; Dill & Soo, 2005; Lomas, 2007).

Within this context, the collection of students' perspectives on the quality of these institutions, along with their participation in assessment, assumes a central role, being converted into routine procedures that increasingly influence institutional decision-making (Green et al., 1995; Harvey, 2003; Lomas, 2007; Kogan et al., 1994; McCulloch, 2009; Menon, 2003; Radcliff, 1996).

Students and quality assessment

Until the 1990s, the collection of students' views on features surrounding higher education and universities was not subject to a systematic procedure (Green et al., 1995; Harvey, 2003). However, the centrality assumed, since that decade, by quality and its assessment, combined with the conception of students as clients or consumers, imposed the need to assemble their opinions on the quality of the 'services' delivered by universities (Green et al., 1995; Harvey, 2003; Popli, 2005; Slaughter & Rhoades, 2004; Wiberg, 2006). Therefore, their participation in quality assessment processes has been increasing, both in quantitative and qualitative terms (Cardoso, 2009; Cardoso & Santos, 2011; Little & Williams, 2010).

Several arguments promote and sustain this participation. One of the most preponderant is that students have the right to be involved in the assessment of higher education because they invest in it and are the major consumers. Therefore, they have a special interest in factors such as quality that guarantee they receive a good 'deal' (Barnett, 2003; Wiberg, 2006). A second justification is that the information given by students on quality is central to assessment, as it results from their experience as clients or consumers of the teaching/learning process and, concomitantly, from both the outcomes of such experience (knowledge and competences, personal and social development, diploma, employment) and the satisfaction derived from it (Dubois, 1998; Green et al., 1995; Harvey, 2003; Leckey & Neill, 2001; Powell et al., 1997; Richardson, 2005; Sarrico & Rosa, 2010). Finally, students' expectations and perceptions on higher education are seen as an important element in shaping universities' quality improvement, namely regarding their competitive potential and students' future employment (Cardoso, 2009; Green et al., 1995; Little & Williams, 2010).

In certain cases, as in Portugal, one can however assume that the integration of students in quality assessment was, to some extent, reconfigured by another (and more relevant) rationale: their centrality as key institutional actors. Indeed, Portuguese students always played a relevant role within universities, namely in their governance[2], being thought of as preponderant actors of institutional decision-making (Cardoso, 2009; Cardoso & Santos, 2011; Cardoso et al., 2011). This means that students tend to be seen as legitimate participants of universities, holding the same responsibilities as the remaining institutional actors (academics, academic managers, non-academic staff) for their operation and the education they provide.

Framed by previous arguments, the participation of students is currently seen to be relevant, among most European countries, at two major levels of the development of assessment – universities (internal level) and quality assessment systems (external level) (Cardoso, 2010; Cardoso & Santos, 2011; Froestad & Bakken, 2004). Despite the specificities assumed depending on the national context, the participation of students generally corresponds to (Cardoso, 2010): (1) integration into the institutional groups responsible for self-assessment and response to questionnaires on the teaching/learning process; (2) presence at meetings with external assessment panels; (3) collaboration in the definition and planning of assessment, namely through the presence in the bodies of the assessment agencies; (4) integration in the external assessment panels and contribution to the composition of the external assessment report; (5) contribution to the development of follow-up initiatives; and (6) involvement in the internal quality assurance systems.

Taking Portugal as reference case, one can state that the forms of student participation in the assessment of quality in higher education and universities, defined by the two legislative[3] configurations of the national quality assessment system, are very similar to those mentioned above. The only exception is that Portuguese students still do not participate in the external assessment panels and, therefore, do not contribute to the composition of those reports (Cardoso, 2009, 2010).

Nevertheless, during the first phase of the history[4] of Portuguese quality assessment (1992–2005) (Rosa et al., 2009), student participation in its development was marked by their significant distance or relevant lack of awareness and experience towards both the features of that development and the forms of that participation (Cardoso, 2009). Students' major complaints in this context relate to the absence of substantive strategies (conceived by universities) aimed at informing them of such features and to the character assumed by such forms of participation, perceived as confining them to less direct and active roles (than, for instance, academics) in assessment (Cardoso, 2009).

To some extent this development can be interpreted as constituting evidence of increasing influence of the conception of students as consumers, also within Portuguese higher education and its assessment. In fact, though student participation in quality assessment tends to be based on their notion as key institutional actors, the aloofness showed towards this process seems to indict that students, as clients or consumers of services, show little involvement and interest in it. This implicitly results in the simplification of their roles and their disempowerment within the process (Cardoso, 2009; Cardoso & Santos, 2011). Students tend to be restricted to a position of mere passive informants, whose opinions and perspectives on the quality of higher education and universities have as their main goal to assist the development of its assessment (Cardoso, 2009).

Next, notwithstanding the shortage of research on the subject, an attempt is made to shed some light on the way students perceive both their involvement in assessment and the process itself, trying to grasp the extent to which these perceptions reproduce ideas denoting their (self-)conception as consumers.

Students' perceptions on quality assessment: translation of a consumerist view?

This part of the chapter aims to theoretically answer the previous question, resorting to research on the way students perceive the assessment of the quality of higher education and universities. It must be mentioned, however, that due to the relative absence of this kind of research, the discussion draws mainly on the studies of Cardoso (2009) and Leite et al. (2007) for its framework while making occasional references to other works. The first study addresses Portuguese students' perceptions of the assessment of the quality of public higher education institutions (between 1994 and 2005), while the second study is based on a comparative analysis of Portuguese and Brazilian students' perceptions of the respective national assessment systems.

In general, it is possible to argue that students' perceptions of quality assessment express, to some extent, their (self-)conceptualization as clients or consumers. This is evident in the way students describe the features and purposes of quality assessment, reveal a predisposition to get involved in the process and actually accomplish this involvement (Cardoso, 2009).

Assessment tends to be perceived by students as a legitimate device of state control and regulation of universities, having as its main aim an increase in the institutions' accountability and quality. Quality assessment is further seen as being focused on the whole operation and performance of universities and, especially, in features such as institutional quality, management, efficiency, effectiveness, results and productivity. To some extent these perceptions seem to be aligned and influenced by the assumptions of the managerial rhetoric legitimizing the existence and development of quality assessment (Cardoso, 2009; Leite et al., 2007).

Students seem to have an instrumental vision of the purposes of assessment. This is evident in its conception as enabling both institutional accountability and quality improvement – namely of education, study programmes and teachers – and graduates' employability, by socially legitimating the external image, prestige and reputation of universities and, thus, the training, competences and skills acquired by graduates (Cardoso, 2009; Leite et al., 2007). These perceptions might be explained by students' increasing awareness about the competitive environment currently framing both higher education and the labour market (Cardoso, 2009; Paivandi, 2006). Perceptions might also be justified by the existence, among students, of an idea of the quality of universities as mainly linked to the quality of the key 'service' offered by these institutions, in other words, the education they provide, as well as of the human and material resources mobilized for its provision (Gatfield et al., 1999). To this extent, one can consider students as positioning themselves as customers of this service, centred on its quality and its future consequences (employment and social recognition of the degrees).

Finally, students also perceive the assessment of quality as aimed at ranking universities. Rankings emerge as a way to recognize and classify these institutions and, thus, to stimulate their improvement and competition for resources and students, based on the quality and institutional capability to respond to the demand and satisfy their consumers (Cardoso, 2009; Leite et al., 2006, 2007).

The next set of statements deriving from students interviewed in Cardoso's (2009) study illustrate some of the aspects previously discussed referring to the influence of the consumer notion on the way students tend to perceive quality assessment:

> [Assessment] is a good way to control the institutions; [...] every institution should be accountable; [...] it is important to have something ensuring [its] quality.

> [Assess] the quality of every dimension of the operation of the university: management, pedagogic, institutional, everything! [...] the performance. [If] the results [...] were accomplished in a efficient and effective way.

> [Assessment gives] the possibility to classify the institutions. [It is a] way for institutions and degrees to demonstrate that they are better or worse. [It] is very important for a person to know that, when she graduates, she will be recognised by the market.

Signs of students' (self-)conception as consumers can also be found in the predisposition they show towards possible involvement in the assessment of the quality of their universities and study programmes. Students tend to present a rather positive predisposition towards this involvement, justifying it through several arguments, such as the central role they can play in the development of the process, namely by enriching it with a unique perspective on the institutional dimensions under assessment; or the opportunity to make the student voice heard and to contribute to change, improvement and the quality of universities. Among these arguments one emerges, however, strictly connected with the notion of students as consumers: the argument that students have the right to be involved and to participate in assessment since they are the main clients or consumers of the services delivered by universities (Cardoso, 2009).

Indeed, the involvement in quality assessment is seen by some students as giving them the opportunity to express their opinions and perspectives as consumers of higher education, as exemplified by the following statement by one student in Cardoso's (2009) study:

> Because we would give our opinion as customers, as someone who is consuming the [higher education] system and education [...] [hoping] to see improvements [...] results.

In terms of their participation in quality assessment, students seem to be relegated to a role of peripheral or secondary actors (Cardoso, 2009). This is made evident by their distance, both socio-cognitive (in terms of knowledge and information) and pragmatic (in terms of practical experience), towards the main features of the process (Cardoso, 2009; Leite et al., 2006, 2007):

[How] the assessment is done, since when, its main features, I don't know.

There is not enough information. I can see that from my case: if it [information] existed, probably I would know. I only would not know if I choose to. But I have never heard of it.

This distance can be explained in two ways: on the one hand, by the less favourable position students tend to assume inside universities (when compared with academics or academic managers, for instance), characterized by the performance of less preponderant roles in regard to institutional decision-making and processes, including quality assessment (Cardoso, 2009; Dubois, 1998; Gueissaz & Hayrinen-Alestalo, 1999; Kogan, 1993); on the other hand, as a result of the increasing tendency, at the level of higher education and universities, to conceive students as consumers (Cardoso, 2009). Such a conception presupposes that students only have the right to limited information and involvement in the chief matters and processes linked with universities' daily operation. This seems to be the case with quality assessment, where the role of students is essentially that of mere passive informants, of producers of opinions and information, with the sole purpose of assisting the development of the process (Bienefeld & Almqvist, 2004; Johnson & Deem, 2003).

However, students also resign themselves to such a role and, consequently, to that of consumers, when they ascribe the responsibility mainly to universities for the provision of information, and promoting their awareness, on the main features characterizing quality assessment, including those related to their participation in it. Students do not seem to make efforts to obtain that information and to use it strategically as a way to enhance their participation and empowerment within universities (Cardoso, 2009).

Students' (self-)conception as consumers is also evident given the fact that they are more interested in the information resulting from the outcomes of quality assessment, than on its development and characteristics. The access to such information is seen as enabling students to accomplish certain instrumental purposes of higher education (namely the choice of and permanence in a given university and study programme), rather than a more effective involvement and participation in quality assessment and university life (Cardoso, 2009).

Other features of students' perceptions can be thought of as providing evidence of their (self-)conception as consumers. That is the case, for instance, of the alignment (though not very strong) with the idea of universities as enterprises or entrepreneurial institutions: (1) developing profitable activities, namely as a way of diversifying financial (re)sources; (2) stimulating demand through marketing and publicity strategies; (3) aiming at the satisfaction of the needs of students as clients or consumers; (4) rationalizing 'supply' (education) based on the needs of the labour market; and (5) granting a central role to, and aiming for, the improvement of institutional quality, efficiency, excellence, image and prestige. In this context, quality assessment is perceived by students both as focused on former features of university operation and as an instrument seeking to stimulate institutional competitiveness, differentiation and attractiveness (Cardoso, 2009).

Moreover, students also tend to see universities as contributing to social and economic development and, therefore, as essentially providing them with a vocational education and training, promoting their future insertion into the labour market. The emphasis on these features appears to be related to a perception of quality assessment as being focused on the vocational and training mission of universities, the social 'demand' for their graduates and their capability to respond to the needs of internal and external consumers (Cardoso, 2009):

> I began to realise that companies are interested in these assessment reports and rely heavily on the bodies responsible for assessment.

To some extent, these perceptions seem aligned with the managerialist rhetoric emphasizing the utilitarian or vocational nature of higher education, the entrepreneurial and responsive character of universities, and of assessment as a device designed to assure their quality, competitiveness and accountability (Barnett, 2003; Clark, 1998; Gibbons et al., 1994; Olsen & Peters, 2005; Scott, 1995; Slaughter & Leslie, 1997). Students' permeability to such rhetoric can be explained by the assimilation of the major transformations higher education has been through over the last decades (Cardoso, 2009).

In summary, it is possible to argue that, at least in relation to the assessment of the quality of higher education and universities, students tend to reproduce ideas and meanings partly translating their (self-)conception as consumers. This seems to indicate that a reconfiguration of the notion of a student might be taking place, reflecting not only the existing external discourse, but also being internally promoted by higher education students.

Students: a multidimensional identity beyond that of the consumer

Throughout the chapter a discussion has developed regarding the way students seem to be perceived and perceive themselves as consumers within the context of higher education quality assessment. In particular, this perception of students is seen as predominant in analysing the way they relate to the assessment process.

Based mainly on the findings of two specific studies (Cardoso, 2009; Leite et al., 2007), it is possible to conclude that, to some extent, students also tend to conceive themselves as consumers when considering their relation to higher education, universities and the assessment of their quality. The presence of this notion is evident in the way students identify the main characteristics and aims of quality assessment as well as their predisposition to get involved in the process. So, at least in relation to quality assessment, the consumer concept seems to be assimilated by students, despite the still predominant notion of them as key-institutional actors, especially at the level of the conception and development of that process.

However, this does not necessarily mean that the consumer notion and presuppositions are being consistently adopted by, or serve as, background to students in their relation to all the remaining dimensions of higher education and universities (access, education and the teaching/learning process, institutional governance and management and so on). Instead, this relation is marked by the (more conscious or unconscious) assumption of multiple identities[5] (Ferrales & Fine, 2005; Tobbell et al., 2010), some closer, some further away from the concept of the student as a consumer. For instance, a recent study of Portuguese students' choices in higher education (Tavares, 2011) shows evidence that, though tending to behave as consumers, especially when deciding whether to participate at this level of education or choosing a given institution, students seem not to act as such when opting for a specific study programme. At this level, they are influenced by a mix of sociological variables linked with the socialization and schooling processes framing the construction of vocation and personality.

Furthermore, the way students conceive the mission and aims of higher education is not completely influenced by consumer logic. Students continue to value features of a more traditional vision of such purposes and mission, emphasizing the need for universities to be oriented towards 'human development' (personal and social growth of individuals) (Cardoso, 2009; Wiers-Jenssen et al., 2002), while criticizing the increasing massification of higher education and its orientation towards the labour market (Cardoso, 2009):

> I have a classic idea of what a university is: [a place] of human development [not] a factory [...] a massification process.

The incomplete subordination to consumer logic may also explain the preponderance of some academic factors, such as those associated with teaching, pedagogical relationships and universities' social environment, in creating student satisfaction and fostering relations towards these institutions (Wiers-Jenssen et al., 2002).

The consumer imagery (and its correlated identity) also seems to act less as a backdrop when the involvement of students in the bodies and processes related with university governance is at stake. In this field, students tend to conceive and assume themselves as active members or participants of university life, holding and sharing responsibility for the diverse dimensions of its operation (Bergan, 2003; Clarke, 2007; Little & Williams, 2010). The prevalent concept of students in this domain seems to be that of institutional actors or active members of the academic community, in other words, crucial actors and legitimate participants in institutional processes and decision-making, holding specific roles, powers, responsibility and extensive involvement in the operation of universities and their quality (Cardoso & Santos, 2011). Authors such as Little and Williams (2010) argue that there seems to be a need for students to gain more awareness of the actual power they have in universities, exercising it through the attribution of a more active role and contribution to the institutions' lives, including the level of quality assessment. This reinforced awareness seems necessarily to imply a (self-)concept of students different from that of a consumer. Instead of empowering students and extending their participation in universities (and, namely, in quality assessment), their concept as consumers results in the oversimplification of their roles, prerogatives and accountabilities within and towards these institutions (Bergan, 2003; Boland, 2005; Harvey, 2009; Little & Williams, 2010; Lizzio & Wilson, 2009). Indeed, under the influence of the consumer rhetoric, students are expected to be mainly focused on (and demand) quality from the courses being delivered by universities, which contributes to a reduction in the sense of themselves both as active contributors to, and participants in, the educational process, the institutional bodies and processes and in the assessment of that same quality (Barnett, 2003; Cardoso, 2009; Harvey,

2009; Little & Williams, 2010; McCulloch, 2009). In this last case, the students' role tends to be conceived as restricted to that of mere users of services and facilities provided by universities (Kotzé & du Plessis, 2003). This can be the origin of students' detachment from quality assessment, as discussed in the third part of this chapter, exhibited by an ignorance of its main features, lack of interest and predisposition to get involved in the process, and in the reduction or restriction of their influence and power towards its provision and development, contrary to what happens with other institutional groups (academics and academic managers, for instance) (Cardoso, 2009; McLaughlin, 2009). Specifically, students' low interest in involvement in quality assessment can be seen as being expressed by the frequently low response rates to question-naires (for instance, on the teaching/learning process) (Cardoso, 2009; Richardson, 2005). Eventually realizing the predominantly indirect and less representative participation enabled by the response to these ques-tionnaires, students seem to withdraw their investment towards their involvement in quality assessment (Cardoso, 2009).

Notwithstanding, students tend to see this participation as important, legitimized by the key role they have in institutional governance and in the teaching/learning process. Such participation is seen as essen-tial to the recognition of institutional problems and their solution as well as to the promotion of improvements. In the same vein, though also justified by their right as consumers of higher education, students' predisposition to engage in such participation is mainly legitimized by the importance of their contribution to the development and enrich-ment of quality assessment as a main feature of university life (Cardoso, 2009). This is especially well supported by the statements of some of the students of Cardoso's study (2009):

> The student is the key element of the whole educational process. As such he should be one of the first ones to be heard [and participate in the assessment].

> Students are the primary way of knowing [if the university or the study programme achieves quality] or to help in the development of assessment.

> [If] we do not participate, [quality assessment] has no validity.

Finally, another dimension of student relation with higher education and universities where the consumer imagery and identity (though present) still does not prevail or, at least, is not linear, is that constituted by the education *tout court*.

Though students can assume (or be increasingly driven to assume) the position of mere purchasers of higher education and, therefore, a more 'distant' and passive role in the educational process and in learning (Barnett, 2003; Bergan, 2003; Harvey, 2009; McCulloch, 2009; Slaughter & Rhoades, 2004), this does not necessarily mean that they passively consume it, as a consumer of any product or service. On the contrary, as mentioned by some authors (Barnett, 1990; Lomas, 2007; McCulloch, 2009; Sharrock, 2000), students tend to actively and personally engage and help to develop ideas and knowledge, namely through their interaction with teachers and other students, participating in a process larger than themselves through which they are provided 'with what they need rather than what they want' (Lomas, 2007, p. 34). Once more, at this level, students tend to act not based on consumerist logic, but rather as institutional actors. This is evident given the fact that students do not behave as mere cooperative participants in the learning process, engaged merely in the production, dissemination and application of knowledge, or as one of the parts of the academic community, contributing to its (re)shaping through the interaction with the remaining parts (Little & Williams, 2010; McCulloch, 2009).

So, by way of a conclusion, one can argue that despite the increasingly widespread (self-)concept and assimilation of student-as-consumer, namely in the context of the assessment of the quality of universities, students still do not behave strictly as such. Changes in this behaviour and in the extent to which they are internalizing the consumer identity should, however, constitute the focus of future research, given the shortage of work on this subject (Johnson & Deem, 2003).

Notes

1. Emergent in the 1970s, the concept of client reflects an objectification of the relation between the deliverer of the service and its recipient, whereby the power is held by the first and the latter assumes a passive role (McLaughlin, 2009). During the 1980s, under the influence of market ideology, two other and interchangeable notions appear – consumer and costumer – translating a relationship where the public service is conceived, respectively, as product to the consumer, managed by a provider mainly accountable to the state; and as a commodity to the costumer, delivered by a provider accountable mainly to the management of the service (Jung, 2010; McLaughlin, 2009). Finally, during the 1990s, the concept of service user emerges with the aim of increasing the voice and action of the recipient of public services, namely as to the way these are developed and delivered (McLaughlin, 2009).
2. In Portugal this role has been formalized since the late 1980s by the University and Polytechnic Autonomy Acts (108/1988 and 54/1990), though its roots date back to the period of the 'Estado Novo' dictatorship (Cardoso et al., 2011).

3. Respectively the Law 38/1994 and Decree-law 205/1998, and the Law 38/2007 and Decree-law 369/2007.
4. In general, the development of Portuguese quality assessment can be considered as being divided in two phases: the first, comprising the period 1992–2005, corresponds to the implementation of the first quality assessment system; the second, begun in 2006, with the dismantlement of the former system, followed by the definition (in 2007) and operation (in 2009) of a new programme (Rosa et al., 2009).
5. Academia is a social field where multiple student identities are constructed and shared (Ferrales & Fine, 2005; Tobbell et al., 2010) as, for instance, the identity of students as learners, as institutional actors, or as future professionals. Depending on these identities, students know how to behave and act according to different contexts and situations (Ferrales & Fine, 2005) or, in other words, how to integrate and participate in the range of communities of practice-composing academia (Tobbell et al., 2010).

References

Amaral, A. and M.J. Rosa (2010) 'Recent trends in quality assurance', *Quality in Higher Education*, 16(1), 59–61.

Barnett, R. (2003) *Beyond all reason: living with ideology in the university*, Buckingham: SRHE/Open University Press.

Barnett, R. (2000) 'University knowledge in an age of supercomplexity', *Higher Education*, 40, 409–422.

Barnett, R. (1990) *The idea of higher education*, Buckingham: SRHE.

Bergan, S. (2003) *Student participation in higher education governance* (unpublished work, 16 p.) http://www.coe.int/t/dg4/highereducation/governance/SB_student_participation_EN.pdf, accessed August 2010.

Bienefeld, S. and J. Almqvist (2004) 'Student life and the roles of students in Europe', *European Journal of Education*, 39(4), 430–441.

Boland, J. (2005) 'Student participation in shared governance: a means of advancing democratic values?', *Tertiary Education and Management*, 11, 199–217.

Brennan, J. and T. Shah (2000) *Managing quality higher education: an international perspective on institutional assessment and change*, Buckingham: SRHE/Open University Press.

Cardoso, S. (2010) *Students' participation in Portuguese higher education institutions: a contribute to its definition* [translated title], online publication: http://www.a3es.pt/pt/estudos-e-documentos/documentos/participacao-dos-estudantes-na-avaliacao-das-instituicoes-de-ensino-superior-portuguesas

Cardoso, S. (2009) *Students' perceptions of the assessment of public higher education institutions* [translated title], PhD Thesis, Aveiro: University of Aveiro.

Cardoso, S., T. Carvalho and R. Santiago (2011) 'From students to consumers: reflections on the "marketization" of Portuguese higher education', *European Journal of Education*, 46(2), 271–284.

Cardoso, S. and S.M. Santos (2011) 'Students in higher education governance: the Portuguese case', *Tertiary Higher Education and Management*, 17(3), 233–246.

Clark, B. (1998) *Creating entrepreneurial universities – organizational pathways of transformation*, Oxford: Pergamon/IAU Press.

Clarke, J. (2007) 'Citizen-consumers and public service reform: at the limits of neoliberalism?', *Policy Futures in Education*, 5(2), 239–247.

Clarke, J., J. Newman, N. Smith, E. Vidler and L. Westmarland (2007) *Creating citizen-consumers – Changing publics and changing public services*, London: Thousand Oaks; New Delhi: Sage.

Clarke, J. and J. Newman (1997) *The managerial state*, London: Sage.

Decree-Law 205/1998 – Creates the National Council for the Assessment of Higher Education.

Decree-Law 369/2007 – Creates the Higher Education Assessment and Accreditation Agency.

Dill, D. and M. Soo (2005) 'Academic quality, league tables and public policy: a cross-national analysis of university ranking systems', *Higher Education*, 49, 495–533.

Dubois, P. (Coord.) (1998) *Evalue – Evaluation and self-evaluation of universities in Europe*, European Community – Targeted Socio-Economic Research Program (TSER), http://www.pjb.co.uk/npl, date accessed April 2006.

Etzkowitz, E. (2003a) 'Innovation in innovation: the triple helix of university-industry-government relations', *Social Science Information*, 42(3), 293–337.

Etzkowitz, E. (2003b) 'Research groups as "quasi-firms". The invention of the entrepreneurial university', *Research Policy*, 32(1), 109–121.

Ferrales, G. and G. Fine (2005) 'Sociology as a vocation: reputations and group cultures in graduate school', *The American Sociologist*, Summer 2005, 57–75.

Froestad, W. and P. Bakken (2004) *Student Involvement in quality assessments of higher education in the Nordic Countries*, Helsinki: Nordic Quality Assurance Network in Higher Education.

Gatfield, T., M. Barker and P. Graham (1999) 'Measuring student quality variables and the implications for management practices in higher education institutions: an Australian and international student perspective', *Journal of Higher Education Policy and Management*, 21(2), 239–252.

Gibbons, M., C. Limoges, H. Nowtny, J. Scheele, P. Scott and M. Trow (1994) *The new production of knowledge: the dynamics of science and research in contemporary societies*, London: Sage.

Green, D., C. Brannigan, P. Mazelan and L. Giles (1995) 'Measuring student satisfaction: a method of improving the quality of the students' experience?' in S. Haselgrove (ed.) *The student experience*, Buckingham: Open University Press, pp. 100–107.

Gueissaz, A. and M. Hayrinen-Alestalo (1999) 'How to integrate contradictory aims: the configurations of actors in the evaluation of universities', *European Journal of Education*, 34(3), 283–297.

Harvey, L. (2009) *A critical analysis of quality culture*, http://www.inqaahe.org/admin/files/assets/subsites/1/documenten/1241773373_16-harvey-a-critical-analysis-of-quality-culture.pdf., date accessed September 2010.

Harvey, L. (2003) 'Student feedback', *Quality in Higher Education*, 9(1), 3–20.

Johnson, R. and R. Deem (2003) 'Talking of students: tensions and contradictions for the manager-academic and the university in contemporary higher education', *Higher Education*, 46, 289–314.

Johnstone, D.B., P. Teixeira, M.J. Rosa and H. Vossensteyn (eds) (2006) *Cost-sharing and accessibility in higher education. A fairer deal?*, Dordrecht, The Netherlands: Springer.

Jung, T. (2010) 'Citizens, co-producers, customers, clients, captives? A critical review of consumerism and public services', *Public Management Review*, 12(3), 439–446.

Kogan, M. (1993) 'The evaluation of higher education: an introductory note' in M. Kogan (ed.) *Evaluating higher education*, London: Jessica Kingsley Publishers, pp. 11–26.

Kogan M., I. Moses and E. El-Khawas (1994) 'The changing framework for the academic profession' in M. Kogan, I. Moses and E. El-Khawas (ed.) *Staffing higher education meeting new challenges*, Report on the IMHE Project on policies for academic staffing in higher education Higher Education Policy Series, 27, Bristol: Jessica Kingsley Publishers, pp. 12–32.

Kotzé, T. and P. du Plessis (2003) 'Students as "co-producers" of education', *Quality Assurance in Education*, 11(4), 186–201.

Law 38/1994 – Establishes the Higher Education Assessment National System.

Law 38/2007 – Juridical Regime of the Higher Education Assessment.

Leckey, J. and N. Neill (2001) 'Quantifying quality: the importance of student feedback', *Quality in Higher Education*, 7(1), 19–32.

Leite D., R. Santiago, M. Leite, M. Genro, A. Braga, M. Polidori and C. Broilo (2007) 'Students and the assessment of the university: a joint study Brazil-Portugal' [translated title], *Cadernos de Pesquisa*, 37(132), 661–686.

Leite, D., R. Santiago, C. Sarrico, C. Leite and M. Polidori (2006) 'Students' representation on the influence of institutional evaluation on universities', *Assessment and Evaluation in Higher Education*, 31(6), 625–638.

Little, B. and R. Williams (2010) 'Students' roles in managing quality and enhancing learning: is there a tension?', *Quality in Higher Education*, 16(2), 115–127.

Lizzio, A. and K. Wilson (2009) 'Student participation in university governance: the role conceptions and sense of efficacy of student representatives on departmental committees', *Studies in Higher Education*, 34(1), 69–84.

Lomas, L. (2007) 'Are students customers? Perceptions of academic staff', *Quality in Higher Education*, 13(1), 31–44.

McCulloch, A. (2009) 'The student as co-producer: learning from public administration about the student-university relationship', *Studies in Higher Education*, 34(2), 171–183.

McLaughlin, H. (2009) 'What's in a name: "client", "patient", "customer", "consumer" "expert by experience", "service user" – what's next?', *British Journal of Social Work*, 39, 1101–1117.

Menon, M. (2003) 'Student involvement in university governance: a need for negotiated educational aims?', *Tertiary Education and Management*, 9(3), 233–246.

Morley, L. (2003) *Quality and power in higher education*, Maidenhead: Open University Press/SRHE.

Neave, G. (1988) 'On the cultivation of quality, efficiency and enterprise: an overview of recent trends in higher education in Western Europe, 1986–1988', *European Journal of Education*, 23(1/2), 7–23.

Neave, G. (1998) 'The evaluative state reconsidered', *European Journal of Education*, 33(3), 265–284.

Neave, G. and F. van Vught (1994) *Government and higher education relationships across three continents: the winds of change*, Oxford: Pergamon Press.

Newson, J. (2004) 'Disrupting the «student as a consumer» model: the new emancipatory project', *International Relations*, 18(2), 227–239.

Olsen, M. and M.A. Peters (2005) 'Neoliberalism, higher education and the knowledge economy: from the free market to knowledge capitalism', *Journal of Education Policy*, 20(3), 313–345.

Paivandi, S. (2006) 'New trends in the sociology of university student in France [translated title]', *Investigar em Educação – Revista da Sociedade Portuguesa de Ciências da Educação, A Organização do Trabalho na Escola*, 5, 261–298.

Pitman, T. (2000) 'Perceptions of academics and students as customers: a survey of administrative staff in higher education', *Journal of Higher Education Policy and Management*, 22(2), 165–175.

Popli, S. (2005) 'Ensuring customer delight: a quality approach to excellence in management education', *Quality in Higher Education*, 11(1), 17–24.

Powell, A., A. Hunt and A. Irving (1997) 'Evaluation of courses by whole students' cohorts: a case study', *Assessment & Evaluation in Higher Education*, 22(4), 397–404.

Radcliff, J.L. (1996) 'Assessment, accreditation, and evaluation of higher education in the US', *Quality in Higher Education*, 2(1), 5–19.

Richardson, J. (2005) 'Instruments for obtaining student feedback: a review of the literature', *Assessment and Evaluation in Higher Education*, 28(4), 387–415.

Robertson, D. (2000) 'Students as consumers: the individualization of competitive advantage' in P. Scott (ed.) *Higher education re-formed*, New Millennium Series, VII, London/New York: Falmer Press, pp. 78–94.

Rothblatt, S. (1993) 'The limbs of Osiris: liberal education in the English-speaking world' in S. Rothblatt and B. Wittrock *European and American university since 1908: historical and sociological essays*, Cambridge: Cambridge University Press, pp. 19–73.

Rosa, M.J., C. Santos, S. Cardoso and A. Amaral (2009) 'The Portuguese system of quality assurance – New developments and expectations', *paper in the 4th European quality assurance forum: challenges for quality assurance beyond 2010*, Copenhagen: Denmark, 19–21 November 2009.

Sarrico, C.S. and M.J. Rosa (2010) 'Student satisfaction with Portuguese public universities', *paper in the 5th European quality assurance forum: building bridges: making sense of QA in European, national and institutional contexts*, Lyon: France, 18–20 November 2010.

Scott, P. (1997) 'The changing role of the university in the production of new knowledge', *Tertiary Higher Education and Management*, 3(1), 5–14.

Scott, P. (1995) *The meanings of mass higher education*, Buckingham: SRHE/Open University Press.

Sharrock, G. (2000) 'Why students are not customers', *Journal of Higher Education Policy and Management*, 22(2), 149–164.

Shattock, M. (2009) 'Entrepreneurialism and organizational change in higher education' in M. Shattock (ed.) *Entrepreneurialism in universities and the knowledge economy*, England: Society for Research into Higher Education & Open University Press, pp. 1–8.

Slaughter, S. and L. Leslie (1997) *Academic capitalism: politics, policies and the entrepreneurial university*, Baltimore and London: The Johns Hopkins University Press.

Slaughter, S. and G. Rhoades (2004) *Academic capitalism and the new economy –
Markets, state and higher education*, Baltimore and London: The Johns Hopkins
University Press.

Tavares, O. (2011) *Students' choices accessing Portuguese higher education: processes
and rationalities* [translated title], PhD thesis, Porto: University of Porto.

Tobbell, J., V. O'Donnell and M. Zammit (2010) 'Exploring transition to postgraduate study: shifting identities in interaction with communities, practice
and participation', *British Educational Journal*, 36(2), 261–278.

Vidler, E. and J. Clarke (2005) 'Creating citizen-consumers: new labour and the
remaking of public services', *Public Policy and Administration*, 20(2), 19–37.

Wiberg, L. (2006) 'The role of students in the external review of QA agencies:
a comparative reflection with the external review of higher education institu-
tions' in H. Aliniska, E. Codina, J. Boher, R. Dearlove, S. Eriksson, E. Helle and
L. Wiberg (ed.) *Student involvement in the processes of quality assurance agencies*,
ENQA Workshop Reports, n. 4, chapter 2, Helsinki: European Association for
Quality Assurance in Higher Education, pp. 8–11.

Wiers-Jenssen, J., B. Stensaker and J. Grøgaard (2002) 'Student satisfaction:
towards an empirical deconstruction of the concept', *Quality in Higher Education*, 8(2), 183–195.

Williams, G. (2009) 'Finance and entrepreneurial activity in higher education in
a knowledge society' in M. Shattock (ed.) *Entrepreneurialism in universities and
the knowledge economy*, England: Society for Research into Higher Education &
Open University Press, pp. 9–32.

Exploring New Academic Identities in Turbulent Times

Mary Henkel

Theories of academic identity: time for a change?

For much of the 20th century the conditions in which academics in Western Europe worked were perceived as conducive to the development and maintenance of distinct, stable and legitimizing professional identities. However, the last 25 years have seen a transformation of academe and its political, economic, cultural and ideological contexts. This raises the question whether in consequence these conditions have been undermined. We might need to think about academic identity formation and development within new conceptual and theoretical frameworks.

This chapter starts from the assumption that social and professional identities are sub-divisions of the broader concept of personal or self-identity (Archer, 2000). Identity incorporates the ideas of both individuation and identification (two key ideas in academe). It has a public as well as a private face but it represents a continuing sense of self through a whole human life, in which there may have been significant, even dramatic, changes but the past, present and future are integrally linked. Questions of identity or 'Who am I?' are also questions of value: What most matters to me and gives me a sense of meaning and self-worth? (Taylor, 1989; Välimaa, 1998; Ylijoki, 2008)

As indicated in Chapter 1, contemporary theory understands social and professional identities as formed and developed through interaction, internal and external, symbolic and linguistic, between the individual and significant others. They give rise to but are also shaped and consolidated by shared sets of practices (Archer, 2000; Delanty, 2008) and the production of recognized goods (MacIntyre, 1981). Significant others include nations, institutions, professions and communities.

They help to ensure that meaning and self-worth are rooted in visible social entities with their own cultures and practices, as well as in private consciousness. Social and professional identities are likely to be legitimizing if those entities are themselves accorded public recognition and authority.

For much of the 20th century, academic identities could readily be understood within communitarian theories (Taylor, 1989; MacIntyre, 1981) of identity (Välimaa, 1998; Henkel, 2000). While by the beginning of that century, the concept of profession had become a strong source of identity for many occupational groups, it was not uncontested in the case of academics (even in the USA and the UK where it was most strongly established), for whom 'community' long remained a significant normative ideal (Clark, 1987).

At the core of academe are the systematic pursuit and the creation, transmission and validation of knowledge by largely self-regulating communities, among which the disciplines have long been recognized as primary sources of academic identities. In the 20th century disciplines were increasingly understood as dualities, not just abstract forms of knowledge, comprising distinct combinations of agendas, theories, methodologies and techniques, but also the socio-epistemic communities that generate, change and regulate them, each with their own intellectual traditions, cultures and associations out of which 'come self [and often dominant] identities' (Clark, 1983, p. 76). Differences in the degrees of and relative importance attached to epistemic coherence and cultural solidarity in different disciplines have been well illustrated in the literature (Becher, 1989; Geertz, 1983).

Clark understands academe as 'necessarily centred in disciplines, but [...] simultaneously [...] pulled together in enterprises', or higher education institutions, thus forming a complex of tangible, local cultures in which academic identities might be consolidated and refined – the basic units. These are 'simultaneously a part of the discipline and a part of the enterprise, melding the two and drawing strength from the combination' (Clark, 1983, p. 32). They can be said to have had a strong role in creating an integrative ideal of academic work, a flexible combination of research, teaching and administration.

Clark and Becher saw commitment to the value of disciplines as uniting and dividing academics, sharing a common field of activity but organized within distinct groups. Becher's characterization of disciplines as tribes with their own territories in what is sometimes termed a map of knowledge has strong connotations of interdisciplinary rivalry as well as diversity. He pays a good deal of attention to disciplinary gate-keeping, equating strong boundaries with tightly knit communities.

Boundaries and boundary maintenance have been key elements of identity theories in higher education and more generally. Taylor (1989) invokes the metaphors of horizons and frameworks, which constitute a bounded and defining moral space within which to forge an identity. For Bernstein (1996) the strength of the boundaries protecting the space between disciplines or discourses constitutes the critical factor. Jenkins (1996) argues that social identity is constructed at and across boundaries between groups, with those outside as well as inside: boundaries are permeable but processes of boundary maintenance are integral to identity formation and sustenance. Polanyi (1962), in elaborating his image of 'the republic of science', draws a clear defining boundary round science itself, while depicting its constituent disciplines as working within overlapping boundaries.

In summary, for much of the 20th century, academics could be said to constitute a small, substantially self-regulating sector of modern societies, a context in which they could form and sustain distinct stable identities over whole and predominantly linear careers. Central to the process of identity development was a continuing interaction between the individual, the discipline, the basic unit and the university carried out within actively regulated boundaries, substantially maintained by peer review. The next section considers how far these ideas about academic identity might now be challenged, if not undermined.

Higher education in turbulent times

We aim here to pinpoint the implications, for academics and the structures and cultures within which they work, of some of the new paradigms of change identified by Guy Neave in Chapter 3.

As expansion gathered pace, the implications for the cultures of higher education institutions (and for their relationship with and status in society) became more evident. The broadening of higher education and research agendas meant the enlargement and diversification of academic staff and the incorporation into institutions of new epistemic communities, some with strong cultures of their own, some rooted in fields or practices where knowledge was less codified and its validity more contested. Academics became a less exceptional and less cohesive occupational group in society. As student populations grew, expectations of higher education became more varied and more explicitly instrumental. Their acceptance of academic authority, values and even definitions of higher education could not be taken for granted (Trow, 1970).

Delanty (2001) notes how from the 1980s a new source of cultural change in universities emerged. Universities became key sites of the 'culture wars' of gender, race, ethnicity and religion and incubators of new cultural and epistemic identities that could and did cut across existing disciplines, knowledge domains and institutions. This was a critical development in that it created alternative knowledge communities rooted in deep affinities and distinctions outside the academy and opened up questions about normative relationships between the cognitive and the emotive.

Meanwhile, the crisis in welfare states and the rising influence of neo-liberalism brought a widespread recasting of relations between the market and the state. Reducing public expenditure became a prime goal of governments. Marketization and new forms of governance and management were introduced into higher education, including, as Neave has indicated, enhanced university autonomy but within a novel and ambiguous definition of its meaning. Universities, now carrying new burdens of responsibility for their futures, were impelled into markets and quasi-markets: for more selective and conditional public funding, for new sources of income, including industry and business, and for new student populations. Engagement in competition was now essential for institutional prosperity and, often, survival, but so also was collaboration.

Institutional futures constituted only one dimension of the additional pressures laid upon them. Concepts of the knowledge economy and the knowledge society were highly profiled in government policies, defining new roles for universities as drivers of innovation, knowledge transfer and skill development and, through these, of national prosperity. However, while universities were, as predicted by Bell (1973), becoming 'axial structures' in their societies, other developments were challenging them. Among the manifestations of the knowledge society was the democratization of knowledge. The more extensive distribution of knowledge in societies erodes distinctions between expert and non-expert actors and organizations and, with them, the authority of professionals (Delanty, 2001). Nowotny et al. (2001) observed how society was beginning to 'speak back to science'; pressures were rising for wider participation in the construction of research and educational agendas, in the production of advanced knowledge and in the evaluation of academic work. Accountability became a key policy theme in the new 'evaluative state'.

Beyond the nation state, the multi-dimensional dynamics of globalization were increasingly evident: economic and political but also technical, structural and temporal. Technological change, notably in communications, information and knowledge, brought about a dramatic compression of time and space and 'a new age of borderlessness' that 'disrupted a variety of nationally organized structures' (Urry, 1988, p. 5). Social theorists identified a significant secular shift into high or late modernity (Archer, 2000; Giddens, 1991) – an era of reflexive modernization (Beck, 1992), in which fixed boundaries or categories and established structures, roles and practices were being overtaken by 'the reorganization of time and space' and 'the expansion of disembedding mechanisms, which prise social relations free from the hold of specific locales...' (Giddens, 1991, p. 2). Together, they were providing the context for a third major influence on the dynamics of contemporary social life, change, now conceived as a continual, reiterative process (see Neave, Chapter 3), or 'reflexivity': 'the susceptibility of most aspects of social activity to chronic revision in the light of new information or knowledge' (Giddens, 1991, pp. 20–21).

Changes in boundaries have particular implications for identity formation, development and sustainment: the shifting, blurring, stretching, permeation and breakdown of different kinds of boundaries and distinctions: geopolitical, institutional and professional boundaries, functional and conceptual divisions between the market and the state and between government, business and universities, traditional epistemic frameworks and accepted divisions of labour in the production of advanced knowledge and the provision of higher education. In some contexts, established organizational structures are giving way in practice or in discourse to the less determinate idea of 'space', constructed, imagined and subject to frequent (perhaps chronic) redefinition. These themes are reflected in the emergence of, for example, 'borderless knowledge' and 'virtual universities' (Gornitzka & Langfeldt, 2008; Middlehurst, 2009), and constructions such as research or education networks, consortia, 'hybrid communities' (Gibbons et al., 1994) and programmes, juxtaposed with or displacing organizational structures such as university departments or basic units. They might be global, international, national, regional, local, inter- or intra-institutional, transdisciplinary, interdisciplinary or intradisciplinary.

It seems that academics, instead of pursuing their careers in tightly connected stable structures and, to a considerable extent, mutually reinforcing cultures, rather clearly separated from other sectors of society, are working in a constantly shifting, multi-level or 'glonacal'

(Marginson & Rhoades, 2002) and multidimensional (collaborative and competitive; public and private) environments with few defined boundaries. This suggests major implications for academic identities, at a point when new theories of identity itself have been emerging, notably in the definition of identity as a process or 'project' (Giddens, 1991) that is 'continuous and reflexive' (Jenkins, 1996, p. 20; Taylor, 2008); a process of individual construction (Beck, 1992) through internal and external conversation (Archer, 2000), dialogue and discourse (Hall, 1992) but also positioning and repositioning (Delanty, 2008), deconstruction and reconstruction (Barnett & Di Napoli, 2008).

However, there have been political and institutional responses to change that present a contradictory picture. With the challenges to the capacity of nation states to protect national interests from economic globalization of markets and the growth and shift in super powers has come the rise of supra-national institutions, policies and organizational frameworks, such as the European Research Area, the Bologna Process and the European Research Council. Academics find themselves in new and enlarged systems of stratification in the form of international league tables, world-class universities, regional, national and local universities.

In European nations, the power, status and functions of higher education institutions have been substantially enhanced. In 1980, a dominant model for the university was still that of a 'holding company' for disciplinary basic units (Becher & Kogan, 1980). By contrast, universities are now pivotal entities in higher education systems. They have become increasingly corporate or strategic actors, obliged to equip themselves collectively to meet multiplying demands and to accommodate or adjust to complexity, novelty and instability. The implications for their modes of governance and operation, for the composition and structures of their workforces (Rhoades, 2006; Middlehurst, 2004; Whitchurch, 2008; Gordon & Whitchurch, 2009) and for academics and their basic units are profound. Universities are managed organizations. Their structures have become more complex but also more hierarchical and less loosely coupled.

For the most part university leadership is still academic. However, academics have lost their monopoly of authority. Universities need to draw upon a greater variety of professional expertise and to recruit personnel with the capacity and experience to fulfil extensive management functions and to work in partnership with or leadership of academics (Henkel, 2007).

Meanwhile, academic labour markets are becoming more flexible and disparities in pay and conditions of employment are growing. Pressures to shrink the primary market for more secure, prestigious and lucrative academic posts and to raise the barriers to it have intensified, while the secondary market has grown substantially. At the same time, new career trajectories have opened up for academics, which we will consider in the next section.

It seems that the contexts of academic identity development have become more ambiguous: less bounded, more variegated, reflexive and individualized but also subject to larger scale governance, stronger institutions and new regulatory regimes. There has been a 'binding and unbinding' of academic careers (Enders & Kaulisch, 2006, p. 85). The rest of the chapter aims to analyse the consequences for the construction of academic identities.

New careers, new academic identities?

Research interest in the impacts of change on academic identities has grown rapidly in recent years (e.g. Archer, 2008; Barnett & di Napoli, 2008; Clegg, 2008; Di Napoli, 2003; Gordon & Whitchurch, 2009; Musselin & Becquet, 2008; Ylijoki, 2005; 2008). The number of empirical studies in or relevant to this field is growing, although many more are needed in order get a stronger grasp of continuities and change in academic identities.

We first focus on the varieties of career trajectories that academics in Europe can now contemplate. The complexity of university organization and the shift from collegial to managerial forms of governance have had significant consequences for career advancement and choice in academe. The roles of dean and head of department or basic unit are now commonly defined as middle management. As this change has become more widely established, accounts of what it means for identities (projected as well as actual) have become more nuanced (Meek et al., 2010). Narratives of alienation, conflict and mutual lack of respect between faculty and academic managers (Henkel, 2000) are giving way to more complex analyses. Whereas initially there was a widespread feeling among the holders of these roles that continuing practice in their discipline was the only way to achieve credibility with faculty and maintain their own sense of identity (Henkel, 2000), new possibilities of identity continuity and enhancement are now emerging for them. Middle management roles in universities are still evolving but there is a growing consensus that success in them must be built on academic achievement and vision, as well as managerial skills. A combination is needed to sustain basic units and institutions that are enabling and not just demanding of faculty (Meek et al., 2010).

Meanwhile there are other challenges to conceptions of academic work. New demands in both research and teaching (including new technologies, quality assurance requirements and the need to secure new resources and engage with varieties of cross-border collaborations) mean growing pressures for new repertoires of skill and new forms of specialization that may entail deconstruction of the research-teaching-administration nexus and thus reconstruction of what it means to be an academic.

A linked development is the emergence of 'blended roles' (Whitchurch, 2009) (e.g. in quality assurance, student and staff development, knowledge transfer), through which academics, often in collaboration with other professionals, move temporarily or permanently into 'third spaces'. Here they may reappraise their authority, self-esteem, values and aspirations in ways that affect how they or others identify them.

The length and shape of academic career trajectories are increasingly varied for other reasons. The broadening academic agendas of universities has meant that many academics are late entrants into the profession, with identities rooted in other professions and occupations of varying status, with different conceptions of the knowledge and educational foundations for work and different hierarchies of value. This may have significant implications for them, as they seek to reconstruct their professional identity in a new context, and for the institutions they have joined.

Meanwhile, a significant casualization of academic work means that relatively high proportions of, particularly, young academics are working 'on the margins of the academy' (Allen Collinson, 2004) on fixed-term contracts, the implications of which are short and uncertain time horizons, shifting or fractured networks and reference groups, limited control of their work and often a search for an alternative identity.

Academic rewards for individuals have long been centred upon research achievements. In the last 30 years, national and international reforms have meant that more and more higher education institutions have come to see research as the main route to institutional rewards: research funding, research commercialization, research networks and, above all, research excellence. Universities driven by the search for research excellence may diminish as well as enhance identities. In accounts of change in higher education, and particularly early accounts, narratives of loss feature prominently (Henkel, 2000; Ylijoki, 2005, 2008): different forms of loss, loss of a shared moral order (Ylijoki, 2008), loss of academic freedom and the linked loss of control over academic time (Neave, 2006; Taylor, 2008), loss of disciplinary identity, and loss of status or role that may equate to loss of professional meaning.

University policies focused on research performance have had particularly severe implications for those who had hitherto defined their professional identities primarily in terms of their teaching role or of an idea of academic work as a combination of research, teaching and administration, the balance between which was determined over time by individuals themselves in negotiation with their colleagues in the basic units. These issues are most sharply exemplified in the UK Research Assessment Exercises, in which only those defined by their institution as 'research active' can be included. Once designated as 'research inactive', individuals acquire a new and undesirable semi-public status from which it is almost impossible to escape. Their teaching and administrative loads are likely to be increased to release their 'active' colleagues to enhance their research productivity and thus their contribution to the institution (Harley, 2002; Henkel, 2000).

Research-centred institutional policies can also impinge upon the time and space in which academics work. The control of academic time is increasingly taken out of academics' hands in the imposition of rigid time frames for academic outputs and agendas, regardless of the diversity to be expected from inquiry, learning and the creation of new knowledge in different disciplines, by individuals at different career points and life stages (Henkel and Pritchard, 2011). Research strategies can result in individuals, whole divisions or departments being relocated to constitute new interdisciplinary or multidisciplinary groupings with a view to improving overall institutional research performance.

The consequences can be individual or collective disengagement from the university and from basic units. Those concerned may feel that they, and also the intellectual tradition and culture in which their academic identity was formed, are no longer valued or that they are alienated from what they perceive their institutions to have become.

All these developments prompt a reappraisal of the implications of change for the *process* of identity formation and construction, in particular the individual-discipline, basic unit institution framework posited early on in the chapter. To what extent are these still the critical elements or forces in identity development? If they are, has the dynamic between them significantly changed?

The processes of academic identity construction

The discipline under question

Examination of process has largely to draw on qualitative and often small-scale empirical studies. It will be necessary to be clear about context in these cases.

The late 20th century saw growing questioning of the value or even validity of the concept of the discipline in the light of the multiplication, diversification, fragmentation and cross-fertilization of epistemic communities in universities and elsewhere and the introduction of new issue-, problem- and occupation-oriented degree programmes (Becher & Parry, 2005). Was the organization of systematic inquiry, learning and teaching becoming so fluid that the idea of distinct disciplines comprising changing but nevertheless shared agendas, theories, methodologies and concepts had little meaning in practice?

Arguments began to emerge for giving primary attention to issues and problems identified outside the academy as against those defined within discipline-based research, and for reconceptualizing and reorganizing research practice. As early as the 1970s, it had been asserted that more and more social research was 'domain-based' (Trist, 1972), that is, neither basic nor applied but 'inherently interdisciplinary', focused on multifaceted societal problems and contributing to theoretical development as well as the improvement of practice. It required cross-boundary collaboration, 'group creativeness and changes in the values and cultures of scientists and scientific organizations' (Trist, 1972). Twenty years later similar arguments were made about the whole spectrum of knowledge production: discipline-based research was being overtaken by multidisciplinary and transdisciplinary modes of inquiry (Gibbons et al., 1994).

Disciplines, in fact, retain significant power in university-based research; indeed, their importance in the advancement of problem-oriented as well as disciplinary research has been strongly re-asserted (Weingart, 1997). However, the analytic value of the concept is questionable, particularly in terms of its epistemic connotations. One reason for this is that 'discipline' has become an umbrella term, co-opted by, among others, governments, funding bodies and newly academized professions and subjects. As such it accommodates but also disguises the differences between the 'knowledges' organized into the basic units of higher education institutions, some of whose activities may be pursued across the boundaries of the academy. Many so-called disciplines thus constitute epistemic communities with different histories, cultures and degrees of coherence, permanence and public recognition, which, in consequence, provide different conditions for identity development and continuity.

Academic identity formation: the doctorate and beyond

There are consequences for the contexts in which individuals become academics. These have become both more diverse and more regulated. As knowledge becomes more broadly defined and less stable, the organizational and pedagogical frameworks within which academic identities are formed have become more systematic. The PhD is now an essential qualification for permanent academic appointment in almost all fields but it is also expected to prepare students for other labour markets. Doctoral education has greatly expanded in terms of numbers of students and the range of subjects incorporated into it. Whereas in many higher education systems, at least in Europe, it was marginal to the education structures and policies of universities, it is now increasingly well incorporated into them, not least under the influence of the Bologna Process (Kehm, 2007). The development of graduate schools or colleges has in many places brought doctoral education within a strong structure. There is now more systematic induction into the discipline, subject or field of study and more collective involvement in it, in the provision of formal teaching, staff and student seminars and also in supervision, now more likely to involve more than one person. However, while in established disciplines, such as physics, chemistry, economics and history, doctoral programmes will be framed within strong paradigms and/or dominant cultures, many others are likely to be far more diverse and context-specific. In areas where there is substantial research collaboration between academics and businesses, the latter may be significantly involved.

Aspiring academics are soon exposed to the performative culture. As doctoral students, they are under pressure to gain early recognition for themselves in their field, through publication and contributions to conferences, and through network identification and participation. They are, therefore, again more exposed to collective influence but also encouraged to exercise more agency in determining the nature of this influence and in constructing their own identities, public and private, in that field (Parry, 2007). This, combined with the necessity of immersion in a specific topic and of completing their own thesis or equivalent in, often, a more compressed and defined period of time than in the past, provides them with conditions in which to begin to build a strong sense of their academic selves. The importance of this is evident, perhaps particularly if their entry to the academic labour market is through the uncertainties of fixed-term contracts in basic units providing little intellectual or cultural support for identity consolidation (Allen Collinson, 2004). Even in apparently more benign contexts, the construction of authentic and robust identities in early career is a struggle, often fraught with compromise and disillusion (Archer, 2008).

Disciplines and identity construction: continuity, change and ambiguity

Despite the scale of change in higher education, there is evidence that the individual-discipline, basic unit institution dynamic is still relevant for understanding identity construction. A strong example of such evidence is provided by a small-scale but highly systematic study of academic work and academic identities in four disciplines (three well-established in academe and one, business studies, more emergent) and three universities in France (Musselin & Becquet, 2008). It shows substantial differences of identity in terms of values, beliefs, academic practices, career trajectories and perceived external threats to identity that derive primarily from interaction between discipline, basic unit and individual. The inter-institutional differences seem more strongly linked to the culture and history of the basic unit than to characteristics of the institutions themselves, but it is notoriously difficult to disentangle these two institutional components.

This suggests that the dynamic persists and continues to provide a convincing framework for the analysis of academic identity. However, in its choice of business studies as one of the disciplines analysed, it reflects how the usage of this concept has changed over time. Business and management studies constitute a leading example of a field of increasing importance to societies that has in consequence been professionalized and academized. But its knowledge base derives largely from recognized disciplines and more or less codified practice. It exemplifies a 'fragmented adhocracy' (Whitley, 2000), exhibiting 'high task uncertainty' and 'low mutual dependence' among its researchers. It is one of a number of professions and semi-professions incorporated into higher education, the identities of whose academic members and, indeed, basic units 'are characterized by divergences and ambiguities' (Musselin & Becquet, 2008), in particular as between the academic and the professional.

A recent two-stage qualitative study of three Australian graduate business schools (Ryan & Neumann, 2010) analyses experimental initiatives aimed at achieving more epistemological coherence, a shared culture and a distinctive academic identity in management studies. Ironically, it shows how they were undermined by national and institutional policies giving priority to research and traditional disciplines. The first stage of the study found multidisciplinary groups of staff, prompted in part by their own views of how postgraduate study could effectively advance management studies and practice and in part by critiques from experienced and demanding students, making collective attempts to develop an interdisciplinary curriculum through collaborative experimentation in the programmes and through consultancy. They seemed to exemplify the kind of group creativeness deemed necessary by Trist (1972) for the development of 'domain-based' research. However, six years later the drive towards interdisciplinarity had been abandoned, graduate business schools had been incorporated into larger business schools, the structures of which were predominantly disciplinary, and the academics concerned had suffered a loss of purpose and identity. The major causes of change were perceived to be the launch of the national Research Quality Framework and institutional responses to it, to pursue research excellence, through strengthening disciplinary specialization and increasing incentives for research as against teaching or consultancy.

A recent comparative study of academic research units' responses to a changing research policy environment in the Netherlands and the UK (Leisyte, 2007) makes it possible to examine quite closely academic processes of identity construction and reconstruction in two contrasting subjects (medieval history and biotechnology).

For the medieval historians, the reforms have an ambiguous meaning. While they, again, endorse a discipline-based organization and evaluation of research, they also threaten long-held disciplinary norms and values: one still shared across a range of disciplines – academic freedom to select and pursue a research agenda – and two particularly associated with history – the value of individual scholarship, supported by a close-knit community of scholars and the production of books (rather than articles) within an individually determined time frame (Becher, 1989). The study analyses the researchers' determined efforts to sustain these norms seen as central to their identity and highlights the role of symbolic compliance with policies in those efforts: the repackaging of their own research to meet funding bodies' criteria; the construction of collaborative programmes that leave the individuals involved free to pursue their own agendas; participation in intra-institutional collaborative activities along with efforts to control the research themes; and the calculation of the time needed to produce the newly required number of articles within a personal programme committed to monographs. The norm perceived to weaken is the research-teaching nexus widely valued in practice as well as in theory by historians. What appears to be strengthened is the dynamic between the individual, the discipline and the basic unit. The relationship with the institution, as the mediator and implementer of research policies perceived as inimical to their identities in significant respects, is one of compromise and, to some extent, manipulation.

This is an example of a traditional disciplinary community struggling to resist change in individual and collective academic identities. However, Leisyte (2007) also examines research units in biotechnology, a contributor to and product of multi-dimensional disciplinary change. Biotechnology has been intricately involved in the reconstruction of the biological sciences. That overarching term can now be understood as constituting an expansive and fluid space within which specialisms are forming, reforming and, in some cases, disappearing at a great pace. Biotechnology itself involves not only biology and chemistry but also physics, informatics, engineering, medical and agricultural sciences; the range and diversity of fields is growing; knowledge obsolescence is an endemic characteristic. University scientists have a key role in it but 'universities are only a base or a part of the whole biotechnology organizational structure' (Leisyte, 2007, p. 140). Its mode of knowledge production is a prime example of transdisciplinarity, relying as it does on large and small firms, private and public research institutes, as well as universities.

This study shows biotechnology researchers adopting some of the same compliance strategies as the medieval historians, particularly in the packaging of research for funding applications. However, the norms of competition and collaboration are central to their culture. Active networking – inter-institutional, international and cross-sector – is essential to their scientific practices. While they regard top-down promotion of this as unnecessary and largely ineffective, and are wary of institutional interference, their overall attitudes to what they perceive as strong and active university management are relatively positive. Earning income is essential to their work and that, in turn, requires strategic thinking, as well as monitoring and maintaining research outputs and reputation. Their own organizational structures are quite hierarchical and research group leaders play key roles in the basic units. At the same time, individuals pursue their own agendas within the collective enterprise. Central to their sense of identity are intrinsic satisfaction in and absolute commitment to academic research but they are also likely to see industry as an intrinsically interesting sector in which to pursue it. This study suggests that identity development is, more obviously than in the case of medieval historians, a matter of continuing and reflexive construction. It is pursued through more complex and varied sets of relationships across less structured or predictable territory. Constant networking, the speed of production and reproduction of knowledge in the field and the frequent entry into it of new epistemic communities mean that positioning and repositioning constitute a significant part of their lives. They, like many scientists and some social scientists now, find no difficulty in maintaining strong disciplinary identities, while also working in mode two forms of knowledge production (Marton, 2005; Nowotny et al., 2001); indeed for biotechnologists, these two are integrally connected rather than distinct ideas. Some find that engagement with the private sector in issues of intellectual property rights, for example, mean that they achieve satisfaction in learning new negotiating skills and competing in a different arena, and in the process stretching their identity in another direction. A minority become entrepreneurs in their own right.

Institutions and identity

There are some striking contrasts in these two accounts of identity work. The two sets of units are very different, epistemologically and culturally. In one account resistance to change in identity is predominant; in the other, change is inextricable from identity. However, in both, the units emerge as agents and as actively engaged with their institutions, as well as their discipline or, in the case of biotechnology, transdisciplinary communities.

Research suggests that such engagement is more likely to occur in institutions with an established culture of academic governance (Shattock, 2002; Clark, 1998) and high academic reputation. There, academics continue to have strong influence on and participation in institutional policies, even if they have had to accommodate a variety of management personnel, functions and values. Such institutions can provide the conditions in which successful academics, particularly in science and technology, can not only maintain but also enhance their existing identities by moving across disciplinary, institutional and sector boundaries, creating new networks, involving themselves in new modes of knowledge production and generating new sources of income. Academic and commercial success can be mutually reinforcing: the most active collaborators with industry are for the most part the highest ranking research universities.

There is some evidence that less academically prestigious institutions with fewer resources are more likely to be dominated by a management ethos and to provide poor conditions for the construction or enhancement of academic identities (Henkel, 2000; di Napoli, 2003). However, other studies, one a recent small-scale exploratory study of academic identity in a post-1992 university in the UK (Clegg, 2008), the other a research project on the implications of gender for career progression in the UK and Germany (Pritchard, 2010) suggest that the issue is more complex.

Research informants in the post-1992 university experienced it as an ambiguous and sometimes conflictual space, in which alien managerialist values had a strong place. Institutional messages about how research and teaching were valued were unclear and constantly shifting. Late entrants into academe from industry or public service professions were not necessarily accepted as serious academics, even if they achieved external academic recognition. Some informants, however, felt the university afforded them freedom for individual identity construction, partly because national research policies were seen as less dominant than in more established universities. Individuals were well aware of their university's relatively low status in a highly stratified national system but there were mixed views about what it would mean for them to be in a 'proper university'. Such institutions were not, it was felt, necessarily more 'intellectual spaces' (Clegg, 2008, p. 339) – only more restrictive ones.

Disciplines or fields of knowledge seemed to constitute equally ambiguous spaces for informants, partly, probably, because the epistemological ecology of the university was not dominated by single or recognized disciplines. Only one person 'identified discipline as having absolute priority in his life project' and 'none identified in any simple way with discipline' (Clegg, 2008, p. 338). However, there was evidence of dialogue and argument with the discipline or socio-epistemic community. There was strong commitment to academic values and a sense of the individual's academic work being central to their identity but 'hybrid identities' were predominant in the study and academic values were not necessarily discipline- or subject-specific. Some individuals were working in fields whose epistemologies were strongly shaped from outside academe. Institutional boundaries were porous and a number of individuals looked outwards to their academic networks or to fields of practice as sources of values, beliefs and identity development.

Overall, it seemed that individuals were shaping self-validating academic identities in an active and 'reflexive project of the self' in an environment rather different from and less strongly framed than most of those in which academic identities and academic work have been researched. The dominant dialogue seemed to be internal and individual or else with collectives such as networks or practitioner groups and individuals selected as significant others. Whether this made for legitimizing identities is much less certain.

However, there were indications that identity construction in this context might, as well as being more fluid, also be more integrated than so far suggested in this chapter. Whereas the interplay between individual, discipline (or perhaps more accurately, subject) and institution emerged as quite uncertain, the interweaving of the personal and the professional in the process of academic identity construction came through more clearly. The way in which individuals thought about academic identity was strongly informed by a deep-seated and continuous sense of self, rooted for some in their gender and class.

This raises issues central to feminist theory, for example, to do with the relationship between personal and professional identity and the distinctions and separation between public and private space. There is some evidence of widening dissatisfaction with the growing conflict between professional and personal lives, and more specifically between academic women's working lives and parenthood. A recent examination of the issue (Pillay, 2009) found 'murmurs of discomfort' about this in writing that reflects a more holistic perspective on female academic identities, a desire to find an alternative in their own lives to the separation of and conflict between intellectual and emotional work (e.g. Ribbens, 1994; Ruddick, 1989).

Jirón King (2005) seems to suggest that it is possible to construct alternatives: 'academic space bends with enough imagination, but it is more versatile when imagined in terms of its relationship to other spaces that are already part of life [...] it overlaps with and redefines the family space as well' (quoted in Pillay, 2009, p. 507). In our own study academic mothers with a more integrated sense of personal and professional identity had either, indeed, succeeded in redefining the family space so as to embrace their academic selves (Pritchard, 2010) or involved themselves in feminist scholarly networks, which had become integral to their sense of what their careers had been about (Henkel & Pritchard, 2011).

Concluding comments

This chapter is centrally informed by a set of contradictions and ambiguities that confront anyone exploring academic identities in current turbulent times. Academics exist in a working environment in which boundaries have loosened or are perpetually shifting and there are different orders of space, macro and micro, which they have to hold in mind and which materially affect their practices. Change is one of the most prominent features of their lives, for many within their disciplines or fields, for most within their institutional context. Individual and collective reflexivity is endemic. Growth and diversification of knowledge in academe have been explosive. Academic career trajectories have multiplied. It is an environment for choice, diversity and uncertainty.

At the same time, higher education institutions are more structured and more powerful and academic lives more regulated. Institutional futures are substantially shaped by economic and reputational competition, fed by national and international performance measurement and ranking. Labour markets are increasingly competitive and academic career trajectories are subject to more rigid temporal and performative frameworks.

The interplay between these trends is complex and highly differentiated; generalization is difficult. The processes of academic identity formation and development are less predictable and, although those most in command of their academic identities are most likely to be in elite universities, such institutions may also be the source of identity loss and uncertainty.

However, while the ideologies, forms of knowledge and epistemic communities accommodated by the academy have diversified, meaning, value and self-esteem among academics remain strongly linked with their commitment to intellectual agendas developed within defined traditions and their individual achievement of principled purposes within them. Academic identities are less stable and the risk of a loss of self-worth has almost certainly increased but so have opportunities for stretching and reshaping identities that are enhancing.

References

Allen Collinson, J. (2004) 'Occupational Identity on the Edge: Social Science Contract Researchers in Higher Education', *Sociology*, 38 (2), 313–329.

Archer, L. (2008) 'The New Neoliberal Subjects? Young/er Academics' Constructions of Professional Identity', *Journal of Education Policy*, 23 (3), 265–285.

Archer, M. S. (2000) *Being Human: The Problem of Agency*, Cambridge: Cambridge University Press.

Barnett, R. and R. Di Napoli (eds) (2008) *Changing Identities in Higher Education: Voicing Perspectives*, Abingdon: Routledge.

Becher, T. (1989) *Academic Tribes and Territories: Intellectual Enquiry and the Cultures of Disciplines*, Buckingham: SRHE and Open University Press.

Becher, T. and M. Kogan (1980) *Process and Structure in Higher Education*, 1st edn., London: Heinemann.

Becher, T. and S. Parry (2005) 'The Endurance of the Disciplines' in I. Bleiklie and M. Henkel (eds) *Governing Knowledge: A Study of Continuity and Change in Higher Education – A Festschrift in Honour of Maurice Kogan*, Dordrecht: Springer, pp. 133–144.

Beck, U. (1992) *Risk Society: Towards a New Modernity*, London: Sage Publications.

Bell, D. (1973) *The Coming of Post-Industrial Society*, London: Heinemann.

Bernstein, B. (1996) *Pedagogy, Symbolic Control and Identity: Theory, Research, Critique*, London: Taylor and Francis.

Clark, B. R. (1983) *The Higher Education System: Academic Organization in Cross National Perspective*, Los Angeles: University of California Press.

Clark, B. R. (1987) *The Academic Profession*, Los Angeles: University of California Press.

Clark, B. R. (1998) *Creating Entrepreneurial Universities: Organizational Pathways of Transformation*, Oxford: Pergamon.

Clegg, S. (2008) 'Academic Identities Under Threat?' *British Educational Research Journal*, 34 (3), 329–345.

Delanty, G. (2001) *Challenging Knowledge: The University in the Knowledge Society*, Buckingham: SRHE and Open University Press.

Delanty, G. (2008) 'Academic Identities and Institutional Change' in R. Barnett and R. Di Napoli (eds) *Changing Identities in Higher Education: Voicing Perspectives*, Abingdon: Routledge, pp. 124–133.

Di Napoli (2003) *Modern Languages: Which Identities? Which Selves?* PhD Thesis. University of London.

Enders, J. and M. Kaulisch (2006) 'The Binding and Unbinding of Academic Careers' in U. Teichler (ed.) *The Formative Years of Scholars*, London: Portland Press, pp. 85–96.

Geertz, C. (1983) *Local Knowledge*, New York: Basic Books.

Gibbons, M., C. Limoges, H. Nowotny, S. Schwartzman and M. Trow (1994) *The New Production of Knowledge: The Dynamics of Science and Research in Contemporary Societies*, London: Sage Publications.

Giddens, A. (1991) *Modernity and Self-Identity*, Cambridge: Polity Press.

Gordon, G. and C. Whitchurch (eds) (2009) *Changing Academic and Professional Identities in Higher Education: The Challenges of a Diversifying Workforce*, London: Routledge.

Gornitzka, A. and L. Langfeldt (2008) *Borderless Knowledge*, Dordrecht: Springer.

Harley, S. (2002) 'The Impact of Research Selectivity on Academic Work and Identity in UK Universities', *Studies in Higher Education*, 27 (2), 187–205.

Hall, S. (1992) 'The Question of Cultural Identity' in S. Hall, D. Held and T. McGrew (eds) *Modernity and Its Futures*, Cambridge: Polity Press in Association with Blackwell Publishers and the Open University, pp. 273–326.

Henkel, M. (2000) *Academic Identities and Policy Change*, London: Jessica Kingsley Publishers.

Henkel, M. (2007) 'Shifting Boundaries and the Academic Profession' in M. Kogan and U. Teichler (eds) *Key Challenges to the Academic Profession*, Paris and Kassel: UNESCO and INCHER-Kassel, pp. 191–204.

Jenkins, R. (1996) *Social Identity*, London, USA and Canada: Routledge.
Jirón-King, S. (2005). 'La estudiante caminante: My Motherwork Is Here, My Otherwork Is There' in R. Bassett (ed.) *Parenting & Professing: Balancing Family Work with an Academic Career*, Nashville, TN: Vanderbilt University Press, pp. 21–33.
Kehm, B. (2007) 'The Changing Role of Graduate and Doctoral Education as a Challenge to the Academic Profession: Europe and North America Compared' in M. Kogan and U. Teichler (eds) *Key Challenges to the Academic Profession*, Paris and Kassel: UNESCO and INCHER-Kassel, pp. 111–124.
Leisyte, L. (2007) *University Governance and Academic Research: Case Studies of Research Units in Dutch and English Universities*, Enschede: CHEPS/UT.
MacIntyre, A. (1981) *After Virtue: A Study in Moral Theory*, London: Duckworth.
Marginson, S. and G. Rhoades (2002) 'Beyond National States, Markets and Systems of Higher Education: A Glonacal Agency Heuristic', *Higher Education*, 43, 281–309.
Marton, S. (2005) 'Academics and the Mode-2 Society: Shifts in Knowledge Production in the Humanities and Social Sciences' in I. Bleiklie and M. Henkel (eds) *Governing Knowledge: A Study of Continuity and Change in Higher Education. A Festschrift in Honour of Maurice Kogan*, Dordrecht: Springer, pp. 169–188.
Meek, V. L., L. Goedegebuure and H. De Boer (2010) 'The Changing Role of Academic Leadership in Australia and the Netherlands: Who Is the Modern Dean?' in V. L. Meek, L. Goedegebuure, R. Santiago and T. Carvalho (eds) *The Changing Dynamics of Higher Education Middle Management*, Dordrecht: Springer, pp. 31–54.
Middlehurst, R. (2004) 'Changing Internal Governance: A Discussion of Leadership Roles and Management Structures in UK Universities', *Higher Education Quarterly*, 58 (4), 258–279.
Middlehurst, R. (2009) 'Developing Higher Education Professionals: Challenges and Possibilities' in G. Gordon and C. Whitchurch (eds) *Changing Academic and Professional Identities in Higher Education: The Challenges of a Diversifying Workforce*, London: Routledge, pp. 223–244.
Musselin, C. and V. Becquet (2008) 'Academic Work and Academic Identities: A Comparison Between Four Disciplines' in J. Välimaa and O-H. Ylijoki (eds) *Cultural Perspectives on Higher Education*, Dordrecht: Springer, pp. 91–108.
Neave, G. (2006) 'On Time and Fragmentation: Sundry Observations on Research, the University and Politics from a Waveringly Historical Perspective' in G. Neave, K. Blückhert and T. Nybom (eds) *The European Research University: An Historical Parenthesis?*, New York: Palgrave Macmillan, pp. 63–76.
Nowotny, H., P. Scott and M. Gibbons (2001) *Re-thinking Science: Knowledge and the Public in an Age of Uncertainty*, Cambridge: Polity Press.
Parry, S. (2007) *Disciplines and Doctorates*, Dordrecht: Springer.
Pillay, V. (2009) 'Academic Mothers Finding Rhyme and Reason', *Gender and Education*, 21 (5), 501–515.
Polanyi, M. (1962) 'The Republic of Science: Its Political and Economic Theory', *Minerva*, 1 (1), 54–73.
Pritchard, R. (ed.) (2011) *Neoliberal Developments in Higher Education: The United Kingdom and Germany*, Bern and Berlin: Peter Lang.
Pritchard, R. M. O. (2010) 'Gender Inequality in British and German Higher Education: A Qualitative Approach', *Compare*, 40 (4), 513–530.

Rhoades, G. (2006) 'The Higher Education We Choose: A Question of Balance', *Review of Higher Education*, 29, 381–404.

Ribbens, J. (1994) *Mothers and their Children: A Feminist Sociology of Childrearing*, London: Sage.

Ruddick, S. (1989) *Maternal Thinking: Toward a Politics of Peace*, Boston: Beacon Press.

Ryan, S. and R. Neumann (2010) 'Interdisciplinarity in Management Education: Tensions Between Curriculum, Profession and the University'. Paper presented at the CHER conference, University of Oslo, 10–12 June.

Shattock, M. (2002) 'Re-balancing Modern Concepts of University Governance', *Higher Education Quarterly*, 56 (3), 235–244.

Taylor, C. (1989) *Sources of the Self: The Making of the Modern Identity*, Cambridge: Cambridge University Press.

Taylor, P. (2008) 'Being an Academic Today' in R. Barnett and R. Di Napoli (eds) *Changing Identities in Higher Education: Voicing Perspectives*, Abingdon: Routledge, pp. 27–39.

Trist, E. (1972) 'Types of Output Mixof Research Organizations and Their Complementarity' in A. B. Cherns et al. (eds) *Social Science and Government: Policies and Problems*, London: Tavistock Publications, pp. 101–138.

Trow, M. (1970) 'Reflections on the Transition from Mass to Universal Higher Education', *Daedalus*, 99, 1–44.

Urry, J. (1988) 'Contemporary Transformations of Time and Space' in P. Scott (ed.) *The Globalization of Higher Education*, Buckingham: SRHE/Open University Press, pp. 1–17.

Välimaa, J. (1998) 'Culture and Identity in Higher Education Research', *Higher Education*, 36 (2), 119–138.

Weingart, P. (1997) 'From Finalization to Mode 2: Old Wine in New Bottles', *Social Science Information*, 36 (4), 591–613.

Whitchurch, C. (2008) 'Beyond Administration and Management: Changing Professional Identities in Higher Education' in R. Barnett and R. Di Napoli (eds) *Changing Identities in Higher Education: Voicing Perspectives*, Abingdon: Routledge, pp. 69–88.

Whitchurch, C. (2009) 'The Rise of the *Blended Professional* in Higher Education: A Comparison Between the UK, Australia and the United States', *Higher Education* (published online: doi.1007/s10734-009-9202-4).

Whitley, R. (2000) *The Intellectual and Social Organization of the Sciences*, 2nd edn., Oxford: Oxford University.

Ylijoki, O-H. (2005) 'Academic Nostalgia: A Narrative Approach to Academic Life', *Human Relations*, 58, 555–576.

Ylijoki, O-H. (2008) 'A Clash of Academic Cultures: The Case of Dr. X' in J. Välimaa and O-H. Ylijoki (eds) *Cultural Perspectives on Higher Education*, Dordrecht: Springer, pp. 75–89, Chapter 6.

Part III

Maintaining Identity Through Organizational Change

10
'That's Dangerous': Autonomous Development Work as a Source of Renewal in Academia

Keijo Räsänen

Introduction

After hearing of my interest in researching and developing our own academic practice, the top manager of our business school, then called 'rector' and now 'executive dean', remarked: 'That's dangerous'. What gave meaning to my work was obviously problematic for him. Unfortunately, I did not then have a chance to ask: 'Dangerous to whom?' In this account I try to continue the broken lunch-table dialogue by articulating the nature of the 'dangerous' activity. I also try to speculate on the possible reasoning behind the manager's remark. However, I don't deal with the possibility that he intended to warn me of dangers threatening me. I play with the idea that he considered our doings dangerous to somebody else and especially to university managers.

This paper outlines a way of understanding the problematic activity as a particular approach to developing academic practices in research and education. I call it autonomous development work and I will identify its general features. This can be done by utilizing the frame of practical activity (Räsänen, 2009, 2010; Räsänen & Korpiaho, 2011) and, in particular, the notion of developmental approach (Räsänen, 2007). Thereafter I will argue for the significance of autonomous development as a basic source of renewal in academic practices. The importance of local activism is understandable by setting local developmental efforts into the context of wider academic movements. Finally, it is possible to discuss why university managers may not like this kind of activity, although it may deliver effectively what they are publicly asking for:

local improvements in the quality of academic work and 'innovative' ways of operating.

This chapter aims to complement the other chapters in this book by focusing on the hopes and worries of ordinary academics. I am here less concerned about the ambitions of university managers and other actors who 'reform' and assess universities. I want to emphasize the local agency of researchers and teachers in the renewal of academic practice. Instead of celebrating management or 'academic leadership' as the major source of development in academia, I would rather warn of the negative, be it often unintended and indirect, consequences of imitating business practices in university governance and development. My warnings may not make a difference, but they may at least remind why some of us are doing academic work and continue to do so in spite of repressive conditions.

The general point that I try to explicate in this chapter concerns the sources of change and development in academia. In contrast to the currently dominant political wisdom, I propose that the work of ordinary academics is one major generator of change in research and education, and also in other activities at universities.

Many politicians and university managers act as if they were the real 'change agents' and ordinary academics were the 'change resisters'. In my view this is a major misunderstanding or ideologically biased rhetoric that cannot accurately describe or explain development in academic practices. This should be evident to any academic trained within a discipline. She or he cannot but try to arrange better education or do better research, because that is what colleagues and the rules of the field demand. It is in our professional *habitus*. Nevertheless, it may be less evident that academics can sometimes collectively renew their academic practices, including the local practices of self-governance, and therefore I will start by telling a local story.

A story of the emergence and decline of local developmental efforts

After the mid-1990s we – an expanding group of colleagues – have been engaged in developing teaching, research and governance practices in our own subject unit (Organization and Management at the Aalto University School of Economics). For instance, we have created new courses, adopted new learning methods and moulded them to our use, renewed disciplinary curriculum, revised research and writing practices, intervened into gendered practices and conference practices, and experimented with various self-governance practices (like new scripts in meetings). This wave of developmental action maintained its momentum for about ten years, but it is still continued with less intensity and lower ambitions.

There is no absolute starting point, because something similar had already been going on in a smaller scale in the 1970s and 1980s. However, the period of more conscious, intensive and collective development work was triggered by an opportunity to change teaching and learning practices. A couple of us participated in a course on cooperative learning. This course was offered as an ad hoc event in the school's staff training programme and the course was run by a consultant who could teach the method by using it. This experience was crucial to a couple of us, because we now knew that we could act differently and that there were alternatives to the traditional format of lecturing and exercises. Soon we created – in two pairs – two totally new courses, which were well received by students. It is not an insignificant aspect of this local story that these new courses were on developmental work. Things seemed to come together in a new way: we were teaching what we were doing; we were researching what we were teaching; students were now learning professionally relevant matters by doing and researching, and we could integrate teaching, research and expert activities. The positive experiences in developing teaching led into further experiments and changes in various academic activities.

The size of the original group of initiators was about four collaborating people. One by one, new people got involved, for instance by teaching with a member of the original group or by joining in a research effort (like the attempt to renew gendered practices by a pair of female doctoral students; Meriläinen et al., 2009). At best, about one third of the unit's staff, in other words about ten people, was active in this development work over and above their own courses. As these people were committed to their work, the rest of the faculty had to take their efforts seriously. Teaching was increasingly taken as an important activity, in which everybody wanted to participate and in which one could gain or lose local respect. Some of us even turned to study academic work and student affairs, and the researcher group Management Education Research Initiative (MERI) was more publicly established in 2004. Thereby we became increasingly aware of what had been done and studied by higher education researchers in other universities all over the world.

The efforts were originally voluntary and based on initiatives of our own. The attempts to develop academic practices were not asked for or resourced by university administrators or 'the management' as we started to call 'them'. We decided ourselves what was in need of development and what would be better than the existing state of affairs. However, the head of discipline did not try to prevent these moves, which would have made the action much more difficult. Moreover, the unit was then pretty autonomous in the matters that we chose to focus on. The university-level management did not prevent us – as long as we could do without extra resources and kept the developmental efforts inside the confines of the subject unit or focused on academic practices outside the university (like conference practices). We also made minor attempts to broaden the action beyond these borders and learned that we would not receive any support from the university if we do not accommodate our work to managerial interests.

The voluntary work over and above expected workloads was not formally remunerated or recognized. The activists were now and then worried about their future. Would they be the losers in rivalry for academic posts and other resources? If one spends time on common interests, would one be considered a less productive and successful academic than those who were 'collecting points' and improving individual reputation by publishing and offering fashionable and likable courses? This is still an acute question. My current assessment would be that at least during the ten-year period, engagement in development work was taken into account when evaluating applicants to various, mainly temporary posts – as far as these evaluations were done by people working in the department. Nevertheless, some of the active (feminist) developers came to the conclusion that it is better to take care of one's publication record first and limit one's effort on common tasks (Meriläinen et al., 2009, pp. 221–222). There was also a consistent majority that did not invest extra time and effort in the developmental tasks beyond their presence in various meetings (often planned by the activists) and beyond taking care of one's 'teaching load'.

Why did people engage in this action and collective effort, in spite of the obvious risks and extra work? Individuals may have different answers to this question. As one of the initiators of the developmental activity, I experienced the first positive responses from students, gained the feeling that my work was finally being integrated across the academic activities and saw positive prospects ahead in regard to the unit's qualitative development. I enjoyed the spirit of collaboration between the active developers. Engagement in autonomous development work made work more meaningful and rewarding. I thought that this would be the right way for me to be an academic. The view of a younger colleague can be found in Räsänen and Korpiaho (2010). She does not regret getting involved in the activities started by others, although it was demanding to start teaching work by creating a new course concept with a senior colleague (on the concept, see Räsänen & Korpiaho, 2007). She still thinks that the way of operating embodied things that she values: collaboration over competition, collegial relationships over supervisor/student hierarchy, participation over withdrawal and belonging over separation.

Why then did the developmental action slow down in the mid-2000s? There must be many reasons for this. Maybe the initiators got somewhat older and more exhausted. Some members of the original group chose to focus on publishing or moved to work at another university (as professors), whereby the action lost energy and key figures. A new head of the unit preferred governance practices that did not invite collective development work and here he was supported by many members of staff. The main topics of meetings were now results, money and prizes. Some decisions, in particular on teaching contracts, did not continue the previous efforts and the profile of the unit's staff started to change. The unit started to take a more positive stance towards the ideas presented by the university management. Internal developments of this kind may be a part of the explanation, but we think that the major influences were external to the group of activists and the unit.

The managerialization of university governance took a big step at the school alongside, but not due to, the Bologna Process in the mid-2000s: new rules were set on degree programmes, the departmental structure was reorganized and the formal position of departmental chair was strengthened (in relation to the head of unit). The school's leaders had earlier chosen the 'strategy of developing the university through evaluations and accreditations' and now the system of a US-accrediting organization started to take effect, after smaller changes demanded by European accreditors. At least these evaluations done recurrently by six external agencies required a lot of work and this work was done mainly by those who cared for education – the former activists. The new, national funding arrangements had made it more attractive to establish projects and alliances in which junior researchers were 'project workers' rather than autonomous researchers working on their own thesis research. The share of instrumentally controlled project researchers grew larger in the unit.

The final blow was the establishment of a new university, into which the business school was merged with two other universities.

The governance of the new university was structured according to a business-based ideal. Its board includes only external members and all the managers are selected top-down. The news of this ambitious, 'world-class' project made everybody uncertain about future prospects and we are witnessing all kinds of 'changes' initiated by the new management.

In sum, this is a story of how a group of academics could collectively develop work practices for a period and of how that was made much more difficult again. This is an example of what I call autonomous development work. Next I turn to elicit the more general features of this way of developing activities in academia.

Autonomous development as a developmental approach

In order to present a more general characterization of autonomous development work in academia, I draw here on the concept of developmental approach. This concept is based on a more general frame of practical activity, which has been developed over the years to study various forms of work, including developmental work in work organizations. Table 10.1 summarizes the framework and approach.

In this frame, academic development and any other work are approached as forms of practical activity. In a practical activity its practitioner unavoidably encounters four basic issues: how to do this, what to accomplish and achieve, why these means and goals, and who to be. Depending on the primary concern, the practitioner may, respectively, take a tactical, political, moral or personal stance to the activity in question. However, the resolution of an issue may be accomplished either consciously or – which is more usual – by default, as the resolution is already embedded in the practices rehearsed and culturally inherited by the practitioner. The world views of various practice theorists similarly prioritize one of these stances and their works can be of help in understanding the respective issues.

Table 10.1 Practical activity: a generic frame for interpretation (revised from Räsänen, 2009)

Issue	Stance	Concretization	Practice theorists
How?	Tactical	Means	Certeau (Goffman)
What?	Political	Goals	Bourdieu (Foucault)
Why?	Moral	Motives/Justifications	MacIntyre (Taylor)
Who?	Personal	Identity	Holland (Dreier, Harré)

This thinking is based on the old concept of praxis and suggests a specific interpretation of it: a group of practitioners are rehearsing a form of praxis when they have resolved all the four issues and in a relatively coherent way. In this sense, actual praxis is rare and the term refers rather to an imaginable possibility – a potentiality – than to what people are actually doing. One advantage of this interpretation is that it allows for the appreciation of various different forms of praxis in emergence, instead of proposing a specific moral and political line of action.

Along with the more general frame of practical activity, the more specific notion of developmental approach has been used in order to identify, describe and compare various forms of developmental work (Räsänen, 2007). This concept provides practitioners with cultural resources that support their attempts to articulate and reflect on their practice. Development work at universities can also be approached with the help of this concept.

Here I want to define academic development in a wide sense, in order to include activities that may easily be ignored or even deprecated. I regard as academic development any intentional efforts to change or improve academic practices, regardless of the activity in question or the actor doing it; my point here is that this work is not done only by managers or staff professionals hired to various developer positions.

Academic development takes various forms and it is practised by a diverse group of practitioners, from various formal positions. These people usually develop education and sometimes other activities in universities. They develop teachers, researchers, administrators and students. They may call their work academic development, staff development or educational development (or development of teaching and learning). Most of them work in specialized units and under the control of university management. These units are more often a part of the administrative hierarchy than academic units with a research and teaching domain of their own. Formal relationships between developers and academics vary from close collaboration to the sale of services and even control functions (as in certifying teachers). This versatility of people, positions and tasks makes it likely that there are significant differences in development practice (see Bath & Smith, 2004; Blackmore, 2009; Land, 2004).

Attempts to professionalize academic development, and thereby advance developers' position and improve the quality of their work, have made the differences in practice visible and made them a matter of politicking. As any professionalization movement, this one has also to deal with the fact that its knowledge base is contested and that there are a number of disciplinary fields that want to claim a dominant role in defining this base, notably psychology, education and sociology. Academics from various substantive fields may also question the ideas and practices of the developers.

It is notable that very few developers say that they are developing 'academic work' as a whole. It is usual that they are developing one of the academic activities or academics in one respect. This indicates that developers – or the discourses of academic development – do not pay much attention to the fact that typical academics are involved in multiple activities and that they have to deal with them all. The one-activity bias may also be partly due to the sources of disciplinary knowledge most often used in development work. Managers, psychologists and educationalists may not be especially prone to talk about work, workers and employers in the university context. 'Learning' is politically a less provocative word, with positive connotations among the relevant parties.

When approaching academic development as a practical activity we acknowledge that practitioners may be only half-aware of what they are doing and that this work is at least partly uncontrollable to them. They may find it hard to sustain a style of working that they would prefer. The logics of development work are, therefore, difficult to grasp and articulate. We should not assume that there is a logic in it akin to any normative statements of how to do it 'rationally and systematically'. Developers may not necessarily have a good or permanent grip on the things and people that are being developed or a good grasp of them. When articulating or describing developmental work we need to take this into account.

While the term 'developmental approach' may sound too general and intellectually empty in English, the Finnish term *kehittämisote* sounds different to native Finnish speakers. The term loses its concreteness in translation. The original term expresses foremost an embodied mode of working and a related stance or orientation as opposed to an intellectual, rationalized approach to work. In Finnish, the word 'ote' also has the meaning of having a 'grip' by hands on something – a tennis racket, for instance. In this sense, one can take different grips on concrete matters, like tennis rackets, and, in an analogical sense, on teachers and teaching in higher education institutions. One can take a grip without conscious deliberation, like a novice tennis player or a university developer in panic with deadlines. And, one can lose one's grip or miss getting it altogether.

Thus, the term 'developmental approach' refers to a deliberate and sustained way of working that may emerge only in special situations.

Yet, as a concept it may serve as an instrument also in articulating less coherent and explicit ways of practising academic development. How can we then articulate or identify a particular approach to development work? This can be done through a set of questions that cover the basic issues of developmental work as a practical activity. This set of questions enables a dialogical articulation of development practice.

Räsänen (2007) presents a list of questions that should make the articulation and description of a 'developmental approach' possible. The list, presented here, is a translation and partial modification of the original list (see Table 10.2). When reading the list, one should bear in mind that the questions have been generated by a logic of multiple perspectives. Thus under a primary concern (e.g. politics) one encounters the other issues or aspects of practical activity (tactics, morals and subjects) but from this specific stance.

In terms of the questions above, one is rehearsing a developmental approach when one has resolved all the basic issues of how, what, why and who in a particular and relatively coherent way. The same questions can, however, be used in describing less coherent and fragmented ways of doing developmental work. Now we can come back to autonomous development and try to specify how the issues have been resolved in this developmental practice.

General features of autonomous development

Table 10.3 summarizes a tentative interpretation of the general features of autonomous development work in academia (Räsänen & Korpiaho, 2010). This interpretation is based on the local case and on the authors' knowledge of the literature on academic development, but in ways that I do not try to articulate in this text. This characterization can hopefully work as a discussion starter and it has to be elaborated in further research. The examples in the table are drawn from the story presented above.

In autonomous development, academics develop academic practices in their own ways in order make their work better according to their own understanding and standards. They are motivated by their conception of the internal goods of the specific disciplinary tradition that they continue and renew (see MacIntyre, 1985; Räsänen, 2010).

How does this approach compare with the other, currently fashionable developmental approaches at universities? In particular, how do the various versions of evaluation, accreditation, quality management and

Table 10.2   Questions for the articulation or description of developmental work

---

1. Who develops, for whom, and with whom (subjects)

   - Who are the 'developers', for example, what are their professional identities (Why I am doing this? What am I trying to accomplish and achieve by this? How I am doing this?)?
   - Who orders (and possibly pays for) this development work?
   - Who participates in it?

2. How is development work carried out? (tactics)

   - How is the object of development constructed, for example, with what basic concepts and methods?
   - How is the developmental work process represented, organized and systematized, for example, with what principles and stages?
   - How are developmental tasks carried out, for example, with what tools and moves, and in what moods; for example, in diagnosing and intervening?
   - How are participation and negotiations arranged and governed?
   - How are the goals and means justified to the relevant actors and outsiders?

3. What is being developed? (politics)

   - What or who is taken as the object of development, for example, whose framing of the object is taken seriously; whose tools are preferred in constructing the object; what is assumed/claimed about people and things under development?
   - What kind of changes are aimed at in the object (as results), for example, whose interests are taken into account in goal-setting; who defines accomplishments and achievements; what is assumed/claimed about the change process in the object and about its possibilities/necessities?
   - What legitimates (more or less routinely) the frameworks and goals?

4. Why these particular means and goals of development work? (morals)

   - Why are these means of development work valuable or at least justified, for example, what is claimed as justification?
   - Why is this direction of change considered development, for example, whose value bases are given priority or taken into account in setting goals?
   - Why do the developers engage in this development work, for example, what (moral) motives drive the developers?

---

change management differ from it? Although a thorough comparison is impossible here, a few striking differences and interactions between the approaches can be identified.

The most important difference is in the assumed subjects of development work. While the developmental methods imported from the

Table 10.3 Autonomous development work as a developmental approach

Issue	General description	Examples
Who?	Academic practitioners	Collaborating teachers/researchers in a disciplinary unit 'I am renewing my own work, and this is my key task.' 'We do it ourselves and together.'
How?	On their own terms and with their own means	Collaborative scripts in events, using academic procedures, modified and complemented with ideas from other contexts, team teaching, participatory work processes; daily reflection with colleagues
What?	Academic practices and practitioners in different academic activities, in order to accomplish improvements in (the quality of) work. The goals defined by the practitioners	Learning to use new learning methods; revising research and writing practices; new meeting practices; changing gendered practices
Why?	In order to redefine and realize the 'internal goods' of a specific form of academic practice	Collegial collaboration; commitment to the long-term development of practices and people; responsibility for student learning

business world presume that managers and the developers hired to advance managerial agendas are the major initiators and leaders of development, in autonomous development it is the academics that act to improve their own practices. The former approaches presume that managers (and politicians) know better than academics and are therefore in a position to define answers to all of the basic questions. Academics are taken as 'objects of change' that have to be induced or forced to accept changes.

Another major difference between the managerial approaches towards autonomous development is in the setting of goals for developmental efforts. Take the example of evaluations: a self-reflective professional is assessing her or his practices, but not according to criteria set by outsiders. Making this professional 'participate' in an evaluation, in which the evaluation frame is set by outsiders, is not the same thing. In an autonomous effort, the renewal of the goals or even the purposes of academic practice may be a central concern. Externally fixed and forced assessment criteria are likely to interfere with these debates or remain invalid to the practitioners. Autonomous development accommodates the case that the criteria of evaluation are in constant change. Academics may be gradually gaining a better and richer grasp of the 'internal goods' of their practice. The criteria are, at least, contest among the professionals.

Staff and educational development are the most promising arenas for the appreciation of autonomous development. Many developers struggle under contradictory pressures: they are hired or funded to advance particular lines of development or to apply a particular development method (like training), they have their own ideas of proper development work and the participants of their operations have their own expectations and doubts. This vocation is also internally divided as various background fields try to gain ground in determining the correct developmental approach within universities. Nevertheless, professional developers encounter academics face to face, which may result in mutual respect and in a realistic understanding of how academic practices can be improved. Although the abundant literature on educational development contains various strands, there are researchers and practitioners who consider teachers to be the prime movers in improving teaching and learning. Some academic developers may thus be receptive towards the idea and practice of autonomous development by academics. Others could be reminded of the fact that what is now called academic development was originally started by activist academics about 40 years ago (Lee et al., 2010).

Finally, a few words about 'change management' in this comparative setting. This term is the most recent entrant to the vocabulary of university development in Finland. At the same time, it is the most radical one in the managerial arsenal of developmental approaches. As it is practised in business firms, it is actually a family of developmental approaches originally based on the behavioural sciences. The destructive potential of this family is large because it legitimates 'top-down' or outside-in changes after changes. It carries with it the presumption that if you are a manager your task is to change things. If somebody does not accept a change he or she is suffering from the condition of 'resistance to change', a pathology that can be healed by better communication, inducements or abrupt measures. As a developmental approach, change management is likely to result in an endless chain of change projects at universities. Even if these projects concerned marginal elements of academic work, they cause disturbances and curb the space for efforts initiated by academics in research and education. This danger is well known by those who work in private corporations or public services, but now this approach has entered universities too.

Why autonomous development matters

As I have now presented a tentative characterization of autonomous development in academia, it is necessary to question the significance of this activity. Is it only a marginal form of activity or does it really make a difference more generally? I suggest that it is actually the major source of renewal in academic practices. This claim finds support from the studies of academic movements.

Groups that rehearse autonomous development can be considered miniature movements or participants in wider academic movements. The logic of mobilization is similar to that of social movements in general. People take initiative and join together to resolve an issue or to correct an injustice. They do not act because they are induced or ordered to do so, but because they see a common cause, and often against the wishes of those who try to discipline or govern them.

In fact, there are many scholars who argue that academic movements create the dynamics in science and, in our terms, renew academic practices of learning and knowing. If this is true, then autonomous development is critical in fulfilling the expectations that academics create new knowledge and educate citizens in the changing societies and natural world.

The role of movements in the change of academic fields has been noticed by a number of scholars, but I can give here only a few examples from recent studies in the sociology of science. Frickel and Gross (2005) focus on intellectual movements within and across academic fields and Arthur (2009) adds that the basis of some changes in academia can be found in wider social movements outside academia.

Frickel and Gross (2005) claim that they have created a general theory of scientific/intellectual movements (SIM). These are defined as collective, political efforts to advance research programmes or projects of thought that meet the resistance of others in an academic community (Frickel & Gross, 2005, p. 206). These movements try to advance a programme of changes in intellectual practices and aim primarily at goals that concern knowledge. SIMs try to change power positions in a field or between fields, and possibly also elsewhere in society. These aims require organized, collective action and coordination from academics with a high status position in the relevant field. These leaders can enrol new members and sources of resources for them, for instance, jobs. Further,

SIMs are episodic and they either disappear or become institutionalized, for example, as new schools of thought or disciplines.

Within this broad frame, SIMs can be very different as regards to their goals: they can bring in a new phenomenon or theme for research, launch a new research approach or set of methods, or revise boundaries between disciplines. Moreover, they can be either progressive or reactive in relation to dominant tendencies: they can advance something new or protect something old against current, harmful biases. Thus the frame accommodates both ambitious and minor goals and efforts. The success of these movements depends on their leaders' abilities to frame the challenge and on structural opportunities to gain access to resources and contexts of micro-mobilization. Frickel and Gross find supportive evidence for these claims from case studies of particular fields like genetic toxicology (Frickel, 2004) and Richard Rorty's pragmatism (Gross, 2003). For a useful, newer review, see Jacobs and Frickel (2009).

Arthur (2009) emphasizes the significance of wider social movements in her study of curriculum changes in US universities. She uses the term 'new knowledge movements' in order to distinguish her approach from the SIM model. In her view, such new disciplines as Gender Studies or Asian-American Studies were not originally advanced by academic leaders but by social identity movements outside of academia. She also pays attention to collaboration between students and the faculty in creating new curricula in these areas.

If we acknowledge the importance of various kinds of movement in the renewal of academic practices, then we can easily find examples of these movements in our own fields (for a list of local examples, see Räsänen, 2008). Think, for instance, of the various 'turns' that we have witnessed in the social sciences and humanities during the latest decennia. Or think about the wide but chronically failing movement aiming to improve university teaching and learning and make it a high priority in academia. Or, think about the impact of feminism in academia. Even if these intellectual turns, developmental programmes and political mobilizations were only partially successful, they can inspire and support local actors in their accomplishment of improvements in the local practices of academic work. Whether these minor, local changes are more significant than those accomplished by managerial orders and techniques is an empirical question. Yet, who would regard major developments in the history of science and education as results from university management – or, in particular, from the managerial approaches to developmental work discussed above? Is it not more realistic to think that researchers and teachers have brought about these 'changes', whereas university administrators have only supported, ignored or complicated such efforts?

Why dangerous, and to whom?

Why then did the rector of our business school consider our way of operating to be dangerous? I do not know what he was thinking, but I can speculate on why university managers in general might find autonomous development problematic or even dangerous. This is not a trivial question, because autonomous development can deliver minor improvements and even more radical innovations and do all this cheaply as outcomes from ordinary, educational and research work in academia, requiring no extra inducements.

The managerial ideology is built on the belief that the world becomes better by letting one profession, the management, rule other professional groups. As the managers are assumed to be the only neutral and non-elitist professional group, they can balance rationally the selfish demands of the other groups. Without going into the debate on the (quasi-) professionalism of management, it is possible to see here one answer to the question of 'why dangerous'. Autonomous development work endangers the position of university managers. If managers are not really needed in the generation of innovative practices, why should they then have the right to decide on who can work at the university, what these academics are to do and how? In this perspective, the rector's comment can be seen as an incidence in an on-going struggle between various professional groups and, in particular, between a university manager and a representative of the academic profession. The same struggle is going on in various other work organizations and has been documented, for instance, in the studies of so called New Public Management.

More concrete answers can be found in how the university management currently operates. Acknowledging the significance of autonomous development work would make the currently fashionable, managerial methods of development work less attractive. This may be hard to accept for a manager who has personally invested a lot of effort and political capital in importing these methods to the university and may even have gained or sustained his or her position by advancing such programmes. Establishing the whole system of accreditation and repeated evaluation has required a lot of work – including in countries that do not necessarily need all of these systems (due to the state's role in granting rights for awarding degrees). In the case of our former business university, university management had declared that evaluations are their – or 'our' – main method of university development.

A crucial challenge to managerial control is in the definition of development goals. The primary concern of university managers seems to be the implementation of policies designed elsewhere. University funding is tied to compliance in Finland and several other countries. Moreover, the managerial ideology presumes that managers determine the goal and others realize it. Autonomous development does not fit into this picture. If academics practice autonomous development, they define their goals themselves and this may result in developments that do not advance the implementation of policy agendas.

A practical problem for managers may also be the fact that autonomous development work results from – and in – such knowledge of the university's activities that is not presented in managerial format and censured by the managers. As managers are expected to control activities that can impact on the reputation of the university, they may not like the idea that academics tell their own stories from the university. In particular, the danger may be felt to be acute if the activists base their developmental efforts on research in their home university, that is, if they rehearse critically reflective practice and – rephrasing Scholarship of Teaching and Learning – 'scholarship of academic work'. Researching one's own workplace is always laden with tensions, but in this case it interferes with the managerial interest in the control of communication. Reports on the local activities unavoidably explicate things that are in need of further development. These reports may also include critical views concerning university governance and higher education or science policies. A minor problem may be that these reports seldom represent managers as the creators of something new.

The foregoing reasoning is political by nature. Alasdair MacIntyre's (1985) distinction between social practice and institution helps in expressing a moral view of the dangers of autonomous development. In his view, a social practice is defined by its specific internal goods, while an institution, established to support such a practice, is after external goods such as fame, status or money. One could imagine that university managers are inclined to think in terms of the external goods and they cannot have practitioner knowledge of the internal goods in the various, for instance, discipline-specific, social practices that they are trying to control. Developmental efforts from within these unknown social practices are not only an intellectual challenge but might also evoke moral turmoil. Conceptions and standards of good practice may be so different that managers may duly be afraid of losing control in conflict situations. The managerial ideology presumes that it is up to managers to resolve both political and moral issues, and the others are left only with the how question. When moral views and points are raised in a debate or negotiation, the situation may become emotionally charged and thereby uncontrollable to all of the parties. This is a managerial nightmare.

Thus, we can conclude that there are several reasons why university managers might consider autonomous development dangerous. However, this developmental approach may cause worries also to academic professionals. As far as the developmental efforts concern educational and research practices, these worries are ordinary in most fields. Academics are used to working among competing schools of thought and debating on alternative theoretical and methodical solutions. Thanks to the teaching and learning movement, negotiations on alternative teaching practices have also become more usual. The situation may become more threatening when developmental efforts concern self-governance practices within a discipline or department. An academic may appreciate creativity in research work and educational affairs, but when somebody wants to revise the everyday routines of collegial governance that academic may become defensive. It is as if the managerial intrusions to academic work were less dangerous.

When autonomous development is extended to self-governance practices, like in the case presented above, the activists are actually proposing or experimenting with new forms of academic professionalism (see Nixon et al., 2001, and compare Adler & Heckscher, 2006). This may feel like a threat to academic autonomy to those who prefer traditional ways of operating, but equally well we could think of these new forms of professionalism as dynamic responses to the old issue of academic autonomy (see Henkel, 2005). Instead of demanding that academics should be left free to continue their activities, this response suggests that academics should have autonomy – and competence – in renewing their own practices, including the practices of collegial self-governance. This slight revision may be needed now as other actor groups are trying to mould academic work as they please. This is the vision behind the approach of autonomous developmental work. It is old wine in a new, redesigned bottle.

Conclusion

This story suggests that the work of ordinary academics is one major generator of change in research and education, and possibly also in the practices of governance in academia. Hopefully, I have given reasons to doubt that university managers and politicians are the only actors capable of renewal and improvement in academic work. I have also suggested a host of reasons why they may not like what I am proposing.

As intentional and organized 'developmental work' has entered universities, it is about time that academics create developmental approaches that sustain academic autonomy and enable new, dynamic forms of academic professionalism. The characterization of autonomous development work presented here hopefully evokes further discussion and draws attention to the diversity of developmental approaches available. The practice-theoretical and practice-based concept of the developmental approach and its background frame of practical activity provide at least one way of framing this diversity or one way of triggering local discussion.

If the practice of autonomous development work is considered dangerous by university leaders, it cannot be entirely insignificant. The dangers and pleasures that it represents to the activists themselves is another story. Maybe the rector was merely expressing his concern over my future at the lunch table...

References

Adler, P. S. and C. Heckscher (2006) 'Towards collaborative community'. In: C. Heckscher and P. S. Adler (Eds) *The Firm as a Collaborative Community*, Oxford: Oxford University Press, pp. 11–105.

Arthur, M. M. L. (2009) 'Thinking outside the master's house: new knowledge movements and the emergence of academic disciplines', *Social Movement Studies*, 8, 73–87.

Bath, D. and C. Smith (2004) 'Academic developers: an academic tribe claiming their territory in higher education', *International Journal for Academic Development*, 9, 9–27.

Blackmore, P. (2009) 'Conceptions of development in higher education institutions', *Studies in Higher Education*, 34, 663–676.

Frickel, S. T. (2004) 'Building an interdiscipline: collective action framing and the rise of genetic toxicology', *Social Problems*, 51, 269–287.

Frickel, S. T. and N. Gross (2005) 'A general theory of scientific/intellectual movements', *American Sociological Review*, 70, 204–232.

Gross, N. (2003) 'Richard Rorty's Pragmatism: a case study in the sociology of ideas', *Theory and Society*, 32, 93–148.

Henkel, M. (2005) 'Academic identity and autonomy in a changing policy environment', *Higher Education*, 49, 155–176.

Jacobs, J. A. and S. T. Frickel (2009) 'Interdisciplinarity: a critical assessment', *Annual Review of Sociology*, 35, 43–65.

Land, R. (2004) *Educational Development: Discourse, Identity and Practice*, Maidenhead: Open University Press.

Lee, A., C. Manthunga and P. Kandlbinder (2010) 'Shaping a culture: oral histories of academic development in Australian universities', *Higher Education Research & Development*, 29, 307–318.

MacIntyre, A. (1985) *After Virtue. A Study in Moral Theory*, 2nd corrected edition, London: Duckworth.

Meriläinen, S., K. Räsänen and S. Katila (2009) 'Autonomous renewal of gendered practices: interventions and their pre-conditions at an academic workplace'. In: S. Andresen, M. Koreuber and D. Lüdke (Eds) *Gender und Diversity. Albtraum oder Traumpaar? Interdisziplinärer Dialog aktueller Tendenzen der 'Modernisierung' von Geschlechter- und Gleichstellungspolitik*, Wiesbaden: Verlag für Sozial-wissenschaften, pp. 209–230.

Nixon, J., A. Marks, S. Rowland and M. Walker. (2001) 'Towards a new academic professionalism: a manifesto for hope', *British Journal of Sociology of Education*, 22, 227–244.

Räsänen, K. (2007) 'Kehittämisotteet: kehittämistyö "käytännöllisenä toimintana" [Modes of developmental work: developmental work as 'practical activity']. In: E. Ramstad and T. Alasoini (Eds) *Työelämän tutkimusavusteinen kehittäminen Suomessa*, TYKES Reports 53, Helsinki: Ministry of Labour, pp. 40–66.

Räsänen, K. (2008) 'Mikä yliopistotyöntekijää liikuttaa?' [What moves university employees?] *Tiedepolitiikka*, 2/08, 17–27.

Räsänen, K. (2009) 'Understanding academic work as practical activity – and preparing (business-school) academics for praxis?', *International Journal for Academic Development*, 14, 185–195.

Räsänen, K. (2010) 'On the moral of an emerging academic praxis: accounting for a conference experience'. In: C. Steyaert and B. Van Looy (Eds) *Relational Practices, Participative Organizing*, Bingley: Emerald, pp. 155–176.

Räsänen, K. and K. Korpiaho (2007) 'Experiential learning without work experience: reflecting on studying as "practical activity" '. In: M. Reynolds and R. Vince (Eds) *The Handbook of Experiential Learning and Management Education*, Oxford: Oxford University Press, pp. 87–104.

Räsänen, K. and K. Korpiaho (2010) Accounting for academic development practice: the concept of developmental approach, the case of autonomous development, and a teacher's story. Paper to the European Conference on Educational Research 'Education and Cultural Change', Helsinki, 25–27 August.

Räsänen, K. and K. Korpiaho (2011) 'Supporting doctoral students in their professional identity projects', *Studies in Continuing Education*, 33, 19–31.

11
The Interplay of Organizing Models in Higher Education: What Room Is There for Collegiality in Universities Characterized by Bounded Autonomy?

Kerstin Sahlin

Coping with a mix of organizational ideals

Many universities and university systems around the globe have recently been subject to extensive organizational and regulatory reforms. A dominating discourse and a trend behind those reform efforts circles around the notions of 'autonomy and accountability' (e.g. see Estermann & Nokkala, 2009; Stensaker & Harvey, 2010). Many national university systems have been reorganized to introduce what will be described here as bounded autonomy. In parallel with these reforms we have witnessed the emergence of new rankings, evaluations and accreditation procedures. These measures are salient aspects of an altered and activated transnational regulatory and organizing landscape in the university sector. A number of international organizations and networks have formed or been mobilized with these developments, as have consultancies and expert groups. Together these changes can be described as forming universities, around the globe, to be part of a more or less global organizational field – or a market – characterized by competition and collaboration.

With these transformations, many universities have developed elaborate organizational structures, including new and strengthened management positions, expanded communication departments, and innovation and technology transfer units. In short we can observe a diffusion of more managerial forms of organizing. However, many of the more traditional traits of universities remain. Traditionally, universities have – in part – been structured as arenas for professions with elected leaders, with a strong emphasis on academic freedom and with decision-making resting on principles of collegiality and meritocracy.

It is clear, when viewing organizational reforms of universities, that the prevalent organizational ideals and reforms are not at all unique to the university sector. Related changes in management and organization have swept through the entire public sector and, to some extent, the entire organizational world. So, even if the organizational reforms clearly impact on university activities and the role of universities in society, changes in university governance and organization can be explained only to a limited extent by changes in research or education policy. Instead, we can see that organizational reforms, as well as ideals and principles of what constitutes good governance and good management, follow more general trends, where certain ways of governing and managing appear ideal at certain times. These ideals then form templates outlining how to assess organizations as well as which reforms of such organizing appear important or even necessary. Hence, there are few eternal truths when it comes to organization. Instead, we can identify eras when certain modes of governance and management appear ideal. However, some reforms go against each other and they rest on different basic conceptions of what universities should do and how they evolve. Thus we can state initially that it is not just one kind of change, or one ideal for how to govern and manage, that affects universities at a given time. For those seeking to manage and cope with university governance at any given time, this is largely a matter of coping with a mix of organizational ideals.

The above-mentioned changes raise questions as to what organizational ideals prevail, but also how the diverse organizational ideals mix and how they translate into a common practice. In this chapter I discuss how university leaders can cope with the kinds of organizational reforms described above. I argue that an important task for leaders in the academic system is to translate all those pressures, demands and expectations that bound the university autonomy and to mix the many diverse organizational ideals that frame universities into a meaningful and working structure. A normative idea that runs through this chapter is the importance of making space for a collegiality. Hence a central question is 'What room is there for collegiality in the university systems characterized by bounded autonomy?'

The chapter focuses primarily on the interplay of organizing models for higher education as they are translated into practice. Before turning

to this main topic of the chapter, I describe various ideal models for organizing universities. I start with the most current changes: the more or
less explosive development of measurements, assessments and rankings.

University management in the Audit Society[1]

A couple of decades ago, rankings of universities and academic disciplines were seldom talked about and did not at all affect the daily
work of most university professors and leaders. At least, this was true
for European universities, although talk about rankings that appeared
now and then on the American scene sometimes caught the attention
of European media reporters. During the past decade, however, we have
witnessed what appears to be an exploding development of rankings.
This development includes three aspects: (1) the number of rankings
has multiplied, (2) rankings have spread globally with the proliferation of international rankings – and with the global attention also paid
to national rankings and (3) the encroachment of rankings into the
very heart of university governance systems. Today, it is no exaggera-
tion to say that rankings are clearly of central concern if not to every
professor at least to every university president, vice-chancellor or dean.
Discussions about, and criticism of, rankings have expanded with this
development. However, most discussions on rankings open with the
remark that they are here to stay.

Ranking lists are based in part on bibliometric measurements. Such
measurements are used not only in the rankings. Nowadays, the Swedish
government resource allocation to universities is partly based on bibliometric measurements. Models of quality-based resource allocation have
been introduced throughout Europe. Well-known examples include the
Excellence Initiative in Germany and the Research Assessment Exercise
in the UK. Even though they differ in their design they are all at least
partly based on bibliometrics. It is actually difficult today to find reviews,
resource allocation models and peer reviews that do not, at least in some
way, use and refer to bibliometric measurements.

Rankings and bibliometrics are two of the many assessment technologies that have proliferated during the past few decades. We can see
a more general diffusion of evaluations and assessments of individual
research performance, universities and various aspects of national systems of higher education. Not only has academic performance increasingly become subject to new kinds of measurements and assessments,
the field of higher education is, like other sectors of organized society, subject to extensive auditing and evaluation. A recent trend in the

Swedish public sector is that new specialized national agencies have been set up, with the task of assessing and evaluating, for example, in the school sector and developmental assistance. In the spring of 2011, a political initiative was announced to investigate whether such a specialized agency should also be formed for the higher education sector. The evaluation, assessment and scrutiny of higher education is already a densely populated organizational landscape where the National Audit Office, the National Agency for Higher Education, individual research councils and a whole set of national and international organizations are scrutinizing and auditing various aspects of universities. An area that has grown dramatically around Europe is the assessment of risk – from which has followed extensive efforts to establish procedures, management units and control measures for the management and control of risk (cf. Power et al., 2009).

This dramatic proliferation of auditing and evaluation took off in the 1990s and has blossomed considerably in the university system since the new millennium. In a fascinating analysis of this development, Michael Power coined the concept 'audit society' (1997). What has evolved is a society characterized not only by a extensive and growing documentation, evaluation, auditing and scrutiny, but also a society in which operations and organizations are increasingly structured in ways that make them 'auditable' (see also Shore & Wright, 2000; Strathern, 2000).

Rankings – and assessments more generally – have spurred extensive organizing efforts. Many universities have responded by setting up special units with the task of following the rankings, suggesting appropriate management responses, and ensuring that fair and favourable data is submitted to the rankers. Some universities have set a goal of climbing the rankings and they have developed strategies for how to do that. We also see tendencies towards further structural reforms among universities, such as the formation of alliances and mergers, as well as reorganizations. For an individual leader, the proliferation of assessments, rankings and evaluations creates demands to favourably present and represent the organization externally, and to translate the organizational operations into measurable results and evaluation criteria – in short to manage the university reputation.

When analysing the rise of the Audit Society, Power and others (see Power, 1997, 2003; Hood et al., 1999; Moran, 2002) propose that the expanded monitoring and auditing activities are associated with a decline in trust. Auditing and monitoring reveal things and make them transparent. Rather than building trust, though, transparency may in fact undermine it further, leading to still more requests for auditing and monitoring (Power, 1997, 2003). Hence, an additional important task for university leaders in the Audit Society is to seek to build and maintain trust in higher education and research, and in the organizational set-ups in which these activities are performed.

In short, the introduction of new measurements, assessments and performance criteria has important consequences for the organizing, management and governance of universities and hence also for the way in which research is performed and for knowledge generation as such.

If we analyse the recent proliferation of rankings and other forms of assessments and evaluations in university systems throughout Europe, it becomes clear that these trends do not originate in policies for higher education and research – but in a more general societal trend of organizing and scrutinizing, and this trend in turn impacts on the reformulation of research and higher education policies on a national as well as a transnational level. As such, they do challenge what could be described as more traditional modes of governing, organizing and managing universities. Hence, to understand the conditions under which academic leaders operate we should continue to look into general organizational trends of the last few decades.

Rankings and audits were not introduced in a vacuum, of course. An extremely powerful proliferation of governing and management principles paved the way, starting in the 1980s, for the more recent management developments. In the next section we turn to this – the rise of New Public Management.

A global wave of organizational reforms

In the mid-1980s, an almost global wave of reforms of the public sector gained momentum. The public sector was transformed to become more business-like. Inspired by business and economic science, more market and more management were introduced. A whole new language for describing and analysing public service emerged. Inspired by management ideas and practices from the private sector, the reforms were referred to as 'New Public Management' (Hood, 1991, 1995). As universities, in Sweden and in most parts of Europe, are state-controlled, these organizational changes affected universities as well as the rest of the public sector. This reform trend is still alive and strong.

New Public Management is a label used both to define a changing style of governance and administration in the public sector and to describe a number of reforms that were carried out in several countries during the 1980s and the 1990s. The transformation of public agencies that falls under the label of New Public Management is well documented and analysed, so I do not need to repeat this at any length here. Let me just mention some of the main features of the transformation. In short, studies have shown that this reform path began as a political project in Britain and North America, was further developed and given a basis in economic theory in New Zealand, was picked up by the Organisation of Economic Co-operation and Development (OECD) as a good example of reform, and was thus circulated around the world in the form of a reform prescription that provided more market, better management, more result measures (in the form of outcomes and outputs) and more evaluations (Sahlin-Andersson, 2001).

A few examples from the Swedish scene remind us of some of the main features of this reform trend. When exemplifying such changed governance and organizing I mention both specific changes in the university system and more general changes introduced in the public sector. Again, this reminds us that changes did not originate in research and higher educational policies, but were part of a more general restructuring of public sector organization and, indeed, of society as a whole. In the early 1990s, management by objectives was introduced in the state administration and what followed was a strong emphasis on outputs and outcomes in planning as well as in the accounts of public sector units. The allocation of resources to the many public activities changed. Funding was increasingly formed as block grants and elements of result-based resource allocation were introduced. Ideas of the market were clearly behind the introduction of a student voucher system, a relative increase in research funding subject to competition and, much later, a performance-driven redistribution of parts of the universities' basic funding. With this development, clearer priorities, management and formulated policies have been requested from the top management of universities. For example, when the state allocated major sums for universities to compete for areas of excellence and for 'strategic research grants', it was not individual groups, but the rector of the university who was the main person responsible for such applications and, when given, for the grants.

The reforms brought with them new ideals of organizing and controlling that had previously existed mainly in the private sector (Power, 1997). In that sense, the various tools embraced by reforms, such as new management accounting models, could be seen as technologies, as concrete practices and as methods with the potential to realize ideals of wider societal programmes (Miller, 1994). These reforms were thus not simply changes in techniques, but represented a more fundamental institutional change. They introduced a new institutional logic that guided, motivated and legitimated activities and gave new meaning to priorities in the field.

Together, these changes have strengthened the top management and hierarchy of universities. This development has been emphasized further through the introduction of accrual accounting. In Sweden this was introduced throughout the whole public sector in the mid-1990s, which meant that all organizations became subject to similar basic principles of accounting. Public authorities should therefore report results, assets and liabilities in the same way as companies. Somewhat earlier, individual pay was introduced throughout the public sector. With changed forms of regulation and governance, many agencies put considerable effort into developing their own missions and strategy documents; many designed or revised logotypes on the grounds that it was important to consider the organization's identity, brand and marketing. The public organizations' communication departments grew, leadership received more attention and leadership courses became increasingly popular. The composition of university boards also changed. Gradually, university boards have gone from being based on collegiate principles, with the rector as chair and representatives of faculty in majority, to having an external person – appointed by the government – as chair and with students, business leaders and representatives from other sectors in society as members in addition to what nowadays is a minority of faculty representatives.

With these changes the organizational design of universities attracted much interest and came to be seen as increasingly important. Indeed, one can claim that all those reforms restructured what used to be seen as a sector of professional groups and activities into a market of organizations (Brunsson & Sahlin-Andersson, 2000). The internal hierarchy and line management was strengthened in universities and the same development could be observed in schools, hospitals and most public authorities. The changes meant that public sector organizations more clearly resembled companies in the business world. It also became more common to make comparisons and draw parallels between public agencies and private companies. With these changes it also became more central for organizations to work for their own development and survival. A general organizational language evolved and the assumption became widespread that there are general principles of management and governance that can be applied to all kinds of organizations.

Is there nothing specific then – in terms of governance, management and performance – to the university? My answer to that question will be yes, and I will come back to it, but first I shall dwell a little further on the proliferation and changed governing and management ideals.

Four eras of governance and management

Based on fieldwork that captured developments in health care in the Bay Area in California during the past 50 years, Richard Scott and his colleagues (2000) showed that reforms in the 1980s introduced a new dominant institutional logic of health care: a managerial market orientation. The two preceding eras were, in turn, dominated by medical professionals and the federal government promoting the logic of professional authority and equity of access to care. Although this particular investigation was carried out in the USA and concerned the governance of health care, I claim that the results of this study have a much broader bearing.[2]

Sometimes organizational trends, such as New Public Management, have been characterized as fashion. Fashion is often associated with something superficial and of short duration.[3] In addition, to many people's ears, the term has a somewhat negative connotation. This understanding may lead to a conclusion that leaders of an organization can choose whether to follow fashion or not. When the above-mentioned eras are characterized as institutional, it is instead stressed that they are fundamental and pervasive. They can be likened to cultures. This also means that we are all part of these eras. It is not just those who are supposed to lead and develop organizations that are picking up the trends I have written about above. Ideals are also picked up by evaluators, auditors and international organizations, including the legislators and many others who set the standard for what is good organization. This means that evaluations, assessments and regulations, too, are framed by those contemporary trends. Therefore, it is undeniably important for leaders and organizers to follow the trend. It is difficult, if not sometimes impossible and probably foolish, to seek to disregard those trends and developments. An organization that does not follow a trend can be seen as unfashionable and as unwilling to change, and it can thus be difficult for such an organization to interact with others. It is, in other words, a matter of being seen as effective and up to date; it is a matter of legitimacy (see Table 11.1).

Even if profound institutional change is demonstrated, developments do not need to follow a straight line with clear-cut phases. Scott et al. (2000) conclude that different modes of governance can be simultaneously active in the field, although to different degrees. In the health

Table 11.1   Institutional eras of governance

Eras	Institutional actors	Institutional logics	Governance structures
1945–1965	*Independent physicians*	*Professional authority* Quality of care	*Professional associations*
	Community hospitals Local/state governments Private insurance	Non-profit, voluntary ethos	State licensure of health occupations Voluntary health planning
1966–1982	*Federal government* State governments Medical profession Multi-hospital systems	*Equity of Access* Consumer health Movement Alternative conceptions of health	*Regulatory Controls* Mandatory health planning Mandatory peer review Rate setting
1983–present	*Health care corporations* Purchasing groups, Specialized health care organizations	*Managerial-market Orientation* Cost-containment Efficiency	*Market building* Selective contracting, Prospective payment

Source: Scott et al. (2000).

care sector, the collegial mode of professional governance is in decline, but health care still largely bears the stamp of professionally dominated governance. Moreover, the market mechanisms have not replaced state control, but rather joined it. Some elements are thus new, but others are merely combinations of elements we knew before. 'The governance structure, logics and actors are altered but many of their components remain recognizable' (Scott et al., 2000, p. 344). The same is true for universities. One example is highlighted by Hedmo and Wedlin, in their research on the Europeanization of higher education of research, where they observe 'more market and more politics' at the same time (see Hedmo & Wedlin, 2008).

Hence, again we can conclude that one of the main challenges for leaders in those reformed sectors is to handle the diverse mix of organizational ideals and the mix of governing modes that rest on this set of ideals. This is true for leaders in health care and it is true for leaders in academia. The framework that Scott and his colleagues developed directs our attention to two models of governing and managing that predated the New Public Management era. Moreover, these models appear to be challenged by more recent governing trends. At least two other governing ideals – administrative and professional – have characterized the health care sector – and the university sector as I will argue below. In a previous study we found similar ideal models when studying changes in the Swedish public sector (Brunsson & Sahlin-Andersson, 2000). In that article we claimed that recent public sector reforms can be understood as an attempt to construct more business-like organizations through measures aimed at strengthening their identity, hierarchy and rationality. In contrast to these recent constructions we claimed that public sector entities were previously more commonly understood as agents or arenas. Agents are formed as instruments for others; thus they do not set their own goals and they have weak identities on their own, but they fulfil the aims that others set. In these kinds of settings the distinction between results in each individual unit are not so clearly distinguished, but a sector as a whole is seen as one bounded entity. This used to be common not only for universities, where many decisions as well as results were identified and summarized at the central governmental level from individual operations and performances throughout the whole university sector. The same logic permeated the health care and the school systems. In this logic, the role of the local management is to follow rules and to fulfil the tasks defined by others, rather than setting its own priorities. The German term *Verwaltung* comes to mind. The administrative era in Scott's table presumes that health care is performed in such entities. As a parallel, the universities rested on such governing ideals in an era of detailed and centralized decision-making and control of higher education. In that model individual organizations are not supposed to strive for their own survival and when individual organizations or individual managers express their own ideals, this is seen rather as distorting governance – as the dysfunction of a well-functioning bureaucracy (cf. Croizer, 1964).

In Sweden – and in the rest of Europe – universities are traditionally, and largely still, seen as agents. They follow the political priorities and the administrative principles set by central government. The call for autonomy, referred to initially, is usually voiced in reaction to what many see as too strong an influence still of this administrative ideal in the governance of universities with a low degree of autonomy as a result.

The third model is also clearly present in the universities of today, but is also challenged by the more recent New Public Management and Audit Society reforms. Traditionally – and especially from the viewpoint of individual researchers and research groups – universities are largely seen as arenas for professional work and professional development. In such a system, local managers have limited control over the work performed. Instead, values, aims and performance criteria develop in the professional arenas that transcend organizational as well as national boundaries. The hiring of professors and the publication of research results are examples of procedures that in most systems rely on peer review rather than on local management decisions. Calls for academic freedom are also expressions of a professionally dominated sector, where managers and politicians should both have limited control. In the professional unit, the individual professional bears a great deal of responsibility for his or her performance.

Similar typologies of ideal types of organizing, managing and governing are also well known in the literature on universities. The three ideal types come close to Clark's (1983) much cited triangle of ideal types of academic authority: market, state authority and academic oligarchy as well as to the one presented in Maassen and Olsen (2006, p. 42).

In my discussion on organizational ideals I choose models based on studies of public sector development because I want to stress, as I have mentioned above, that even if the organizational reforms clearly impact on the university activities and the role of universities in society, the changes in university governance and organization can be explained only to a limited extent by changes in research or education policy. Instead, we can see that organizational reforms, as well as ideals and principles of what constitutes good governance and good management, follow more general societal trends where certain ways of governing and managing appear ideal at certain times. Another reason for basing my presentation about ideal organizing models on Scott rather than on the university-specific models is that I want to stress that organizational ideals emerge as generations, building on each other, but also challenging each other.

Hence, it is not the case that one kind of governance disappears or is abandoned when a new type of governance is introduced. Instead it is rather a question of new ideals and principles being added to the old – they complement and challenge previous principles. That is precisely why it is important for leaders to learn to cope with and act under multiple governance principles. It is, in fact, a very important leadership skill to mix different governance and organizing principles wisely. If new kinds of governance and organizing are merely added to the old, management and organizing easily become too complex and thus virtually incomprehensible.

However, the newly introduced principles tend to be more clearly formulated, while the earlier principles are easily taken for granted: 'that's what we've always done', 'this is what we usually do', and so on. The fact that the new organizational principles tend to be more clearly formulated partly follows from how ideas spread. Moreover, once established in a context, certain organizational ideals easily become institutionalized – taken for granted – and hence it is perhaps not always perceived to be so important to document and explain them. International organizations are important carriers, developers and distributors of new governance ideas and ideals. Other important carriers of such ideas are consultants, organizational researchers, the media and professional networks. All these groups are involved in disseminating, creating and transforming ideas so that they become presentable in appealing, simple and clear ways. When existing or previously dominating governing principles are not described and explained to the same extent, but rather referred to as old habits, there is the risk that they will be considered passé, uninteresting, unimportant and simply not very relevant. This reasoning leads to the conclusion that there may be reason to highlight and formulate those older governing and organizing principles – at least if we are eager to retain them.

We can find support for the arguments above when we read through many recent public acts and investigations, consultants' reports and books on university governance and organization. One gets the impression, when glancing through this rich and diverse mix of publications, that while public reports and consultancy reports write more about the agency ideals and the business organization ideals, collegiality may be mentioned but not much spelled out. Many books written by previous deans, vice-chancellors and presidents, on the other hand, based on their own experiences as university leaders, devote considerable space and thought to professional and collegial systems and to matters of academic freedom and academic duty (a couple of recent examples are Cole [2009] and Sundqvist [2010]).

Universities as professional and collegial arenas

The above observations show that collegiate and professional principles are still fundamental to universities and for their capacity to produce high-quality research and teaching. However, individual leaders often appear to learn about these principles largely through experience when seeking to manage, despite newly introduced systems of governance that are often based on other governing principles. Surprisingly often collegiality is not described in detail but only mentioned in current reports and investigations of university governance and control. This is true, for example, in relation to discussions on quality assurance. In many universities and university systems, new models of quality assurance are imported from the business world (e.g. see Westerheijden et al., 2007). In contrast, one can claim that the academic system as a whole – with peer reviews, seminars and the constant questioning and testing of research results – is a quality system, but this is seldom brought into the picture when new models for quality assurance are being introduced. It is not uncommon, especially among university colleges in Sweden, to introduce quality assurance packages that are taken from the business world, rather than building on collegial models, with peer review and critical scrutiny, that have characterized university systems for decades.

Something similar applies to academic freedom. Now that many countries are in the midst of major change in the regulation of the organization of universities, there is every reason to express clearly the principle of collegiality and academic freedom; the above-cited books by Cole and Sundqvist include excellent discussions on these principles and on their value to higher education and research. There are many who find that collegiality has been undermined in recent years – partly due to the business-inspired reforms and the emphasis on universities' line management and leadership. It is also easy to find texts critical of collegiality and academic freedom. Bo Sundqvist wrote, in the book in which he summarized some of his experiences of his duties as vice-chancellor of Uppsala University, that collegial ways of working are often the target of criticism against the university. Many, he wrote, perhaps primarily outside the academy, seem to suggest that academic freedom and collegial organization stand in the way of effective governance and development. Viewed in the light of the governance eras that I have presented above, this is a typical criticism that comes with management principles as a starting point. In addition, criticism is often levelled against a pillar of collegiate forms of organizing – peer review (e.g. see Lamont, 2009).

The collegiate organizing principle ideally includes a management structure with elected leaders (elected as *primus inter pares*), peer review, on-going and critical seminars and a continuous critical dialogue among academics – all based on the belief that knowledge should be continually tested and reviewed. It is through peer review – and critical dialogue – that high-quality teaching and research can be ensured. To avoid personal conflicts and dependencies, peer review transcends organizational boundaries and thus limits management control within organizations.

I have highlighted three important bases in the collegial work mode: the election of leaders, peer review and the critical dialogue or seminar. Collegiality, I maintain, should therefore be defined as a work process.

Collegiality will not work just because the university's organizational chart is drawn in a certain way. Collegiality is as much a culture of how work should be pursued as it is a structure for planning, decision-making and follow-up.

When writing about university expansion and the associated transition from elite universities to mass universities, Halsey (2004/1992) emphasized that collegiality assumes close relationships among colleagues. Collegiality presupposes, of course, that there are colleagues who can listen and talk to each other. Furthermore, collegiality requires decision-making processes that build on and support the peer review and critical dialogue. This brings the formal organizational design into the picture. Formal organizational bodies such as faculty boards, senates, boards of trustees and so forth – and the composition of them – can support or, if composed largely of non-academics rather than academics, challenge collegiality. Again, for individual leaders it is usually a matter of managing collegiality together with the other logics of management and governance that I have described above.

If we bear in mind that the background and rationale for collegial decision-making and collegial bodies is that scientific knowledge and scientific discourse must be given space, it is also important to keep in mind that the representatives of these bodies represent the scientific community and professional life in general – they are not representatives of special interests. In practice this is of course often confused. In practice many members of such bodies see themselves as representatives of a particular group, not as academic representatives who should draw conclusions from critical discussions regardless of whether 'their own group' benefits or loses. Collegial leadership is, of course, as is the case with all leadership, rarely perfect and it has in many places become subject to criticism. Certainly it is legitimate to criticize and to critically examine peer leaders, but I believe that the criticism frequently spills over onto the principle. If this is the case, if much criticism of individual leaders does in fact spill over into critiquing the organizing and governing principle, it is important that we also let this principle, as such, have a say in the on-going debate on how to manage and organize universities.

The common criticism and questioning of collegiate organizing principles can be further illuminated if we look at the debate and research on the professions. In this research, we find a similar tension, as described above, between, on the one hand, professionals as representatives of the general knowledge and, on the other hand, professionals as guardians of their own group interests. Let me start by summarizing, very briefly, some of the elements of the most common definitions of professionals. Professional work is ideally based on theoretical knowledge. This means that there is education and research within the professional domain. Since professionals base their work on scientific knowledge, their work cannot or should not be controlled in detail. Scientific knowledge provides the basis and guidelines for the way work is conducted. Closely linked to such views, it is often cited, as in Richard Scott's table above (Table 11.1), that professional practice is performed for the public good – directed by a voluntary ethos. This is further supported through ethical codes and professional associations. Legitimacy and professional integrity are further backed with state licensing and authorization. I have given a very brief summary of the classical professional ideals. In contrast, though, critical research on the professions has also largely developed contrasts to these ideals, not least through results showing how professional groups work with closure mechanisms to guard their own interests and status (e.g. Larson, 1977).

The critical research on professionals has also served as a basis for criticism of professional organizations, which in turn has led to more regulations and more management of the kinds displayed in the two lower rows of Table 11.1. Again, we can see parallels with the kind of criticism of collegial organizing principles described above. As in all groups, groupthink and group interests can also prevail in collegial organizations and, in the worst case, collegiality can turn into confrontations of cliques driven to protect their own interests and status. However, if we return to my discussion above on collegiate organization, I would like to conclude that these problems can be caused by too little rather than too much collegiality. The strengthening of collegiality – the election of leaders, peer review, critical dialogue and argumentation – can serve as protection against the problems pointed out above. In other words, the medicine for poorly functioning collegial organizations may not at all be just more business-like management or more regulation, but more collegiality. I do not have the space here to expand this discussion further. However, my brief remarks come close to Cole's (2009) important reasoning around disinterestedness (pp. 62–63) and the threats to this important collegial principle in the university landscape of today (Cole 2009).

Four eras and four management ideals

The role of a university leader is profoundly different depending on the four governing and organization ideals. In the Audit Society I pointed to the importance of reputation management; in New Public Management, internal hierarchical control is strongly emphasized; in the administrative era, a local leader is seen rather as an administrator (or *Verwalter*). In the professional arena, the leader is limiting local control; here he or she is partly an administrator, but primarily the leader is expected to coordinate and follow professionally set priorities and performances rather than follow rules set by higher levels in the hierarchy. In a professional arena then a leader should have the required skills for such coordination of professional work. These, of course, are the common principles behind the ideals of leaders as *primus inter pares* that prevail in professional systems.

The typology that I have discussed here is of course far from unique. As stated above, the diverse ideals of governing higher education and the missions of universities that connect with those diverse ideals have, of course, been much discussed and analysed – in much more sophisticated and deeper ways than I have done here. My motives for bringing them up here – and for doing so based on typologies largely developed outside of universities – are threefold. First, I want to stress that the management principles described above are not primarily based on ideas or discussions on the role and missions of universities, but they have been developed and disseminated in the organizational world as a whole. This is especially true for the last two eras in Table 11.2. This indicates that

Table 11.2   Four institutional eras and four ideal styles of management

Eras	Institutional actors	Institutional logic	Governance structure	Leadership ideal
Professional	Independent professional	Professional authority	Collegiality	*Primus inter pares*
Administrative	Political system	Equity of access	Regulatory controls	Administrator
New Public Management	Corporation	Market and management	Market building	Manager
Audit Society	Students, employers and other 'end users'	Transparency and accountability	Standards, performance measures, guidelines	Reputation management and translator of performance measures

Revised table based on Scott et al. (2000)

in those latter governance eras, general organizing principles need to be adapted and translated when applied to universities. Second, I want to emphasize that governing, organizing and management ideals follow on from each other; they both build on and challenge each other. Thus it is the task – in practice – for individual leaders to mix and blend these ideals into a management model that works. Because I want to focus on individual leaders and how they may cope with change, I have added the fifth column to Table 11.2, in which I summarize the role of the individual leader. And third, I want to make clear that the most recent changes in the university sector – with the expansion of rankings, bibliometrics and assessments – constitute an institutional ideal that both challenges the other ideals and puts additional tasks on university management.

Bounded autonomy: coping with the interplay of multiple organizing principles

In this chapter I have discussed four principles of university governance, organization and management. Even if Table 11.2 gives the impression that the principles are distinct and follow on from each other, I have stressed that it is not the case that one era is followed by the next. Rather, all four principles are institutionalized in the environment and operation of today's universities. This means that a university leader cannot choose whether to follow or ignore such a principle. The demands and expectations of universities are characterized by all four principles. Universities and university leaders are, in other words, subject to multiple and conflicting demands when it comes to governance, organization and management. In the introduction to this chapter I referred to current talk about autonomy in many countries. This can partly be understood as evolving with New Public Management, where the view of universities as organizations – or as actors on a market – has prevailed. Such autonomy may in fact be a kind of autonomy for universities as organizations, as with the Swedish example of deregulation of how universities are to be organized internally. This does not necessarily mean more autonomy for the individual researcher or for research and education as such. Rather, with much dependence on external funding, strengthened top management and the proliferation of assessments and measurements, autonomy is clearly bounded. Audits, assessments and measurements are not chosen by the individual university, but flow both nationally and internationally, so that autonomy is also clearly bounded for the university as a whole. I have referred above to recent developments not only as 'more market' but also as 'more politics'. This topic would require a paper of its own – here I can only state that universities are also clearly politically bounded. Finally, even if each organizational ideal described above stresses certain forms of autonomy – as they are all present in today's university landscape – the various ideals do bound each other.

An important task for leaders of universities is to handle this mixture and interplay of organizing principles in addition to the important task of handling the translation of general principles into a working practice. One obvious way to handle this tension between the principles is to try to play down or disregard one principle at the expense of another or to subordinate some principles to a leading governing and organizing model. We find this in many places where, for example, much more top management control has been introduced, while collegiate principles have been played down. For instance, I am thinking of cases where the system of elected leaders has been abolished or clearly compromised and managers, sometimes with limited experience of the university sector, have been hired. However, we also find that such measures have not been without problems and, even if some of the ideal models described above are disregarded in individual units or individual activities on the whole, it appears to be difficult to completely ignore them.

Another way to deal with conflicting demands, which is clearly identified in organization theory, is to separate or decouple these demands. When university representatives reserve the talk of collegiality to formal rhetoric, but in practice limit management to a hierarchical, sometimes called top-down, management, this is a form of decoupling – between talk and action.[4] Another form of decoupling can occur between different levels of an organization so that top management works according to certain principles, and thus meets certain requirements, while lower levels of the hierarchy are working according to other principles. Specific units can be formed as a way to take care of certain demands in the environment and thus to protect the core business from these pressures (cf. Meyer & Rowan, 1977). One example may be if certain units are formed as a way to take care of rankings, evaluation and assessments while the rest of the university does not deal with these issues. However, such responses to the Audit Society seem to have their limits. For example, with the introduction of performance measurements, the evolving media society and the introduction of performance-based resource allocation, the Audit Society has come to permeate all aspects of universities, so that it appears difficult or even impossible to buffer core operations from these new measures (see Strathern, 2000). Another way of decoupling may be when collegial bodies are formed but are given a very limited mandate. I have argued that collegiality is equally important at all levels. Collegiality is made possible and facilitated by some structural organization solutions, but should be seen primarily as a culture that permeates all activities and processes of the organization.

Decoupling between different demands that follow from partly conflicting principles can also be done between different occupational groups. A traditional distinction is usually made in universities between, on the one hand, the academic organization – supposedly operating primarily along collegiate principles – and, on the other hand, the university administration – working as an administration according to the above-described ideals. There are many reasons to maintain such a clear division of roles, not least to preserve the collegial forms of work. Too much conflation and confusion between these groups and roles may add to ambiguous organization and control. However, it is equally important that these two groups develop in a continuous dialogue, that they interact and have great confidence in each other. Only then can the two groups – and the two governing principles – support, complement and correct each other. We can generalize the picture further. Different groups and different work processes in organizations are usually designed more clearly in accordance with one of the four principles. If we accept this diversity of governing principles and still maintain a dialogue between them, I believe that diversity can lead the different governing principles to serve as correctives and complements to each other.

The various ways of decoupling assume that different requirements and different organizational principles can be separated. The above reasoning, however, indicates that the principles are interwoven in each other and are in part based on each other. With New Public Management, for example, the administrative principles were being reshaped as they were clearly influenced by more business-like ideals of governing and organizing. Corporate ideals and New Public Management have further paved the way for the performance measures, audits and evaluations that shape the Audit Society. Collegiate principles and the Audit Society are also blended and build on each other in practice. For example, bibliometric measures make clear distinctions between peer-reviewed journals and others. Meanwhile, a too-frequent use of standardized measures is sometimes referred to as a reason for cutting down on peer reviews of various kinds. I have mentioned a few examples, demonstrating the possibilities but also the limitations of decoupling strategies, and I have emphasized the importance of balancing and blending the various principles in a sensible way. Further studies of how such a mixing of demands is carried out in different contexts and in different places should give us a better understanding of the role of university leaders in a complex and turbulent environment.

The conflicting demands do not reach the university with the same force. When the university landscape has come to be characterized by more market and more politics, these build on but also emphasize further the business management and political administrative models. To these must be added the evolving Audit Society with its many measurements, audits and evaluations. The elaborate formal organizational structures of universities and the many new organizational units such as communication departments, technology transfer offices, ranking committees and risk management groups are all responses to the enhanced emphasis on management, politics and the Audit Society. They are shaped as reflections of an institutional line of thinking and thus add strength to these governing models. The collegial model is challenged and is easily left behind. This, I have tried to argue, largely has to do with the fact that principles of collegial processes tend not to be so clearly expressed. They are sometimes seen as obvious, since they are institutionalized, and they are sometimes criticized for being outmoded and not working according to the ideals. I have devoted much space in this chapter to discussing collegiality and I have tried to make clear that collegiality is essential for universities in order for them to meet their basic missions of high-quality research and education and to fully contribute to society with the generation and critical review of such knowledge. With this as a background I have argued for the importance of keeping the discussion and development of collegial models alive. Only then can we see that some of the problems attached to collegial models of leading and organizing may be a sign of the fact that universities may be characterized by too little, rather than too much, collegiality.

In the previous section, I discussed decoupling practices as a way to cope with the diverse mix of organizing principles of universities, but I also pointed to the limitations of such decoupling strategies. Another way to manage the interplay of organizational ideals is to translate the diverse demands into a common working practice. With the developments outlined above, the organizational design of universities has come into focus to a much larger extent than before. This has meant a focus on internal hierarchy, organizational boundaries and organizational identity (Brunsson & Sahlin-Andersson, 2000). It has also meant that universities are not seen as unique, but as variants of a larger group of units – named organizations. I have stressed that the management principles described above are not primarily based on ideas or discussions on the role and missions of universities specifically but have been developed and disseminated in the organizational world as a whole. This is especially true for the two latter eras in the table above. In arguing for the importance of acknowledging the uniqueness of higher education, Burton Clark wrote

> It does not make much sense to evaluate business firms according to how much they act like universities, nor economic systems according to their resemblance to higher education systems. Neither does it make any sense to do the reverse; yet it is built into current common-sense and management theory that we do so. [...] The 'imagery of "organization" and "system" ', the very terms themselves, lead us to expect simplicity – simplicity that must be there if we are only intelligent enough. But if the higher education system was ever simple, it will not be again. We are looking at an inordinate and uncommon complexity.
>
> (1983, pp. 275–276)

One conclusion to draw from this insightful reasoning is that in the latter governance eras, the general organizing principles needed to be adapted and translated when applied to universities and, further, such translation most likely involves a complication of those generalized organizing principles. In the Audit Society, translation needs to go in the other direction too. Specific operations and results need to be translated so that they can be assessed by widely used assessment criteria. An important task for managers is to make the operations 'auditable'.

I would like to end by pointing to a few challenges for university leaders in this important editing practice. First, there may be a temptation for leaders to apply just widespread success criteria. I provided one example of this initially – the formulated aim among universities to climb the rankings. In contrast, I would claim that a university leader cannot simply apply the often generalized and simplified measures of bibliometrics and rankings as their own success criteria. This again points to the importance of supporting critical discussions internally, in other words to support such internal and external reviews – and active seminars – that are core aspects of collegiality. In times when research is largely financed and assessed as projects, one may need to take special action in order to protect and/or support novel research with 'long term perspective'. This may need special translation both of the measures applied and of the activities to be measured.

Second, I noted above that the Audit Society has been shown to be driven by and to drive distrust. A main task for university leaders – in the Audit Society – then is to build trust in universities and in university systems, even in the basic idea of what universities are and what universities are for. I noted above that the Audit Society requires that leaders engage in reputation management. However, the building of trust goes beyond the individual leader and the individual university. To be effective, such reputation management needs a base and a context of trust in the needs and missions of universities in society more generally. This points to the urgent need for much research on research, on reforms of university systems and on the role of universities.

Notes

1. This section is based in part on Wedlin et al. (2009).
2. In previous work I have used this framework to analyse the fundamental changes in management and governance of Swedish health care (see Blomgren & Sahlin, 2007). The description of Scott et al.'s framework is based on Blomgren and Sahlin.
3. This view of fashion as superficial can itself be seen as superficial, however. Much research has shown that fashion is much more fundamental and pervasive. Fashion is a basic social process. See, for example, Czarniawska (2005).
4. In several publications Nils Brunsson has developed models, analyses and understandings of such decoupling between talk and action. See, for example, Brunsson (1989).

References

Blomgren, M. and K. Sahlin (2007) 'Quests for Transparency: Signs of a New Institutional Era in the Health Care Field', in T. Christensen and P. Laegreid (eds) *Transcending New Public Management*, Aldershot: Ashgate, pp. 155–177.

Brunsson, N. (1989) *The Organization of Hypocrisy: Talk, Decisions and Actions in Organizations*, Chichester: Wiley.

Brunsson, N. and K. Sahlin-Andersson (2000) 'Constructing Organizations: The Example of Public Sector Reform', *Organization Studies*, 21(4), 721–746.

Clark, B. R. (1983) *The Higher Education System. Academic Organization in Cross-National Perspective*, Berkeley: University of California Press.

Cole, J. R. (2009) *The Great American University: Its Rise to Preeminence, Its Indispensable National Role, Why It Must Be Protected*, New York: Public Affairs.

Croizer, M. (1964) *The Bureaucratic Phenomenon*, Chicago: University of Chicago Press.

Czarniawska, B. (2005) 'Fashion in Organizing', in B. Czarniawska, Barbara and G. Sevón (eds) *Global Ideas. How Ideas, Objects and Practices Travel in the Global Economy*, Malmö: Liber and Copenhagen Business School Press, pp. 129–146.

Estermann, T. and T. Nokkala (2009) *University Autonomy in Europe – Exploratory Study*, Brussels: European University Association.

Halsey, A. H. (2004/1992) *Decline of Donnish Dominion: The British Academic Professions in the Twentieth Century*, Oxford: Oxford University Press.

Hedmo, T. and L. Wedlin (2008) 'New Modes of Governance: The Re-Regulation of European Higher Education and Research', in C. Mazza, P. Quattrone and A. Riccaboni (eds) *European Universities in Transition: Issues, Models and Cases*, Cheltenham: Edward Elgar, pp. 113–132.

Hood, C. (1991) 'A Public Management for All Seasons?', *Public Administration*, 69(Spring), 3–19.

Hood, C. (1995) 'The New Public Management in the 1980s. Variations on a Theme', *Accounting, Organization and Society*, 20(2–3), 93–109.

Hood, C., C. Scott, O. James, G. Jones and T. Travers (1999) *Regulation Inside Government*, Oxford: Oxford University Press.

Lamont, M. (2009) *How Professors Think: Inside the Curious World of Academic Judgment*, Cambridge: Harvard University Press.

Larson, M. S. (1977) *The Rise of Professionalism: A Sociological Analysis*, Los Angeles: Univ. of California Press.

Maassen, P. and J. P. Olsen (eds) (2006) *University Dynamics and European Integration*, Berlin: Springer.

Meyer, J. W. and B. Rowan (1977) 'Institutionalized Organizations: Formal Structure as Myth and Ceremony', *American Journal of Sociology*, 83(2), 340–363.

Miller, P. (1994) 'Accounting as a Social and Institutional Practice: An Introduction', in A. G. Hopwood and P. Miller (eds) *Accounting as a Social and Institutional Practice*, Cambridge: Cambridge University Press, pp. 1–39.

Moran, M. (2002) 'Understanding the Regulatory State', *British Journal of Political Science*, 32, 391–413.

Power, M. (1997) *The Audit Society: Rituals of Verification*, Oxford: Oxford University Press.

Power, M. (2003) 'Evaluating the Audit Explosion', *Law & Policy*, 25(3), 115–202.

Power, M., T. Scheytt, K. Soin and K. Sahlin (2009) 'Reputational Risk as a Logic of Organizing in Late Modernity', *Organization Studies*, 30(02&03), 165–188.

Sahlin-Andersson, K. (2001) 'National, International and Transnational Constructions of New Public Management', in T. Christensen and P. Laegreid (eds) *New Public Management: The Transformation of Ideas and Practice*, Aldershot: Ashgate, pp. 43–72.

Scott, W. R., M. Ruef, P. Mendel and C. Caronna (2000) *Institutional Change and Healthcare Organizations*, Chicago: University of Chicago Press.

Shore, C. and S. Wright (2000) 'Coercive Accountability. The Rise of Audit Culture in Higher Education', in M. Strathern (ed.) *Audit Cultures: Anthropological Studies in Accountability, Ethics and the Academy*, London: Routledge, pp. 57–89.

Stensaker, B. and L. Harvey (eds) (2010) *Accountability in Higher Education: Global Perspectives on Trust and Power*, London: Routledge.

Strathern, M. (2000) *Audit Cultures: Anthropological Studies in Accountability, Ethics and the Academy*, London: Routledge.

Sundqvist, B. (2010) *Svenska universitet: Lärdomsborgar eller politiska instrument?*, Stockholm: Gidlunds.

Wedlin, L., K. Sahlin and T. Hedmo (2009) 'The Ranking Explosion and the Formation of a Global Governing Field of Universities', in L. Wedlin, K. Sahlin and M. Grafström (eds) *Exploring the Worlds of Mercury and Minerva. Essays for Lars Engwall*, Uppsala: Acta Universitatis Upsaliensis. Studia Oeconomiae Negotiorum, 51, pp. 317–334.

Westerheijden, D. F., B. Stensaker and M. J. Rosa (eds) (2007) *Quality Assurance in Higher Education: Trends in Regulation, Translation and Transformation*, Berlin: Springer.

12
The Management of Academic Culture Revisited: Integrating Universities in an Entrepreneurial Age

David D. Dill

Introduction

Some 30 years ago I published a paper, 'The Management of Academic Culture: Notes on the Management of Meaning and Social Integration' (Dill, 1982a), which has been frequently cited in the subsequent higher education literature addressing the concept of 'organizational culture'. Like other early contributions to the general literature on organizational culture, my paper was inspired in part by growing knowledge at that time about management processes in Japanese industries, which placed an emphasis on increasing worker interdependence and on developing a special organizational identity or culture as a means of enhancing worker loyalty and productivity. My paper also reflected a distinctive line of research on 'academic culture' then emerging within the field of higher education through the contributions primarily of Burton Clark (1970, 1972, 1983) and Tony Becher (1981, 1984, 1987, 1989, 1994) as well as my personal experiences with the symbols and ceremonies of the University of North Carolina at Chapel Hill, the US's oldest public university. In this chapter I would like to revisit the concept of academic culture as I defined it, further clarifying what I meant by this term as well as relating the concept to more recent theory, research and the contemporary challenges of universities.

Modes of culture in higher education

In the years since I wrote my paper research on organizational culture, as suggested by the two most recent comprehensive reviews of the topic (Ashkanasy et al., 2000; Cooper et al., 2001), has become much more diverse, with significant differences among researchers as to the definition of the concept and appropriate levels of analysis as well as contentious debates over the legitimacy of relevant research paradigms. Studies of organizational culture in higher education have experienced a similar evolution (Välimaa, 1998). To provide an interpretive context for discussing my earlier contribution to the topic, I briefly review the related literature in higher education employing Clark's much cited categorization of the role of 'belief' in academic life (Clark, 1983). After first suggesting the importance of the symbolic side of higher education and arguing for greater emphasis on the normative dimension and its impacts on academic behaviour in future research, Clark outlined three levels of culture in higher education: the culture of the discipline, the culture of the enterprise (in other words, organizational culture) and the culture of the academic profession and/or national system.

Of these three the concept of a shared culture of beliefs among the members of the academic profession in a particular national system has received less attention in subsequent research. Clark (1983) himself provided an important example of this concept with his description of the national influence of the shared belief in academic freedom as articulated by the American Association of University Professors (AAUP) when it was founded after the First World War.[1] Over many decades, through the public identification and celebration of professorial 'martyrs' to academic freedom (in other words, dismissed faculty members), through rigorous, objective evaluations of the circumstances surrounding each supposed transgression of academic freedom (in other words, a 'ceremony' or 'ritual'), and through the 'black-listing' of universities that violated its beliefs (i.e. the sanctioning non-believers), the AAUP significantly reshaped the framework conditions of universities in the USA. Eventually the boards of control of all major public and private universities formally adopted the AAUP's beliefs as a basis for institutional policy. More recently the important role played historically by academic beliefs in other national systems in shaping 'academic identity' has been exposed by the implementation of major policy reforms in a number of countries (Henkel, 2000). For example, in the UK and other 'Westminster' systems of higher education, the extent to which academic identity was shaped by collective academic beliefs in the required autonomy of publicly financed universities and in a necessary 'gold standard' of university performance has been dramatically revealed by national reforms influenced by a different set of beliefs derived from the new institutional economics (Dill & van Vught, 2010).

One very valuable contribution to the limited research on the culture of the academic profession is the national survey of college and university faculty members in the USA regarding ethical beliefs about teaching by Braxton and Bayer (1999).[2] Their study discovered that the strength of professional norms with regard to responsibilities for teaching, advising and grading, obligations for the planning and design of courses, and commitments for the governance of the department and university are weakest among faculty members in US research universities. They also studied differences in disciplinary cultures and noted that there was greater agreement on ethical standards for teaching and their enforcement in more paradigmatic fields such as the sciences than in the social sciences and humanities. These observed differences in professional norms across disciplines have not received the scholarly attention they deserve. The intriguing approach to the study of academic culture by Braxton and Bayer (1999) is certainly worthy of replication in other countries.

The larger body of research on culture in higher education has been on the topics that Clark termed the culture of the enterprise (or organizational culture) and the culture of the disciplines. While there were progenitors, arguably Clark's (1970, 1972) own study of the organizational 'sagas' of distinctive American liberal arts colleges was the defining contribution to the concept of organizational culture in the social sciences.[3] In this study Clark examined the evolution of several well-regarded liberal arts colleges in the USA. He discovered that their reputation was achieved in part because each developed over time a unique saga or story of triumph over challenging circumstances, an integrated self-belief in a history of hard work and struggle leading to uncommon achievement. Anticipating the focus of organizational culture research that followed, Clark's study examined the nature and impacts of the social context of organizational life: the role played by language, symbols, ceremonies and institutional legends as well as the influence a shared set of beliefs had on the loyalty, commitment and effort of organizational members. Clark also identified some of the critical variables affecting the strength of organizational culture: institutional size, complexity and control. For example, symbolic bonding may be more significant in small, liberal arts colleges than in large research universities, in private institutions that must compete for their own funds than in public institutions with more predictable sources of financial support and so on. Finally, while Clark examined in his study the influence of founders and administrators on the development of a saga, his perception of the role of human agency in the development of an organizational culture was clearly more collective and collegial than managerial.

The research that followed Clark's contribution, both in the field of higher education and in the social sciences more generally, focused to a much greater extent on the role of administrators and managers in organizational culture. With regard to colleges and universities these studies included analyses of how the specific behaviours of institutional leaders may help embed or transmit organizational culture (Tierney, 1988) and how strategies, practices and processes characteristic of the general management literature may influence organizational culture and adaptation in higher education (Sporn, 1996; Kezar & Eckel, 2002; Bartell, 2003; de Zilwa, 2007). In a review of much of the recent research on organizational culture in higher education Silver (2003), echoing a number of the constraints Clark identified in his early research on organizational sagas (see above), concluded that '(u)niversities do not now have an organizational culture' (Silver, 2003, p. 167). While Silver believed there was evidence to support the view that the academic disciplines were an influential source of belief, professional identity and loyalty, he argued that attempting to amalgamate these sub-cultures into a common institutional identity was impossible and ignored the reality of the value conflicts and lack of coherence that characterized contemporary universities.

As Silver noted, the culture of the disciplines has been the most studied and affirmed component of Clark's cultural typology. The early research by Biglan (1973a, 1973b) provided empirical support for the influence of disciplinary structures on many aspects of academic behaviour including: the amount of social connectedness within disciplines; the degree of commitment to teaching, research and public service; the quantity and type of publishing; and the number of dissertations sponsored. Biglan's disciplinary classification has been validated in numerous subsequent studies and is primarily responsible for the inclusion of academic discipline as an important control variable in studies of higher education.[4] In a related series of studies Becher (1981, 1984, 1987, 1989) expanded the previous research on the academic disciplines to focus on the influence of the social and cultural aspects of subject fields. Becher's research helped to emphasize the normative aspects of academic behaviour, the means by which the values and beliefs guiding appropriate and inappropriate professional behaviour are communicated and enforced in subject fields (Braxton, 1986, 2010). Becher emphasized that the shared way of thinking and collective manner of behaving that makes it possible to integrate the teaching and research activities of largely autonomous academics is significantly shaped by social interactions within each discipline such as the recruitment and initiation of academic staff.

Given this brief review of the related literature as background, let me now revisit my original paper to clarify its contribution to the field.

Managing academic culture

In my original article, consistent with the research reviewed above, I focused on the normative aspects of academic institutions. I argued that since universities were value-based organizations (Long, 1992), they needed to actively manage their academic culture and that this involved two interrelated and significant mechanisms of coordination and control in professional organizations: the management of meaning and the management of social integration.

My emphasis on coordination and control through norms and values was informed by traditional sociological perspectives on professional organizations including universities. From this perspective the complexity of tasks in universities requires that the academic staff, as in other professional organizations, be granted a substantial amount of individual autonomy in teaching and research in order to function effectively. Traditional hierarchical methods of coordination and control are therefore ineffective in professional settings and the necessary integration of autonomous professionals must be achieved instead primarily through socialization to common norms and values. For example, in applying his model of the 'professional bureaucracy' to universities, Mintzberg (1979) similarly argued that long years of educational training supplied future faculty members with the standardized skills and knowledge characteristic of their particular subject. Their approach to teaching, to their subject content and to their research was therefore influenced by these ingrained norms. As a consequence, faculty members could teach individually and independently because the professor lecturing on physics to engineering students could successfully predict what the professor lecturing on calculus to the same students was covering. The norms of professional socialization thereby permitted faculty members to effectively coordinate their teaching and research while working in a largely autonomous fashion. In a related study Hage (1974) provided important insights into the role on-going communication plays with organizational peers in further socializing professionals to necessary values and norms. He argued that this communication is not vertical, as with administrators, not primarily written, as in reports and procedural documents, and not episodic. Rather, the communication is horizontal, with respected peers, largely verbal and face-to-face, continuous and focuses on the exchange of information about means of improving core professional tasks.

My concept of the management of academic culture therefore had similarities and dissimilarities with the literature that followed. It was similar in that I drew attention to the need for universities to attend to the language, symbols and ceremonies that help clarify and give meaning to academic work. Obvious examples included the communal designation of outstanding teachers and researchers (i.e. what I termed 'the canonization of exemplars') as well as ceremonies that demonstrate and reinforce the values essential to the academic craft, such as public PhD defences and Festschrift celebrations. My concept of academic culture was also similar to the studies of organizational culture and the culture of the disciplines in its analysis of the culture within universities. It was particularly similar to Becher's approach to the culture of the disciplines in that I emphasized, as noted above, the need to achieve social integration within universities by attending to mechanisms of collegial communication and control that help socialize faculty members to the values essential to academic work.

However, my concept of managing academic culture differed from the literature on the culture of the disciplines in that I addressed mechanisms of socialization that influenced the values of all or most members of the academic staff, not just socialization processes within a particular subject field. My concept also differed from most of the organizational culture research on higher education that followed in that I focused less on the actions of university administrators or the processes of academic management and more, as suggested by Hage (1974), on the language and symbols expressed by peers and on the collectively organized socialization mechanisms of the university that influence the core activities of teaching, scholarship and research.

There are a number of collective mechanisms in the disciplines by which the norms or values that guide appropriate and inappropriate behaviour in teaching, scholarship and research are communicated and controlled. These include collegial processes for the selection of academic staff, peer observations of teaching, peer review of research proposals, peer review of scholarship and research submitted for publication, and ultimately peer decisions on promotion and tenure in subject fields. In line with Silver's (2003) challenge to the existence of a unifying university culture, it may be fairly asked whether it is meaningful in the modern university to assume that there are also broadly shared values on teaching and research that can be communicated and controlled through the collective actions of academics themselves. In my original paper I proposed a hypothetical response to this question by recommending the creation of 'guilds' of outstanding teachers to define and preserve the values essential to teaching. That is, while most universities attempt to manage the meaning of good teaching by identifying and celebrating outstanding individuals who embody the values necessary for good teaching ('the canonization of exemplars'), these universities had as of the time I wrote my original paper failed to manage the social integration of these values by developing appropriate means for communicating and embedding these norms among all members of the academic staff. Creating a guild-like mechanism composed of these 'sanctified' teachers and awarding to this group responsibility for socializing other members of the academic staff to the values essential to good teaching could, I suggested, be one means of achieving the necessary integration. Since I published my paper a number of US universities have in fact created such collegial bodies with institution-wide responsibilities for fostering good teaching. At the University of North Carolina at Chapel Hill, for example, following the recommendations of a faculty task force, an Academy of Distinguished Teaching Scholars was created.[5] The Academy's mission is to 'promote excellence in teaching through short-term and long-term educational and scholarly initiatives, [provide] advocacy and support for teaching, [and develop] financial resources to encourage teaching excellence.'[6] The members of the Academy are drawn from those individuals on the academic staffs who have won one of the university's distinguished teacher awards.

A more definitive example of the articulation and enforcement of shared academic values in modern universities, that illustrates my conception of the management of social integration, is the creation of collective processes for communicating and controlling the norms necessary to protect human subjects in academic research (King et al., 1999). In recognition of atrocities perpetrated by medical researchers under the Nazi and Imperial Japanese regimes during the Second World War, as well as inhumane research studies conducted by academic researchers in the USA and other countries, many professional societies have developed norms and ethical guidelines for the protection of human subjects in academic research. Partially from the influence of members of the academic profession who share these values (cf. Clarks' conception of the culture of the academic profession) and partially from the influence of government agencies that fund research involving human subjects, contemporary universities in a number of countries have created collective mechanisms (e.g. in the USA so-called Institutional Review Boards [IRBs]) to communicate and embed ethical norms (in other words, values) guiding behaviour in research with human subjects. These processes often involve attempts to socialize all relevant academic staff to these guidelines through workshops and research manuals, as well as collegial mechanisms for enforcing these values through peer reviews of research protocols and proposals. The focus of these processes on the communication and control of broadly shared academic values is clearly indicated by the scope of the processes, involving not only researchers in the medical and biological sciences, but also some experimental studies involving human subjects in the social sciences as well as some interview- and observation-based studies on sensitive issues in the social sciences and humanities. The extent to which these collective processes actively manage and reshape existing norms of research and scholarship is evident in the sometimes sharp debates among university faculty members over perceived conflicts between the value of protecting human subjects and the core academic values of freedom of inquiry and the unfettered pursuit of the truth.

There is also contemporary evidence of attempts to manage the symbolic side of universities – what I termed the management of meaning. The emergence of a global rivalry among academic institutions and of a related market competition among universities for outstanding researchers, able students and funds from all sources has created strong incentives for university administrators to try to sharpen or clarify an institution's identity, reputation or 'brand' (Toma et al., 2005). This is obvious in institutional self-designations as 'world class', 'entrepreneurial' or 'international', as well as in the ubiquitous emphasis on university logos or mottos. Much of this emphasis on language and symbols reflects efforts at external marketing rather than the nurturance of an organizational saga (cf. Clark, 1972) that develops loyalty and commitment among university members. Nor does the current emphasis on university 'branding' address my conception of an academic culture that defines, communicates and helps embed the values essential to effective teaching, scholarship and research within universities.

In contrast, changes in the framework conditions of universities suggest that the management of social integration may be of greater importance now than when I first wrote. The rapid expansion and fragmentation of academic knowledge has lessened prior agreement on academic norms, standards and content at the subject level.[7] Disciplinary cultures now appear to play a lesser role in the coordination and control of academic behaviour (Becher & Trowler, 2001). Achieving integration at the subject level is made even more challenging by the development of new multidisciplinary and interdisciplinary subjects. Designing and teaching academic programmes that provide effective student learning in these fields necessarily requires even greater coordination than in traditional disciplines, but ironically existing disciplinary norms frequently act as a brake on cooperation in multidisciplinary subjects. At the same time university reforms in many countries are creating a more 'corporate' university, in which the individual institution will have greater control over the development and approval of its academic programmes, the appointment and promotion of academic staff, and the management of research (Dill & van Vught, 2010). Therefore the need to develop collective processes for managing academic culture in the contemporary university – understood as the communication and control of the values and norms affecting teaching and research – has likely become even more significant.

Managing social integration in the contemporary university: the case of academic quality

One clear contemporary instance of the management of social integration, in the terms I have described it, is the development within many universities of new collective mechanisms for assuring quality in academic programmes (Dill, 2007; Dill & Beerkens, 2010). Attempting to develop a stronger culture in support of effective teaching, student learning and the assurance of academic standards provides a good example of the problems associated with communicating and controlling the essential values to guide academic behaviour. With the declining influence of disciplinary cultures, universities themselves must find more effective means of promoting integration within academic programmes. It is after all at the subject level that academic quality is demonstrably assured and improved. Along these lines a series of studies on successful self-governing organizations by the Nobel Prize–winning political economist Eleanor Ostrom (Ostrom, 1990, 1998, 2000; Ostrom & Walker, 1997) provides additional support for the ideas already outlined regarding the design of mechanisms for promoting social integration within universities.

An example of a collective mechanism for transmitting and embedding essential values is the process developed in a number of universities for addressing marking standards. Grade inflation, or more accurately grade compression in which few low marks are awarded to students in a subject, is receiving increasing attention in many universities (Yorke,

2008). With the adoption of modular instruction and continuous assessment, the traditional discipline-based process of external examining employed in a number of countries has become less reliable as a means of assuring equity of marking standards within as well as across subject fields (Lewis, 2010). In addition, the wide spread implementation of student surveys and of department funding based upon student enrolment and/or graduation rates increases the incentives for academic staff to be more generous in their marking standards.

A number of universities have therefore taken collective action to address the grade inflation issue. At one university I have visited the faculty senate created a standing committee to develop and implement university-wide marking standards. The committee defined and published general grade distribution guidelines for the university as a whole and monitored departmental grade distributions for each term. Members of the committee met with departments, which varied significantly from the grading guidelines, and asked them to provide supporting arguments and evidence for the observed exceptions. While the committee actively pursued fairness in grading across units, it was equally concerned with promoting the value of educationally defensible grading policies within each academic programme.

A second example of an effective collective mechanism for assuring academic quality was implemented, ironically, in one of the most research-intensive institutions I have ever visited. Within this university the academic quality assurance process was not in the hands of administrators, but the responsibility of a committee of faculty members elected from across the university, who were respected researchers and scholars committed to assuring academic standards. It was this committee, not an administrative office, which was actively pressing each department to demonstrate the effectiveness of its processes for improving teaching and student learning. The committee required initial reports from each department on its quality assurance processes, but followed up these reports with meetings with the members of each department to provide criticism and suggest needed improvements. This committee was a formal standing committee of the university, an integral part of the university governance process, with close linkages to the academic deans.

The design and conduct of these collective processes of quality assurance illustrate a number of the points I have suggested about the management of social integration in universities. First and obviously, these processes were designed and carried out by academics themselves (Ostrom, 2000). They are core processes of each university's academic governance system, not temporary task forces or procedures delegated to administrative offices or staff members. Second, monitoring is applied to all academic units and addresses factors known to affect student learning – grading standards and collective processes for assuring academic quality. Research suggests that a social norm of cooperation is most likely to evolve in an organization when its members believe that rules will produce collective benefits and when monitoring is fairly and systematically applied to all, that is 'free riders' will not be rewarded (Ostrom, 1998). Third, the processes included written reports, but the committees avoided the danger of empty 'proceduralism' by emphasizing collective discussions. Thus the committees met face to face with the members of each academic unit as a means of reinforcing collective norms, changing expectations and fostering group identity. Through this direct communication there is also the greater possibility of disseminating information on means for improving core academic processes including the transfer of best practices developed in other academic units of the university.[8] Both laboratory and field research suggests that face-to-face communication in social dilemmas is the most effective means of producing substantial increases in cooperation over time (Ostrom & Walker, 1997).[9]

At the same time, as noted in the earlier discussion about the norms governing research on human subjects, collective debates about core academic values are unlikely to proceed smoothly or without rancour. Discussions about the definition of academic quality, about the specification of student outcomes and about essential academic responsibilities in teaching will necessarily engage legitimate professorial concerns regarding academic freedom, intellectual autonomy and managerial control. The degree to which these types of issues are under discussion and vitally debated within universities may be the best measure of the extent to which necessary social integration is being effectively engaged within modern universities.

Conclusion

As Burton Clark (1983) made clear, universities are 'culturally loaded' organizations, in which values such as objectivity, academic freedom and respect for students and human subjects guide academic behaviour and are therefore reflected in the language, symbols and ceremonies of academic life. In recent decades the emergence of a more competitive international market among universities has been interpreted as threatening core academic values (Teixeira et al., 2004) and the symbolic life of universities now appears to be more focused externally on marketing the institution than internally on clarifying and embedding the values necessary to sustain the integrity of academic work. In the new world of the corporate university, where many institutions are being accorded greater autonomy over their internal affairs, the successful management of academic culture may well determine whether the university fully meets its responsibilities to society. As I have tried to suggest, this will involve strengthening the collective processes by which the academic members of the university communicate and enforce the norms and values essential to teaching and research.

Notes

1. See also Dill (1982b).
2. See also my more recent analysis of academic ethics (Dill, 2005).
3. However, though Clark's (1972) study was based on systematic field research and appeared in the premier journal of organizational theory of the time (i.e. *The Administrative Science Quarterly*), outside of the field of higher education the significant contribution Clark made to the concept of organizational culture appears to have been lost. For example, none of the papers written by leading researchers in the field that appear in the two most recent collections on organizational culture (Ashkanasy et al., 2000; Cooper et al., 2001) cite Clark's article. A number of years ago I once quipped, when given the privilege of introducing Bob Clark to a professional audience, that because of his rich vocabulary he may be passed over as the 'father' of the concept of organizational culture, because he chose to use the more evocative term 'saga' rather than the more pedestrian term 'culture' to describe his concept. Sadly, perhaps because of the current influence of digital search systems, this comment appears to have come true.
4. For a very thorough and informative review of the research on academic disciplines, including the studies verifying Biglan's (1973a, 1973b) classification, see Alise (2007). Lodahl and Gordon's (1972) related research suggesting the influence on academic behaviour of the level of consensus about theory, methodology, techniques and problems within a scientific field was published before Biglan's work and offered a rival framework. But following Cole's (1983) systematic study questioning the validity of disciplinary consensus as a measure of significance, empirical research on disciplinary variation no longer includes consensus as an independent variable.
5. The actions taken to form this Academy, and similar actions taken at other US universities, were motivated to the best of my knowledge by collegial concerns and values, and were not inspired by anything I said or wrote!
6. See http://www.unc.edu/depts/adts/index.html
7. Commenting on the contribution that increased specialization makes to disciplinary fragmentation, Clark (1996) observed

> In mathematics, 200,000 new theorems are published each year, periodicals exceed 1000, and review journals have developed a classification

scheme that includes over 4500 subtopics arranged under 62 major topic areas. In history, the output of literature in the two decades of 1960–1980 was apparently equal in magnitude to all that was published from the time of the Greek historian Thucydides in the fourth century B.C. to the year 1960. In psychology, 45 major specialties appear in the structure of the American Psychological Association, and one of these specialties, social psychology, reports that it is now comprised of 17 subfields. [...] In the mid-1990s, those who track the field of chemistry were reporting that 'more articles on chemistry have been published in the past 2 years than throughout history before 1900.' *Chemical Abstracts* took 31 years to publish its first million abstracts, 18 years for its second million, and less than 2 years for its most recent million. An exponential growth of about 4 to 8 per cent annually, with a doubling period of 10 to 15 years, is now seen as characteristic of most branches of science. (pp. 421–422)

8. Research on 'learning organizations' – that is, organizations skilled at creating, acquiring and transferring knowledge, as well as adapting their behaviour to reflect new knowledge – has identified a number of activities that are necessary conditions (Dill, 1999). The identified activity least in evidence in a study of contemporary universities was a process or structure encouraging the transfer between programmes of implemented innovations for improving teaching and student learning.
9. In their study of academic ethics, Braxton and Bayer (1999) also argued that effective deterrence and detection of proscribed academic behaviour is more likely to occur in departments that have frequent social contact. Departmental meetings, face-to-face informal interactions and performance reviews related to teaching and student learning provide the social ties necessary for the communication, observation and enforcement of ethical standards.

References

Alise, M. A. (2007) *Disciplinary Differences In Preferred Research Methods: A Comparison of Groups in The Biglan Classification Scheme.* PhD diss., Louisiana State University and Agricultural and Mechanical College: http://etd.lsu.edu/docs/available/etd-02222008-085519/unrestricted/alisediss.pdf
Ashkanasy, N., C. Wilderom and M. Peterson (2000) *The Handbook of Organizational Culture and Climate*, Thousand Oaks, CA: Sage.
Bartell, M. (2003) 'Internationalization of Universities: A University Culture-Based Framework', *Higher Education*, XLV, 43–70.
Becher, T. (1981) 'Towards a Definition of Disciplinary Cultures', *Studies in Higher Education*, VI, 109–122.
Becher, T. (1984) 'The Cultural View'. In B. R. Clark (Ed.), *Perspectives on Higher Education: Eight Disciplinary and Comparative Views*, Berkeley, CA: University of California Press, pp. 165–198.
Becher, T. (1987) 'The Disciplinary Shaping of the Profession'. In B. R. Clark (Ed.), *The Academic Profession: National, Disciplinary and Institutional Settings*, Berkeley, CA: University of California Press, pp. 271–303.

Becher, T. (1989) *Academic Tribes and Territories: Intellectual Enquiry and the Cultures of Disciplines*, Milton Keynes, England: Open University Press.

Becher, T. (1994) 'The Significance of Disciplinary Differences', *Studies in Higher Education*, XIX, 151–161.

Becher, T. and Trowler, P. R. (2001) *Academic Tribes and Territories: Intellectual Inquiry and the Culture of Disciplines* (2nd edn.), Buckingham, England: Open University Press.

Biglan, A. (1973a) 'The Characteristics of Subject Matter in Different Academic Areas', *Journal of Applied Psychology*, LVII, 195–203.

Biglan, A. (1973b) 'Relationships between Subject Matter Characteristics and the Structure and Output of University Departments', *Journal of Applied Psychology*, LVII, 204–213.

Braxton, J. M. (1986) 'The Normative Structure of Science: Social Control in the Academic Profession'. In John C. Smart (Ed.), *Higher Education: Handbook of Theory and Research* (Vol. 2), New York: Agathon Press, pp. 309–357.

Braxton, J. M. (2010) 'The Criticality of Norms to the Functional Imperatives of the Social Action System of College and University Work', *The Journal of Higher Education*, LXXXI, 416–429.

Braxton, J. M. and Bayer, A. E. (1999) *Faculty Misconduct in Collegiate Teaching*, Baltimore: Johns Hopkins University Press.

Clark, B. R. (1970) *The Distinctive College: Antioch, Reed & Swarthmore*, Chicago, Aldine Publishing Company.

Clark, B. R. (1972) 'The Organizational Saga in Higher Education', *Administrative Science Quarterly*, XVII, 178–184.

Clark, B. R. (1983) *The Higher Education System: Academic Organization in Cross-National Perspective*, Berkeley, CA: University of California Press.

Clark, B. R. (1996) 'Substantive Growth and Innovative Organization: New Categories for Higher Education Research', *Higher Education*, XXXII, 417–430.

Cole, S. (1983) 'The Hierarchy of the Sciences?', *The American Journal of Sociology*, LXXXIX, 111–139.

Cooper, C. L., S. Cartwright and R. C. Earley (2001) *The International Handbook of Organizational Culture and Climate*, New York: Wiley.

de Zilwa, D. K. (2007) 'Organisational Culture and Values and the Adaptation of Academic Units in Australian Universities', *Higher Education*, LIV, 557–574.

Dill, D. D. (1982a) 'The Management of Academic Culture: Notes on the Management of Meaning and Social Integration', *Higher Education*, XI, 303–320.

Dill, D. D. (1982b) 'The Structure of the Academic Profession: Toward a Definition of Ethical Issues', *The Journal of Higher Education*, 53, 255–267.

Dill, D. D. (1999) 'Academic Accountability and University Adaptation: The Architecture of an Academic Learning Organization', *Higher Education*, XXXVIII, 127–154.

Dill, D. D. (2005) 'The Degradation of the Academic Ethic: Teaching, Research, and the Renewal of Professional Self-Regulation'. In R. Barnett (Ed.), *Reshaping the University: New Relationships Between Research, Scholarship and Teaching*. Buckingham: McGraw-Hill/Open University Press, pp. 178–191.

Dill, D. D. (2007) 'Are Public Research Universities Effective Communities of Learning?: The Collective Action Dilemma of Assuring Academic Standards'.

In R. L. Geiger, C. L. Colbeck, R. L. Williams and C. K. Anderson (Eds), *Future of the American Public Research University*, Rotterdam: SensePublishers, pp. 187–203.

Dill, D. D. and M. Beerkens (2010) *Public Policy for Academic Quality: Analyses of Innovative Policy Instruments*, Dordrecht, The Netherlands: Springer.

Dill, D. D. and F. A. van Vught (2010) *National Innovation and the Academic Research Enterprise: Public Policy in Global Perspective*, Baltimore, MD: The Johns Hopkins University Press.

Hage, J. (1974) *Communication and Organizational Control: Cybernetics in Health and Welfare Settings*, New York: John Wiley.

Henkel, M. (2000) *Academic Identities and Policy Change in Higher Education*, London: Jessica Kingsley Publishers.

Kezar, A. J. and P. D. Eckel (2002) 'The Effect of Institutional Culture on Change Strategies in Higher Education: Universal Principles or Culturally Responsive Concepts?', *The Journal of Higher Education*, LXXIII, 435–460.

King, N. M. P., G. E. Henderson and J. Stein (1999) *Beyond Regulations: Ethics in Human Subjects Research*, Chapel Hill, NC: University of North Carolina Press.

Lewis, R. (2010) 'External Examiner System in the UK'. In D. D. Dill and M. Beerkens (Eds), *Public Policy for Academic Quality: Analyses of Innovative Policy Instruments*, Dordrecht, The Netherlands: Springer, pp. 21–38.

Lodahl, J. B. and G. Gordon (1972) 'The Structure of Scientific Fields and the Functioning of University Graduate Departments', *American Sociological Review*, XXXVII, 57–72.

Long, E. L. (1992) *Higher Education as a Moral Enterprise*, Washington, DC: Georgetown University Press.

Mintzberg, H. (1979) *The Structuring of Organizations: A Synthesis of the Research*, Englewood Cliffs, NJ: Prentice Hall.

Ostrom, E. (1990) *Governing the Commons: The Evolution of Institutions for Collective Action*, New York: Cambridge University Press.

Ostrom, E. (1998) 'Institutional Analysis, Design Principles, and Threats to Sustainable Community Governance and Management of Commons'. In E. Berge and N. C. Stenseth (Eds), *Law and the Governance of Renewable Resources: Studies from Northern Europe and Africa*, Oakland, CA: ICS Press, pp. 27–53.

Ostrom, E. (2000) 'Collective Action and the Evolution of Social Norms', *Journal of Economic Perspectives*, XIV, 137–158.

Ostrom, E. and Walker, J. (1997) 'Neither Markets nor States: Linking Transformation Processes in Collective Action Arenas'. In D. C. Mueller (Ed.), *Perspectives on Public Choice: A Handbook*, Cambridge: Cambridge University Press, pp. 35–72.

Silver, H. (2003) 'Does a University Have a Culture?', *Studies in Higher Education*, XXVIII, 157–169.

Sporn, B. (1996) 'Managing University Culture: An Analysis of the Relationship Between Institutional Culture and Management Approaches', *Higher Education*, XXXII, 41–61.

Teixeira, P., B. Jongbloed, D. Dill and A. Amaral (2004) *Markets in Higher Education: Rhetoric or Reality?*, Dordrecht, The Netherlands: Kluwer.

Toma, J. D., G. Dubrow and M. Hartley (2005) 'The Uses of Institutional Culture: Strengthening Identification and Building Brand Equity in Higher Education'. *ASHE Higher Education Reports*, XXXI(3), 1–105.

Tierney, W. G. (1988) 'Organizational Culture in Higher Education: Defining the Essentials', *Journal of Higher Education*, LIX, 2–21.

Välimaa, J. (1998) 'Culture and Identity in Higher Education Research', *Higher Education*, XXXVI, 119–138.

Yorke, M. (2008) *Grading Student Achievement in Higher Education: Signals and Shortcomings*, New York: Routledge.

13
Conclusion: New Practices and Identities as Drivers of Cultural Change

Jussi Välimaa, Bjørn Stensaker & Cláudia S. Sarrico

The aim of this book was to analyse the functioning of higher education from different insiders' perspectives on higher education institutions, in a social context of accelerating speed of reforms (see Guy Neave in this book). 'Insiders' in our case are academic leaders, academics or students. We have also aimed to look at academia from the point of view of leadership, quality management, strategic thinking and academic work. Changes and reforms are discussed in a number of chapters in the context of collegiality and other central cultural characteristics of higher education. These continuously under-estimated structuring principles create a context for all the reforms and changes taking place in academia. Reform is one of the forms of change, as Taina Saarinen and Jussi Välimaa discuss in their chapter. With these different perspectives we have aimed to feed discussion on the difference between reform attempts and actual changes taking place in higher education and higher education institutions.

What we have tried to underline through the title of our book 'Managing Reform in Universities: The Dynamics of Culture, Identity and Organisational Change' is the ambiguity relating to how reforms are adapted in universities. While managing reform can be understood as a controlled and quite instrumental way of adapting to reform, managing reform can also be interpreted as a more naturalistic and less deterministic mode of adaptation – where changes are coped with rather than strictly controlled.

One of the key insights found in a number of the chapters in our book is that reforms have opened up new practices and new identities in higher education institutions. New practices can be found in relation to the organization of research and education, in how decisions are taken regarding strategy or how information on performance is collected and analysed. New possible identities have also appeared, influencing students, academics and the leadership of universities. Such new identities compete with the existing making it more difficult to find appropriate responses to the challenges caused by reform. As such, one can argue that the new practices and identities found are the key drivers for change in higher education institutions. However, as also underlined in our chapters, the result is rarely pure adaptation of the 'new' at the expense of the 'old'. Rather than controlled adaptation, we find compromises – characterized by partial adaptation, by mixing new practices with old, often resulting in more hybrid institutions. Such compromises have also been found in other recent studies focusing on the relationship between reform and change in higher education (e.g. see Amaral et al., 2003; Teixeira et al., 2004; Huisman, 2009; Gordon & Whitchurch, 2010).

While our empirical data does not allow us to answer the question of whether the noticed compromises could be characterized as a substantial transformation of higher education, they do indicate that different explanations can be offered as to how we should portray change. While one certainly can see how new reform-inspired structures influence the cultures of higher education, one can also see how cultural artefacts, norms and traditions influence the new structures being implemented. However, while the use of the word 'compromise' suggests that higher education finds its practical solutions in a state of harmony, our data do indicate that the changes undertaken are not free of conflict and tension.

On change, reform and tension

Typical of many higher education reforms is the fact that reformers share an ideologically inspired starting point for their actions. Normally, this ideological starting point not only dictates their assumed and hoped outcomes of the reform but it also prevents them from seeing higher education and higher education institutions as they are in reality. Higher education as a national system or as higher education institutions are a complex social entity with many organizational layers of governance and decision-making processes, with conflicting interests between teaching and research and third mission, and with poorly defined clients and stakeholders. Instead of acknowledging this complexity the reformers often, and normally, define higher education institutions as they wish to see them – either as state organizations (as was the case in the 1960s and 1970s) or as business-like enterprises (which has been the case during the 21st century). These politically idealized perceptions of higher education institutions as certain kinds of organizations try to force higher education institutions into social dynamics defined and hoped for by the reformers. Defining higher education in this way serves the needs of the reformers because it gives the political rationale for action. However, it creates problems for the implementation of reforms because reforms normally affect only some parts of the complex nature and processes of higher education while many of the previous practices and practicalities remain as they have always been. This is one of the reasons why there may exist many parallel academic and administrative cultural layers in higher education institutions (see Sahlin in this book). Cultural characteristics embedded in the basic processes in and of higher education institutions are not easily overturned even by new practices and identities.

Of course, some reform attempts may be more successful than others and change can take place in different forms. Hence, it is important to emphasize that there can be different underlying assumptions on the nature and causes of changes in the field of higher education research and policy-making. In their chapter, Taina Saarinen and Jussi Välimaa define four main types of changes depending on whether changes are caused by internal or external factors, or whether the nature of change is continuous development or radical discontinuation. These distinctions are important because higher education policy is legitimated with a continuous need for change. The question is, therefore, whose view of change becomes the dominant one? As Guy Neave points out in his contribution, the acceleration of higher education policy-making at the macro level is a fact in Europe. Essential also is the fact that from the early 1990s onwards and at the macro level, this 'stop/go' rhythm mutated into a reiterated cycle of continuous adjustment, occasionally amplified by new initiatives from government, often to correct what earlier national strategy had enacted and which, in the meantime, had revealed unwelcome and perverse effects.

The implication of this development – regardless of the nature of change as such – is that higher education institutions most likely are destined to enter into a more permanent state of tension, as Cláudia Sarrico and Ana Melo note in their chapter. There are forces both pushing universities in the direction of the mass university and forces pushing it in the direction of the ivory tower serving the needs of the elites of societies.

The increasing number of identity options found in modern universities is without doubt an important factor that provides fuel for such tensions. As Mary Henkel underlines in her chapter, academic career trajectories have multiplied in an environment for choice, diversity and uncertainty. At the same time, the balance of power is shifting towards higher education institutions which have become more managerial and more structured and thus more powerful actors than before. In a globalized world, institutional futures are substantially shaped by economic and reputational competition, fed by national and international performance measurement and rankings. In this environment the processes of academic identity formation and development are difficult to predict even though Mary Henkel suggests that those most in command of their academic identities are most likely to be in elite universities – although one could also imagine greater diversity among the academic staff within elite institutions as a result of this development. For sure, new practices related to research funding will lead to expectations for academics to interact in new ways with both those that fund and administer research programmes – again challenging traditional academic identities (see the chapter by Metcalfe). At the same time, meaning and value and self-esteem among academics remain strongly linked with their commitment to intellectual agendas developed within defined traditions and their individual or principled purposes within them.

The definitions of students are also challenged by increasingly global and consumerist expectations. According to Sónia Cardoso, the identities of students are influenced not only by traditional images of students as institutional actors but also by the perceptions of students as consumers. However, despite the (self-)concept of student as a consumer being increasingly widespread and assimilated, students still do not strictly behave as such. There are tensions to be found between their traditional student identities and their expected consumer behaviours.

From traditional to extended forms of collegiality?

The accelerating cycle of reform, and the new practices and identities established, have challenged the university in new ways, as Kerstin Sahlin discusses in her chapter. She describes four different ideal types of governance and organization: professional, administrative, New Public Management and Audit Society. Crucially, the role of a university leader is profoundly different according to the four governing and organizational ideals. According to Kerstin Sahlin, an important task for leaders of universities is to handle this mixture and interplay of organizing principles in addition to the important task of handling the translation of general principles into a working practice. Kerstin Sahlin emphasizes the importance of collegiality as a culture of working and as a way to reach decisions in academia.

David D. Dill also emphasizes the need to take collegial practices seriously as the core processes within higher education institutions. Without considerable collegial decision-making powers and academic autonomy the processes of teaching, research and recruiting academic staff will result in poor quality. Thus the processes of efficient leadership in academia require the respect of principles and values of collegiality, academic freedom and autonomy. In this regard he comes close to Keijo Räsänen, who in his chapter stresses the fact that the work of ordinary academics is one of the major generators of change in research and education, and possibly also in the practices of governance in academia. Why should we believe that university managers and politicians are the only actors capable of renewal and improvement in academic work? A similar argument is launched by Maria J. Rosa and Alberto Amaral, who emphasize the need for academics to get involved and motivated in institutional quality assurance practices. There is a real danger for institutional quality if the members of the higher education community consider that quality assurance has nothing to do with quality enhancement. In the same manner, Nicoline Frølich and Bjørn Stensaker show that unorthodox, broader or even anarchic ways of organizing strategic processes, in which competing sensemaking processes are confronted, can create new ideas and ways to think forward, sometimes leading to more dynamic translations of ideas and possible practices to undertake. Finally, Amy Scott Metcalfe underlines that network approaches extending beyond disciplinary and institutional boundaries are becoming more important both when initiating and undertaking research projects, perhaps paving the way for a new understanding of 'collegiality' in contemporary higher education.

It is on these arenas that tensions are often played out, that problems have to be addressed and that decisions have to be taken. While established and more traditional forms of collegiality can indeed be said to be important processes in handling these challenges, our different contributions also point to emerging or perhaps extended forms of 'collegial' arenas – arenas where administrative and academic staff are jointly to reach decisions, arenas integrating different vertical levels in the university or arenas expanding beyond institutional borders. Whether such arenas could indeed be characterized as 'collegial', is, of course, another issue, which also leads us to some final reflections on the underlying themes in our book – the interactions and dynamics of culture, identity and organizational change.

On future research agendas

Overall, this book has helped to paint a picture of change in higher education as interactive and quite dynamic where the result of reform can take surprising twists, where change is complex and where adaptation is not seen as passive, a response to external cues. We think three elements are vital in explaining such outcomes.

A first element, central in reform, but also central as paving the way for new practices in higher education is what we can label cultural entrepreneurs. These people are not necessarily the formal leaders in the organization, but people who see reform and change as opportunities and not only as threats. They can sometimes be found within the academic staff, as emphasized in the chapter by Keijo Räsänen, or be part of more developmental processes such as strategy developments, as shown in the chapter by Nicoline Frølich and Bjørn Stensaker. This suggests that studies of academic leadership should perhaps be broadened beyond the current focus on managers and the formal positions they hold. Of interest here is the study of how formal management and informal leaders can interact and open up new insights into organizational change in higher education. Such informal interaction could shed light on how modern forms of collegiality play out in higher education, also following up the plea for a renewed emphasis on the classical academic practices underlined by Kerstin Sahlin and David D. Dill.

A second element, central to higher education institutions, although often overlooked during reform, is the symbolic and cultural capital of a given university. Currently one can detect some ambiguity as to the role of the reputation and other cultural artefacts in higher education, not least due to the role such artefacts play in external rankings of higher education institutions. However, within academe itself, such cultural artefacts are also frequently used in a variety of ways – from selecting research collaborators to legitimizing procedures, decisions and positions. Reputation is in itself a cultural element that blurs the distinction identified in our introductory chapter between culture as something an organization is or something an organization has. Reputation is often conceived as something an organization is, not least underlined in a number of classical studies by Burton Clark in the 1960s and 1970s. However, in modern higher education it also seems that reputation and other cultural artefacts are something an organization can use for different purposes, transforming the element into a manipulative feature – something an organization has. How such cultural capital plays out in reform processes is an under-studied phenomenon in higher education, although several of the chapters in this book touch upon the subject. As shown by Mary Henkel in her chapter, inherent academic identities are still quite persistent in higher education and even paid tribute to in some reform rhetoric related to concepts such as quality and excellence. As further underlined by Maria J. Rosa and Alberto Amaral, and visible even in the chapter by Sónia Cardoso, cultural capital can also be used to mobilize resistance and in blocking reform. But, as highlighted by David D. Dill, cultural capital can also be weakened, opening up for the hollowing out of key cultural characteristics of higher education. Hence, a key issue for further research is analysing the relationship between reform and cultural capital in more depth.

A final element we see as vital in creating interesting adaptation processes in higher education is what we would label cultural transmitters – found in existent and new practices exposed to reform. In this book, a number of such practices have been analysed ranging from new ways to organize research (Metcalfe) and how leadership is executed (Sahlin) to new ways of performance reporting (Sarrico and Melo). What we do know is that such transmitters are open for cultural influences, but we know less about how such transmitters function in relation to each other, and how and in what form they are institutionalized in the sector. The spread of such transmitters makes it harder and harder to see them as merely symbolic practices, not least because these practices are occupied and undertaken by academic and administrative staff stepping in and out of these practices. As such, academics and administrative staff can be expected to carry such cultural transmitters into other arenas they are participating in. Here, there is a need for more holistic in-depth and close-up analysis of academic work and academic practice. There is indeed much research that focuses on certain dimensions of academic work – that being teaching, research or innovation – but there is a lack of research analysing how all dimensions of academic work and academic practice are affected by reform. Hopefully, our book has been an inspiration to those that want to take up these challenges.

References

Amaral, A., L. Meek & I.M. Larsen (eds) (2003) *The Higher Education Managerial Revolution?*, Dordrecht: Kluwer Academic Press.

Gordon, G. & C. Whitchurch (eds) (2010) *Academic and Professional Identities in Higher Education*, New York: Routledge.

Huisman, J. (ed.) (2009) *International Perspectives on the Governance of Higher Education*, New York: Routledge.

Teixeira, P., B. Jongbloed, D. Dill, & A. Amaral (eds) (2004) *Markets in Higher Education. Rhetoric or Reality?*, Dordrecht: Kluwer Academic Press.

Index